WATER
CONSCIOUSNESS

HOW WE ALL HAVE TO CHANGE TO PROTECT
OUR MOST CRITICAL RESOURCE

Edited by Tara Lohan

"Summer" by Josh Harbison, age 17 of Fultondale, Alabama. Josh was a 2008 Finalist in the River of Words environmental art and poetry contest. River of Words is a nonprofit organization dedicated to promoting literacy, creative expression, and community awareness of our most critical environmental concern: water. It was co-founded by U.S. Poet Laureate (1995-1997) Robert Hass and writer Pamela Michael to help young people make a personal and lasting connection to the environment.

THIS BOOK IS DEDICATED TO ALL THE ARTISTS WHOSE WORK EMBODIES A WATER CONSCIOUSNESS

At Blackwater Pond
By Mary Oliver

At Blackwater Pond the tossed waters have settled
after a night of rain.
I dip my cupped hands. I drink
a long time. It tastes
like stone, leaves, fire. It falls cold
into my body, waking the bones. I hear them
deep inside me, whispering
oh what is that beautiful thing
that just happened?

AlterNet Books
77 Federal Street, 2nd Floor
San Francisco, CA 94107
www.alternet.org
books@alternet.org

Watershed Media
513 Brown St.
Healdsburg CA 95448
www.watershedmedia.org
info@watershedmedia.org

Cover and interior designed and co-produced by Watershed Media.

A version of "Why We Need a Water Ethic" (Chapter 16) by Sandra Postel was previously published as "The Missing Piece: A Water Ethic" by *The American Prospect* in 2008.

A version of "The Crisis and Solutions: A Conversation with Peter Gleick" (Chapter 3) by Roger D. Stone was previously published as "Freshwater Politics" by *The American Prospect* in 2008.

A version of "Sacred Waters" (Chapter 14) by Vandana Shiva was previously published in *Water Wars* by South End Press in 2002.

A version of "Making Water a Human Right" (Chapter 15) by Maude Barlow was previously published in *Blue Covenant* by McClelland & Stewart Ltd. in 2007 and The New Press in 2008.

Library of Congress Cataloging-in-Publication Data

Water consciousness : how we all have to change to protect our most critical resource / edited by Tara Lohan.
     p.   cm.
Includes bibliographical references and index.
ISBN 978-0-9752724-4-2. Water conservation--Citizen participation. 2. Water-supply--Management--Citizen participation. 3. Water resources development--International cooperation. I. Lohan, Tara, 1977-

TD388.W248 2008
333.91'16--dc22
               2008023995

First printing, 2008
Printed in Canada
1 2 3 4 5 6 7 8 9 10 – 12 11 10 09 08

This book is printed with soy-based ink by a union Canadian printer using 10% post-consumer fiber, which is Forest Stewardship Council certified.

Mixed Sources
Product group from well-managed forests, controlled sources and recycled wood or fibre
www.fsc.org Cert no. SW-COC-000952
© 1996 Forest Stewardship Council
FSC

Cover photo by Ben Roberts shows an "acequia" in New Mexico, a communal irrigation system that dates back thousands of years to the peoples of present day India, the Middle East, and the Americas. Acequias embody the principles of democracy, equity, and sustainability, and provide a model for water use in the United States.

TABLE OF CONTENTS

WE ALL LIVE DOWNSTREAM

Introduction by Tara Lohan

In this book, you'll see a phrase repeated, "We all live downstream." We are connected to each other by our dependence on water and our participation in its use. Over time, water has been our world's architect–carving and sanding stone, breathing life into forests, testing the patience of deserts. But water has also been the architect of our communities, enabling us to put down roots along the banks of rivers and build lives as deep as our wells.

How we use or abuse our water resources has shaped the kinds of communities we live in and the land that surrounds them. Today, as our world heats up, as pollution increases and population grows, and as our globe's resources of freshwater are strained, we are faced with an environmental and humanitarian problem of mammoth proportions.

Demand for water is doubling every 20 years, outpacing population growth twice as fast. Currently 1.3 billion people don't have access to clean water and 2.5 billion lack proper sewage and sanitation. According to estimates, demand for freshwater will exceed the world's supply by over 50 percent in less than 20 years.

We need to change. Now. This problem affects every one of us, and to implement solutions we need help from every one of us. That means rethinking our individual water habits. It also means mobilizing communities and put-

ting the brakes on a system that is hurtling us towards ecological disaster. We cannot continue our current rates of mass consumption and pollution or the increasing commodification of water. We need a new consciousness. We need to change the way we think about water.

But how does change happen? How do we change individual and government behavior? And more importantly, what will it take to motivate the major shifts in attitudes and operations of the huge corporations and leaders of countries that are mostly responsible for creating the crisis we face?

Some think that change happens only when people are scared by grim reality. Others insist that we must think positively. The truth is we need both. In this book there will be times when you will likely feel discouraged, such as when you read Wenonah Hauter's writings in Chapter 6 about the enormous waste and devastation produced by factory farms and agribusiness, the world's thirstiest water users.

But at the same time, great movements for change are gaining momentum each day. As Deborah Kaufman and Alan Snitow write in Chapter 4, a grassroots movement is spreading across the globe that has already won some major victories, especially against powerful international water companies that are trying aggressively to take over local water supplies.

This book is a journey along the path for change as well. As water makes its way through

Previous page: A boy drinks from a water pump in a village near the Yemeni capital Sanaa.

our world, from ice-capped mountains to rivers to oceans, we will also travel in our understanding of the water crisis and what we can do.

The first step is to truly grasp the extent of the crisis, to learn the hard facts—however difficult it may be to face them. The book is divided into four sections—the first is *Water Scarcity*. Chapters in this first section provide an overview of how much water we have left and how we got ourselves into this mess. This section also explores tough questions about how prepared we are for facing drought, and what tools we can use to get ourselves onto a more sustainable path.

The second part of the book, *Water Inc.*, looks at how this crisis is being exacerbated by the commodification of water. This includes the growing threat to public control of water by the privatization of municipal systems and the ballooning bottled water industry. Authors also detail the rise of grassroots movements against these forces.

This growing corporate threat also extends to the food we eat and how it is grown, as well as the construction of massive infrastructure like dams, which are worsening our water crisis, displacing communities, and destroying ecosystems.

These first two sections are that part of the change equation that has more to do with facing the hard facts. But in the third section, *Water Solutions*, we present the solutions that are already being put into practice and how we can take part, beginning with first understanding the watershed that we each live in.

This section also examines a number of communities that are proactively working on solutions—including ancient techniques, basic conservation measures, new technology, and the best help nature has to offer.

In the final section, *Water Future*, we take these tools and combine them with some of the most important principles for water consciousness—recognizing the sacredness of water, working to ensure water as a human right for all people, and developing a water ethic to guide us in our actions.

Combined, the authors lay out the hard road ahead of us, but they also provide a road map to get us to a better place—a new consciousness that will enable us to protect and preserve our most important resource. Woven throughout the text are images of what this crisis, and its solutions, look like across the world.

Of course, we can only do so much reading and so much looking. Then it is time to put down the book and get busy doing. The end of this book contains a list of necessary actions for a healthy water future. But these are nothing without people behind them.

Readers of this book, we are counting on you to become water warriors, change agents—people who know the facts and are willing to step up to reverse our direction. Help us get back to respecting water and its deep and inspiring role as the architect of our communities and ecosystems. It may very well be the most important thing you do.

GLOBAL WARMING AND WATER SHORTAGE: DIFFERENT FACES OF THE SAME DILEMMA

Foreword by Bill McKibben

For years now there's been a discussion among some environmentalists about which of the many crises bearing down upon us will strike us first. The answer, it appears, may be a kind of tie between global warming and water shortage—and with it a new understanding that in many ways they're different faces of the same dilemma. That's why this book is so singularly important.

I remember, for instance, traveling the country north of Beijing and talking to angry people in village after village whose wells had gone dry. No great mystery why—the huge diesel pumps sucking irrigation water had dropped the water table too far.

Indeed, the fields around us were showing that even the farmers were feeling the effects. What would once have been wheat fields were now filled with corn, which can fare a little better with rainfall instead of irrigation. But the total amount of grain that China produces is dropping steadily—even as America begins to use its great plains to grow gasoline, partly because global warming is calling petroleum into disrepute.

Meanwhile, that same warming was evaporating ever more of the water that was still available for irrigation—say, in Australia, where farmers were abandoning whole agricultural districts because the rain no longer fell, or in Georgia, where Atlanta city officials watched in horror as the reservoirs dropped ever lower.

The way these kinds of effects twine and intertwine mark the boundaries of human and political potential in this century. If you want to understand foreign policy, for instance, don't spend too much time fretting about ideology and religion. Look at aquifers and oil wells.

If you want to understand what a globalizing economy really means, look at the fights over privatization of water.

And if you want the perfect symbol for the high-consumption 21st century, look at a plastic bottle of water, fast replacing the SUV as the ultimate metaphor for our craziness. To take a product that is freely available to everyone in the West, and to turn it into a commodity, and to burn incredible amounts of energy shipping it around the world, and to create small mountain ranges of empty bottles—that is enough to tell you how out of control our consumer society has become.

The traditional antidote to insipid enchantment, of course, has been a bucket of water over the head. And as this book shows, water can still play that role. It's the one commonality on this planet that could bring us back together, to unite against the rise of sea level and the decline of glaciers, against the end of irrigation and the spread of desert, against the privatization of the one central human necessity and instead advocate for the graceful communion that a glass, a splash, a spray, a wave of water represents.

The world is running dry, but only because of our folly. There is time, just, to head it off. But only if we begin. This volume is the place to start.

For two miles the Childs Glacier encroaches directly on the channel of the Copper River in Alaska, sometimes dropping house-sized icebergs into the deep current.

WATER

TODAY, ONE-THIRD OF THE WORLD'S POPULATION IS LIVING WITHOUT ACCESS TO ADEQUATE SUPPLIES OF FRESHWATER. BY 2025 UP TO TWO-THIRDS OF PEOPLE IN THE WORLD MAY BE FACING SERIOUS WATER SHORTAGES, INCLUDING PEOPLE IN 35 PERCENT OF CITIES IN THE UNITED STATES.

ARIZONA, CALIFORNIA, NEW MEXICO, AND NEVADA ARE ALREADY FACING WATER SHORTAGES. IN THE FARM BELT STATES OF THE MIDWEST, THE OGALLALA AQUIFER, WHICH IS THE LARGEST UNDERGROUND BODY OF WATER ON THE CONTINENT, IS BEING DRAINED FOURTEEN TIMES FASTER THAN NATURE CAN REPLENISH IT. MUCH OF TEXAS, AS WELL AS THE SOUTHEAST REGION FROM FLORIDA UP THROUGH THE CAROLINAS, IS EXPERIENCING SERIOUS DROUGHT.

SCARCITY

IN THE UNITED STATES AND ACROSS THE WORLD, PEOPLE ARE RUNNING OUT OF DRINKING WATER. THOSE WITH ACCESS TO AQUIFERS ARE FORCED TO SUPPLEMENT WATER RESERVES BY MINING ANCIENT GROUNDWATER THAT, IN THE LONG RUN, WON'T BE ENOUGH TO QUENCH OUR THIRSTY HOMES, INDUSTRIES, AND FARMS.

IN ORDER TO UNDERSTAND THE MESS WE'RE IN, WE NEED TO FIND OUT HOW WE GOT TO THIS PRECIPICE, PEER OVER THE EDGE TO SEE WHAT THIS CALAMITY MIGHT LOOK LIKE, AND THEN FORMULATE A PLAN TO STEER OURSELVES TO SAFETY.

Chapter 1

HOW MUCH IS LEFT?
AN OVERVIEW OF THE CRISIS

By Eleanor Sterling and Erin Vintinner

The first full views of Earth from Apollo 8—a brilliant blue oasis in a vast black matrix—graphically showed how water distinguishes our world from other planets and underscored our planet's misnomer. Indeed, given that over 70 percent of its surface is covered in water, Earth should have been named "Planet Ocean" or the "Blue Planet." Water defines our world, from shaping its surface to fostering the evolution and complexity of life as we know it.

Water not only surrounds us physically but also inspires our art and music, our literature and dance. Access to freshwater has driven the emergence of societies, and loss of water has brought them crashing down.

All life on Earth is linked through water as it cycles at different scales across the planet, from wetlands to rain clouds to rivers to oceans. It is a finite and powerful force, and both its presence and absence have profound implications at every level, from global climate patterns to ecosystems to the processes within living cells.

Some of nature's most interesting vignettes stem from species adapting to the astonishing variety of water habitats, both fresh and marine.

Children drink water from a broken pipe in a dumpsite in Baghdad's Sadr City.

While the human body—60 percent of which is water, on average—is not as capable of adapting easily to extreme water environments, our ingenuity makes it possible for us to live in very wet and very dry surroundings.

Because our livelihoods and lifestyles are completely dependent on freshwater, in a global sense, we are all downstream from someone else in the world's water cycle. Which is why, as we face a global water crisis, we must all work together—water-rich and water-poor regions alike. While we cannot control the uneven natural distribution of freshwater, we have direct responsibility for the ways in which we use water in agriculture, industry, municipalities, and domestic capacities. We have the ability to turn this crisis around, for the sake of all life on our blue planet. But first, we must understand the scope of the problem. How much water do we have left, and which areas will be hardest hit? Why are we faced with global shortages, and how can we equitably share what remains?

Where in the World Is Our Water?

Even though we live on a planet covered by water, 97 percent is salty, and the majority of what's fresh is stored in glaciers or deep underground aquifers. That means that all freshwater-

Eleanor Sterling and Erin Vintinner

dependent life forms must share less than 1 percent of the water on Earth.

This precious fraction of freshwater is truly our most valuable resource and is renewable at the local scale. Yet as water passes through the water cycle, it is not evenly distributed across our landforms, rendering some regions water rich and others water poor. Hydrologist Malin Falkenmark noted that we "live under the tyranny of the water cycle."[1]

Only six countries (Brazil, Canada, China, Colombia, Indonesia, and Russia) hold over half of the world's freshwater.[2] Other statistics reveal the disparity in freshwater distribution. While Asia and the Middle East have about 60 percent of the world's population, they have only about 36 percent of river runoff (one main indicator of freshwater). In contrast, only 6 percent of the world's population lives in South America, yet the region has one-quarter of all of the world's runoff.[3]

These regional disparities translate into harsh conditions for people living in areas where freshwater supplies are scarce and populations are increasing. Most of the world's megacities are in water-stressed regions where periodic water shortages may occur. These include Mexico City, Calcutta, Cairo, Jakarta, Beijing, Lagos, and Manila,[4] whose residents can anticipate chronic water shortages that threaten food production, hinder development, and negatively impact species and ecosystems.[5]

By 2025 the United Nations estimates that 2.8 billion people in 48 countries will be living in areas facing water stress or scarcity.[6,7,8] These areas will be concentrated mainly in Africa, West Asia, and the Middle East—including the countries of Ethiopia, Kenya, Nigeria, India, and parts of China.

It is important to note that calculations of water stress and scarcity are based on estimates of a country's renewable freshwater supplies and do not include water withdrawn from non-renewable groundwater. A country may temporarily alleviate the effects of water stress by mining ancient aquifers, which are underground reservoirs of water stored within interconnected spaces in the soil, sand, gravel, and rock. Groundwater plays a central role in the water cycle, because it is a major contributor to flow in streams, rivers, and wetlands. However, since groundwater can take a long time to recharge from surface waters draining into the soil, the practice of mining aquifers is often not sustainable, especially if population and freshwater demands increase.[9]

There are numerous water-stressed areas in the United States, particularly in the dry Southwest, where water shortages are now chronic. Current trends such as declining groundwater levels, increasing population, and growing demand for public water supplies indicate that the amount of freshwater in many areas of the country is reaching its limits. Alarmingly, water managers in 36 U.S. states anticipate that they will face local, regional, or statewide water shortages during the next 10 years.[10] These water shortages would lead to severe restrictions in water usage in all areas (agriculture, industry, and domestic) and prompt exploration into new water-management strategies or freshwater sources that are more expensive and have a

---

FACT

If all the world's water were fit into a gallon jug, the fresh water available for people to use would equal only about one tablespoon.

greater impact on the environment.

Already, the United States Geological Survey has reported groundwater depletion in the Southwest and Great Plains, which in some cases has resulted in land subsidence. A further risk in the depletion of groundwater is saltwater intrusion, which occurs when saltwater creeps into the aquifer when the water table is lowered too far, rendering freshwater unusable for drinking or irrigation. This has already been reported in coastal areas of Florida, Georgia, South Carolina, New Jersey, and even inland Arkansas.[11]

Even regions that have historically been water rich, such as the southeastern United States and cities such as Chicago and New York, have been increasingly facing unexpected water shortages due to groundwater depletion, drought, and increasing demands on freshwater resources.[12] A rare prolonged dry spell in the southeast United States that began in 2006 and continued into 2008 was the area's worst drought in more than 100 years.

A 2003 report by the General Accounting Office anticipated water shortages occurring that could result in severe economic, environmental, and social impacts for the United States. It is difficult to measure the nationwide economic costs of water shortages, but an analysis by the National Oceanic and Atmospheric Administration estimated that eight water shortages that occurred during the last 20 years cost $1 billion or more in monetary losses.

Water shortages can harm water-dependent animal and plant species, wildlife habitat, and water quality. They also impact communities by creating conflict between water users over decisions on how water is consumed in homes and businesses, and who is subject to inequalities in levels of relief from water shortages.[13]

How Did We End Up With So Little Left?

We make many choices in the allocation and use of our finite freshwater resources, and these decisions each have consequences for human societies as well as other life on Earth. The ability to deliver water wherever it is wanted has been one of the most important factors in the growth of civilizations and cities. But over time our ingenuity has wrought schemes of larger- and larger scale, often with concurrent heavy social and environmental costs that we are just beginning to understand.

Once delivered to where we want it, water is often wasted or degraded, undermining its renewable nature. Effective water management to ensure a sustainable supply of healthy water for all Earth's creatures (including ourselves) and ecosystems will demand a shift in the way we use, manage, and value our water wealth.

To begin to place a value on water, we need to understand how we are using it. Currently, our water crisis is being exacerbated by a number of factors. Climate change is altering precipitation patterns and affecting freshwater sources such as glaciers and snowpack. We are diverting and polluting surface waters, overmining groundwater, and deforesting, degrading, and paving over essential natural systems that help with water collection.

Through instream uses (such as hydropower dams) and the withdrawal of water from surface and ground sources, humans appropriate over 50 percent of the Earth's renewable freshwater.[14] While this water is renewable at a local scale, it often carries heavy pollution loads following usage, affecting some of the most threatened freshwater ecosystems and species in the world. Scientists estimate that half of the world's wetlands, which act as natural water treatment

Eleanor Sterling and Erin Vintinner

systems, may have been lost in the last 100 years. As our numbers continue to grow, competition for freshwater between humans and the negative consequences of our actions for other species will only intensify.

Agriculture: Our Biggest Water User

Of all the water that humans use, on a global scale the majority goes to large-scale agriculture—about 70 percent—while industry (mainly hydropower or nuclear power) accounts for 22 percent, and municipal and personal use 8 percent. But these numbers vary greatly by country, with the United States for instance, allocating more (46 percent) to industry than agriculture (41 percent), while domestic use lies at 13 percent. In contrast, 96 percent of Bangladesh's water is used for agriculture, with just 1 percent for industry and 3 percent for domestic use. A remarkably different profile emerges for Poland, where only 8 percent of the country's water is used for agriculture, 79 percent is used in industry, and 13 percent used domestically.[15]

Agriculture's large global water footprint is the result of the huge number of acres of land that are irrigated, the inefficient water delivery systems used for that irrigation, and the cultivation of "wet" crops in dry places.

We've always had a rather complex relationship with agriculture and water, going back about 10,000 years to when crops were rainfed. Then the Egyptians introduced irrigation techniques about 7,000 years ago along the Nile River. Much of the early irrigation techniques consisted of creative wheels or levers for lifting water from streams and rivers into higher-lying fields or diverting water via canals into lower-lying fields.

Later, the invention of dams facilitated the upstream diverting process. Irrigated crops are generally higher yielding than rainfed crops, so over time farmers have developed a variety of systems for irrigation, including flooding fields— as for rice—and elaborate sprinkler systems, as used for feed crops such as alfalfa. Today, 40 percent of the world's food is grown in areas where irrigation is necessary—where crops wouldn't flourish with rainfall alone. And by using irrigation, some farmers can raise two or even three crops each year instead of only one.

However, our water delivery systems are often inefficient, with at times up to 50 percent of the water lost to leaks and evaporation.[16] Farmers are increasingly using more efficient systems, such as "drip irrigation," which has been particularly effective in arid regions such as Israel, where a high technology version was first invented in the 1950s, as well as in California's Central Valley. However, drip irrigation is not a panacea. Some drawbacks to this method include high installation costs and technical issues such as clogging. Other advances for irrigation efficiency include laser-leveling of fields to prevent pooling, increasing organic matter in the soil to foster its ability to absorb water, planting cover crops that slow down water movement, retiring land that has high rates of erosion, and, in particular, planting a diversity of crops and those most suited to the soil and rainfall of the region.

Unfortunately, this commonsense approach

FACT

By 2050, the U.S. population is expected to increase by over 100 million people, and the global population is expected to increase by 50 percent to 9 billion people.

Nearly **97 percent** of the world's water is salty

or otherwise undrinkable. Another **2 percent** is locked in ice

caps and glaciers. Only **1 percent** is left for all agricultural,

residential, manufacturing, community and personal needs,

as well as other freshwater-dependent species.

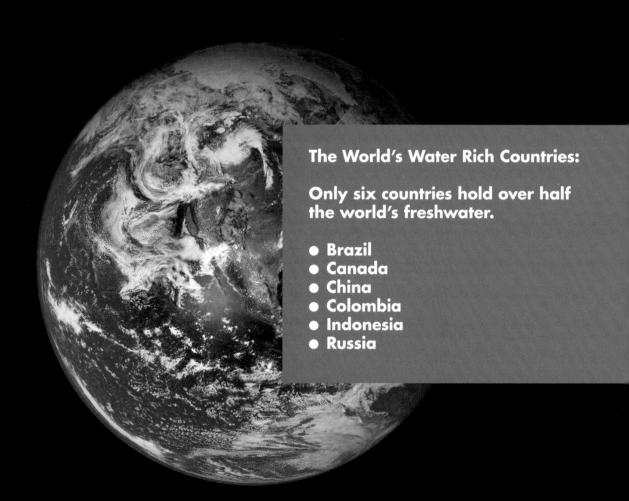

The World's Water Rich Countries:

Only six countries hold over half the world's freshwater.

- **Brazil**
- **Canada**
- **China**
- **Colombia**
- **Indonesia**
- **Russia**

to agriculture is not yet in practice in many parts of the world. "Thirsty" crops–those needing large quantities of water to grow–are often grown in areas where water supplies are low in general or where the crops need the most water during the dry season.

Thirsty crops are surprisingly voracious consumers of water. A grain-fed cow eats mostly corn. It takes 600 gallons of water to grow the amount of corn needed to produce one third of a pound of beef for one hamburger. The production of one pound of cotton by irrigated agriculture requires over 2,000 gallons of water.[17] Rice, which is the main source of directly consumed calories for about half of the world's population, is one of the thirstiest crops, taking more than 400 gallons of water to grow one pound.

Advances in technology have unlocked hidden sources of water for agriculture. Well drilling has afforded access to underground aquifers where water is stored in porous rock and soil. But at times these advances have outstripped the ability of water systems to renew themselves.

As one example, drilling into the Ogallala Aquifer underlying much of the Great Plains region from Texas to South Dakota has turned the High Plains from a Dust Bowl region, where farmer after farmer failed in the early 20th century, to one of the most productive agricultural regions of the world. However, as smaller farmers are now learning, this productivity results from borrowed water and is not sustainable in the long term. The Ogallala Aquifer was formed over 20 million years ago, and much of the water has built up and been held within it for millions of years. Deep wells in the Ogallala still bring up ancient water, laid down at the end of the last Ice Age over 10,000 years ago.

But we are currently consuming this "fossil" water at a rate of 10 times the natural recharge rate. From the early 1900s, when the Ogallala was first tapped for irrigation, to 2005, the water table in parts of the High Plains dropped by more than 150 feet.

Elsewhere in the world, the overmining of groundwater is also taking its toll. Europe relies on groundwater for 65 percent of its drinking water,[18] and the practice is increasing across Asia, particularly in India, Pakistan, and China.

Dams, Pollution, and Consumption

As consumers and members of a democratic society, we have choices in how our agricultural systems are run. Every day we use products whose "water footprint"–the amount of water used in its production, packaging, and distribution–is unexpectedly large. It takes 74 gallons of water to produce a single cup of coffee and over 750 gallons to produce a fast-food meal, including a one-third-pound hamburger, French fries, and orange juice. Diets that include large amounts of meat and other animal products require more water than diets that consist mainly of vegetables and grains. Similarly, diets that are made up of highly processed foods require more water than those consisting of whole foods like fruits and vegetables.

Not only food products but everything, including the cars we drive and the computers we use, takes water to produce. A single medium-sized cotton T-shirt takes over 700 gallons of "virtual water" to produce. Acting on this information does not mean we should go without, but by consciously thinking about our consumer

A sign on a New Zealand beach warns a young boy that the water is too polluted for swimming.

HARBOUR AREA POLLUTED by RAW SEWAGE

Today's sophisticated sewage systems treat biodegradable food, human waste, and metals, but they are not designed to capture the massive amounts of synthetic chemicals used to manufacture consumer products or the chemical ingredients in agents used in our bathrooms and kitchens.

practices and focusing on what we need more than what we want, we can each contribute to water sustainability around the world.

To support our water use in agricultural, industrial, and domestic sectors, we rely on a massive water infrastructure anchored by dams. Built through the ages to control, contain, and divert water, dams have provided a wide range of significant benefits. But in taming the world's rivers, these massive marvels of engineering have also had negative impacts by blocking migration routes for many fish species and altering river habitat. The reservoirs behind large dams have also displaced millions of people. And large dams often don't live up to expectations–delivering less water and less profit than expected, and some hydropower dams generate less power than predicted, too.

Significant water withdrawals for agricultural, industrial, and municipal use also have downstream affects. Ten of the world's major rivers, including the Colorado, Ganges, Jordan, Nile, Rio Grande, and Yellow regularly run dry before reaching the sea.

The continual threat of water pollution reinforces the need to address both characteristics of the water crisis: quantity and quality. While we must consider our impacts on the supply of water, we must also take into account how we are polluting these same supplies.

"The true nature of the water crisis is not that there is too little freshwater on Earth, but that humans fail to respect water as a resource and manage it so that every living being dependent on it has a safe and adequate supply."

As Maude Barlow reports in *Blue Covenant*, water is also polluted from industrial and domestic use, including inadequate sanitation. This combination of factors has had disastrous results worldwide. Currently, 90 percent of the groundwater under China's cities is contaminated;[19] 70 percent of India's rivers and lakes are unsafe for drinking or bathing;[20] 40 percent of the rivers and streams in the United States are too dangerous for drinking, fishing, and swimming;[21] 75 percent of people in Latin America and the Caribbean suffer from chronic dehydration because they don't have access to safe drinking water;[22] and all of Africa's 677 major lakes are now threatened to varying degrees by unsustainable use, pollution, and climate change.[23]

The environmental concentrations of many pharmaceuticals and personal care products (PPCPs) indicate that the occurrence of these chemicals in municipal sewage effluent could negatively impact the health of humans and other species. Endocrine-disrupting chemicals are a class of emerging environmental pollutants that encompass a wide range of industrial and household chemicals. The environmental occurrence of these chemicals has been implicated in the feminization of fish and hormone-related cancers in humans.

Today's sophisticated sewage systems treat biodegradable food, human waste, and metals, but they are not designed to capture the massive amounts of synthetic chemicals used to manufacture consumer products or the chemical ingredients in agents used in our bathrooms and kitchens. Scientists have found levels of pollutants such as pesticides, organic pollutants such as PCBs (polychlorinated biphenyls), and heavy metals such as lead and mercury in the tissues of polar bears, seals, and sea birds living in remote areas of the Arctic where none of these pollut-

HOW MUCH WATER WE CONSUME

600gal.

It takes 600 gallons of water to grow the amount of corn needed to produce one third of a pound of beef for a hamburger.

74gal.

It takes 74 gallons of water to produce a single cup of coffee.

The average person in Kenya uses only 3 gallons per person per day while the average U.K. resident uses around 30. Residents of the United States and Canada use 150 gallons per person per day for domestic and municipal purposes.

KENYA

U.K.

U.S.A. CANADA

3gal. a day

30gal. a day

150gal. a day

ants are used. The pollutants travel via long-range atmospheric transport, ocean currents, and run-off passing through the Arctic drainage basin.

Sharing What's Left

Our overconsumption and increasing levels of pollution suggest that in some of the more water-rich parts of the world, the value we place on water is extremely low. But in other parts of the world, water is a luxury few can afford. In 2004, the World Health Organization and the United Nations Children's Fund estimated that more than one-sixth of the world's population lacked access to safe drinking water, and more than twice that number lacked access to safe sanitation, exposing billions of people to potential waterborne diseases.[24]

On a daily basis, humans require a minimum of about 13 gallons per person per day to maintain an adequate quality of life: 10 percent for drinking, 40 percent for sanitation, 30 percent for bathing, and 20 percent for cooking. The average person in Kenya uses only 3 gallons per person per day while the average U.K. resident uses around 30. These numbers stand in stark contrast to the 150 gallons per person per day used for domestic and municipal purposes by residents of the United States and Canada.[25] Imbalances in water abundance and access at the individual and regional levels have far-reaching implications not only for economic productivity and political stability but also for public health and ecosystem integrity.

The true nature of the water crisis is not that there is too little freshwater on Earth, but that humans fail to respect water as a resource and manage it so that every living being dependent on it has a safe and adequate supply. Therefore, while water scarcity can be a product of physical limitations due to competing demands, unequal water distribution, pollution, environmental stresses, and unpredictability of access to water, many people experience water scarcity due to flawed management policies, poverty, inequality, and unequal institutional power structures.[26]

Access to adequate supplies of clean water is central to human development and many of the United Nations Millennium Development Goals. One such goal is to reduce by half the proportion of people living without access to safe and sustainable drinking water by 2015. Yet the biosocial roots of the water crisis persist. Addressing the politics of water scarcity is an essential part of the effort to reduce the proportion of the world's population lacking clean water.

As Benjamin Franklin noted in *Poor Richard's Almanac* (1733): "When the well is dry, we learn the worth of water." Water, so unevenly, spatially, and temporally distributed, is fast becoming our most valuable, and most contested, resource. There are numerous opportunities to address the global water crisis. This chapter has noted the promise of more efficient irrigation schemes and of raising consumer awareness of our water footprint as examples. Other chapters in this book go in depth about agriculture, dams, and privatization, and will also examine other efficient and cost-effective solutions, including appropriate technology, conservation, and a new ethics around water policy.

Even in water-rich areas, water should not be taken for granted. There is inherent uncertainty in climate patterns, and good conservation habits can help make water supplies last. But by 2050, the U.S. population is expected to increase by over 100 million people, and the global population is expected to increase by 50 percent to 9 billion people. This population growth and corresponding increase in food and energy production and urban expansion has serious implication for freshwater resources.

As noted above, we are already seeing the evidence of freshwater scarcity around the globe, and water pollution is a continual problem. Humans also share the fraction of freshwater on Earth with all other freshwater-dependent species. As these species and ecosystems are threatened and degraded by human actions, we are losing the precious functions that they provide worldwide.

It is essential, therefore, to recognize our roles as stewards of the world's water so we can begin to find solutions to the challenges presented by the water crisis. These solutions can include exploring conservation measures; working with nature to manage water resources; incorporating social, environmental and more accurate economic costs into the value of water; reducing waste in our water-delivery infrastructure; addressing the social and political roots of water stress and scarcity; and investing in appropriate and efficient technological approaches to increase water recycling and reduce water use and contamination.

Our Blue Planet is our only home and it contains all the freshwater that humans and other species rely on to survive. We must raise our water consciousness by recognizing the vital role of water in our lives. We must resolve to value and protect the most valuable resource of all.

SOLVING THE WATER CRISIS

- Exploring conservation measures
- Working with nature to manage water resources
- Incorporating social, environmental, and more accurate economic costs into the value of water
- Reducing waste in our water-delivery infrastructure
- Addressing the social and political roots of water stress and scarcity
- Investing in appropriate and efficient technological approaches to increase water recycling and reduce water use and contamination

Star Wash

Automatic Soft Cloth

SORRY NO WATER

VACS STILL OPEN

Chapter 2

IS THERE A PLAN FOR DROUGHT?

By Tom Engelhardt

Georgia's on my mind. Atlanta, Georgia. It's a city in trouble in a state in trouble in a region in trouble. Water trouble. In November of 2007, backed up by a choir singing "Amazing Grace" and accompanied by three Protestant ministers and 20 demonstrators from the Atlanta Freethought Society, Sonny Perdue, Georgia's Baptist governor, led a crowd of hundreds in prayers for rain.

"We've come together here," he said, "simply for one reason and one reason only: to very reverently and respectfully pray up a storm." It seemed, however, that the Almighty was otherwise occupied, and a regional drought continued to threaten Atlanta, a metropolis of 5 million people (and growing fast), with the possibility that it might run out of water in as little as 80 days or as much as a year if the rains didn't come. Here's a little summary of what the situation was like:

Water rationing has hit the capital. Car washing and lawn watering are prohibited within city limits. Harvests in the region have dropped by 15 to 30 percent. By the end of summer, local reservoirs and dams were holding 5 percent of their capacity.

A sign outside a car wash lets patrons know that the facility is closed. Water restrictions were ordered by Maryland governor Parris Glendening due to the drought that hit the Mid-Atlantic area of the United States.

Oops, that's not Atlanta, or even the southeastern United States. That's Ankara, Turkey, hit by a fierce drought and high temperatures that also have held southern and southwestern Europe in their grip.

Sorry, let's try that again. Imagine this scenario:

Over the last decade, 15 to 20 percent decreases in precipitation have been recorded. These water losses have been accompanied by record temperatures and increasing wildfires in areas where populations have been growing rapidly. A fierce drought has settled in—of the hundred-year variety. Lawns can be watered, but just for a few hours a day (and only by bucket); four-minute showers are the max allowed. Car washes are gone, though you can clean absolutely essential car windows and mirrors by hand.

Sound familiar? As it happens, that's not the American Southeast either; that's a description of what's come to be called "The Big Dry"— the unprecedented drought that has swept huge parts of Australia, the worst in at least a century on an already notoriously dry continent, which is also part of the world's breadbasket, where crops are now failing regularly and farms are closing down.

In fact, on my way along the parched path toward Atlanta, Georgia, I found myself taking any number of drought-stricken detours. There's Moldova. (If you're like me, odds are you don't even know where that small, former Soviet republic falls on a map.)

Like much of southern Europe, it experienced baking temperatures in the summer of 2007, exceptionally low precipitation, sometimes far less than 50 percent of expected rainfall, failing crops and farms, and spreading wildfires. The same was true, to one degree or another, of Albania, Bulgaria, Croatia, Macedonia, and—with its 100-year record scorching of Biblical proportions—Greece, which lost 10 percent of its forest cover in a monthlong fiery apocalypse, leaving large tracts of countryside at risk for depopulation.

Or how about Morocco, across the Mediterranean, which experienced 50 percent less rainfall than normal? Or the Canary Islands, those Spanish vacation spots in the Atlantic Ocean known to millions of visitors for their year-round mild climate which, also in the summer of 2007, morphed into 104-degree days, strong winds, and fierce wildfires. Eighty-six thousand acres were burnt to a crisp, engulfing some of the islands in flames and smoke that drove out thousands of tourists.

Or what about Mexico's Tehuacán Valley, where, thousands of years ago, corn was first domesticated as an agricultural crop? Even today, asking for "un Tehuacán" in a restaurant in Mexico still means getting the best bottled mineral water in the country. Unfortunately, the area hasn't had a good rain since 2003, and the ensuing drought conditions have made subsistence farming next to impossible, sending desperate locals northward and across the border as illegal immigrants. Some have gone to Southern California, itself swept by monstrous Santa Ana–driven wildfires fanned by prolonged drought conditions and fed by new communities built deep into the wild lands where the fires gestate.

And Tehuacán is but one disaster zone in a growing Mexican catastrophe. As Mike Davis has written, "Abandoned ranchitos and near-ghost towns throughout Coahuila, Chihuahua, and Sonora testify to the relentless succession of dry years–beginning in the 1980s but assuming truly catastrophic intensity in the late 1990s–that has pushed hundreds of thousands of poor rural people toward the sweatshops of Ciudad Juarez and the barrios of Los Angeles."

According to the "How Dry I Am" chart of "livability expert" Bert Sperling, four cities in Southern California (not parched Atlanta) top the national drought ratings: Los Angeles, San Diego, Oxnard, and Riverside. In addition, Pasadena had the dubious honor, through September 2007, of experiencing its driest year in history.

Resource Wars in the Homeland

"Resource wars" are things that happen elsewhere. We don't usually think of North America as water poor or imagine that "resource wars" might be applied as a description to various state and local governments in the Southwest, Southeast, or upper Midwest now fighting tooth and nail for previously shared water. And yet, "war" may not be a bad metaphor for what's on the horizon.

According to the National Climate Data Center, federal officials have declared 43 percent of the contiguous United States to be in "moderate to extreme drought." Sonny Perdue of Georgia became embroiled in an ever more bitter conflict–a "water war," as the headlines said–with the governors of Florida and Alabama, as well as the Army Corps of Engineers, over the flow of water into and out of the Atlanta area.

He's hardly alone. After all, the Southwest is in the grips of what, according to Davis, some climatologists are terming a "megadrought," even the "worst in 500 years." More shockingly, he writes, such conditions may actually represent the region's new "normal weather."

The upper Midwest has also been in rainfall-shortage mode, with water levels in all of the Great Lakes dropping unnervingly. The water level of Lake Superior, for instance, fell in 2007 to the "lowest point on record for this time of year." (Notice, by the way, how many "records" are being set nationally and globally in these drought years; how many places are already beginning to push beyond history, which means beyond any reference point we have.)

And then there's the Southeast, 26 percent of which, according to the National Weather Service, is in a state of "exceptional" drought, its most extreme category, and 78 percent of which is "drought affected." We're talking here about a region normally considered rich in water resources setting a bevy of records for dryness. The driest year on record for North Carolina and Tennessee, for instance, was 2007, while 18 months of blue skies led Georgia to break every historical record, whether measured by "the percentage of moisture in the soil, the flow rate of rivers, [or] inches of rain."

Atlanta was hardly the only city or town in the region with a dwindling water supply. David Bracken of Raleigh, North Carolina's *News & Observer*, reported in the fall of 2007 that "17

North Carolina water systems, including Raleigh and Durham, have 100 or fewer days of water supply remaining before they reach the dregs." Rock Spring, South Carolina, he said, "has been without water for a month. Farmers are hauling water by pickup truck to keep their cattle alive." The same was true for the tiny town of Orme, Tennessee, where the mayor was turning on the water for only three hours a day.

And then, there's Atlanta, its metropolitan area "watered" mainly by a 1950s manmade reservoir, Lake Lanier, which, in dramatic photos, is turning into baked mud. Already with a population of 5 million and known for its uncontrolled growth (as well as lack of water planning), the city is expected to house another 2 million inhabitants by 2030. And yet, depending on which article you read, Atlanta is essentially running out of water—the only question may be when.

OK, so let's try again:

Across the region, fountains sit "bone dry"; in small towns, "full-soak" baptisms have been stopped; car washes and laundromats are cutting hours or shutting down. Golf courses have resorted to watering only tees and greens. Campfires, stoves, and grills are banned in some national parks. The boats have left Lake Lanier, and the metal detectors have arrived.

This is the verdant southeastern United States, which, thanks in part to a developing La Niña effect in the Pacific Ocean, now faces the likelihood of drier weather. And, to put this in context, keep in mind that 2007 was "the warmest on record for land [and]...the seventh warmest year so far over the oceans, working out to the fourth warmest overall worldwide." Oh, and up in the Arctic Sea, the ice pack reached its lowest level in September 2007 since satellite measurements were begun in 1979.

FACT

Twenty-six percent of the Southeast U.S. is in a state of "exceptional drought" and 78 percent is drought affected.

29

And Then?

And then there's the question that has been nagging at me, the question that seems so obvious that I can't believe everyone isn't thinking about it, the one you would automatically want to have answered or at least gnawed on by thoughtful, expert reporters and knowledgeable pundits.

I've googled around, read scores of pieces on the subject, and they all—even the one whose first paragraph asked, "What if Atlanta's faucets really do go dry?"—seem to end just where my question begins. It's as if, in each piece, the reporter had reached the edge of some precipice down which no one cares to look, lest we all go over.

We can take it for granted that the Bush administration hasn't the slightest desire to glance down, that no one in FEMA who matters has given the situation the thought it deserves, and that, on this subject, as on so many others, top administration officials are just hoping to make it to January 2009 without too many more scars. But if not the federal government, shouldn't somebody be asking? Shouldn't somebody check out what's actually down there?

So let me ask it this way:

And then what exactly can we expect? If the Southeastern drought is already off the charts in Georgia, then, whether it's 80 days or 800 days, isn't there a possibility that Atlanta may

---

FACT

Four cities in Southern California top the national drought ratings: Los Angeles, San Diego, Oxnard, and Riverside.

---

one day in the not-so-distant future actually be without water? And what then? OK, they trucked water into waterless Orme, Tennessee, but the town's mayor, Tony Reames, put the matter well, worrying about Atlanta. "We can survive. We're 145 people, but you've got 4.5 million there. What are they going to do?"

What indeed? Has water ever been trucked in for so many people before? And what about industry, including, in the case of Atlanta, Coca-Cola, which is, after all, a business based on water? What about restaurants that need to wash their plates or doctors in hospitals who need to wash their hands?

Let's face it: with water, you're down to the basics. And if, as some say, we've passed the point not of "peak oil" but of "peak water" (and cheap water) on significant parts of the planet... well, what then? What exactly are we talking about here? Someday in the reasonably near future could Atlanta or Phoenix, which in winter 2005–2006, went 143 days without a bit of rain, or Las Vegas, another place with questionable sources of water, become a Katrina minus the storm? Are we talking here about a new trail of tears? What exactly would happen to the poor of Atlanta? To Atlanta itself?

Certainly, you've seen the articles about what global warming might do in the future to fragile or low-lying areas of the world. Such pieces usually mention the possibility of enormous migrations of the poor and desperate. But we don't usually think about that in places like the United States.

Maybe we should.

Or maybe, for all I know, if the drought continues, parts of the region will burn to a frizzle first, *à la* parts of Southern California, before they can even experience the complete loss of water. Will we have hundred-year fire records in the South, without

Drought hits Georgia's Lake Lanier. Parts of the lake bottom were revealed that had not been seen since the lake was constructed by the Army Corps in the 1950s.

a Santa Ana wind in sight? And what then?

Mass Migrations?

I found one vivid, thoughtful piece on this subject: "The Future Is Drying Up," by Jon Gertner, written for the *New York Times Magazine*. It focused on the Southwestern drought and began to explore some of the "and thens," as in this brief passage on Colorado in which he quotes Roger Pulwarty, a "highly regarded climatologist" at the National Oceanic and Atmospheric Administration:

The worst outcome...would be mass migrations out of the region, along with bitter interstate court battles over the dwindling water supplies. But well before that, if too much water is siphoned from agriculture, farm towns and ranch towns will wither. Meanwhile, Colorado's largest industry, tourism, might collapse if river flows became a trickle during summertime.

Mass migrations, exfiltrations...Stop a sec and take in that possibility and what exactly it might mean. After all, we do have some small idea, having, in recent years, lost one American city, New Orleans, at least temporarily.

Or consider another "and then" prediction: What if the prolonged drought in the Southwest turns out, as Mike Davis wrote in *The Nation* magazine, to be "on the scale of the medieval catastrophes that contributed to the notorious collapse of the complex Anasazi societies at Chaco Canyon

Tom Engelhardt

and Mesa Verde during the 12th century"?

What if, indeed.

I'm not being apocalyptic here. I'm just asking.

As the World Burns

As we've seen, the Southeastern drought, unlike the famed cheese of childhood song, does not exactly stand alone. Such conditions, often involving record or near record temperatures, and record or near record wildfires, can be observed at numerous places across the planet. But it is rare to hear them compared.

An honorable exception would be a *Seattle Times* column, "Fire, Water and Denial," by Neal Peirce, that brought together the Southwestern and Southeastern droughts as well as the Western "flame zone," where "megafires" are increasingly the norm, in the context of global warming in order to consider our seemingly willful "myopia about the future."

But you'd be hard-pressed to find much information in the mainstream media that puts all (or even a number) of the extreme drought spots on the global map together in order to ask a simple question (even if its answer may prove complex indeed): Do they have anything in common? And if so, what? And if so, what then?

Amy Goodman of *Democracy Now!* interviewed Tim Flannery, paleontologist and author of *The Weather Makers: The History and Future Impact of Climate Change*, on the topic of a "world on fire." Flannery offered the following observation:

It's not just the Southeast of the United States. Europe has had its great droughts and water shortages. Australia is in the grip of a drought that's almost unbelievable in its ferocity. Again, this is a global picture.

We're just getting much less usable water than we did a decade or two or three decades ago. It's a sort of thing again that the climate models are predicting. In terms of the floods, again we see the same thing. You know, a warmer atmosphere is just a more energetic atmosphere. So if you ask me about a single flood event or a single fire event, it's really hard to make the connection, but take the bigger picture and you can see very clearly what's happening.

I know answers to the "and then" question are not easy or necessarily simple. But if drought– or call it "desertification"–becomes more widespread, more common in heavily populated parts of the globe already bursting at the seams (and with more people arriving daily), and if whole regions no longer have the necessary water, how many trails of tears, how many mass migrations or civilizational collapses are possible? How much burning and suffering and misery are we likely to experience? And what then?

I'm no expert on this. These are questions I can't answer, that our elected leaders seem to be desperately unwilling and unprepared to face, and that, as yet, the media have largely refused to consider in a serious way. And if the media can't face this and begin to connect some dots, why shouldn't we be in denial, too?

It's not that no one is thinking about, or

> *"Let's face it: with water you're down to the basics. And if, as some say, we've passed the point not of 'peak oil' but of 'peak water' (and cheap water) on significant parts of the planet...well, what then?"*

Southern California wildfires blaze above a neighborhood.

doing work on, drought. I know that scientists have been asking the "and then" questions (or perhaps far more relevant ones that I can't even formulate), that somewhere people have been exploring, studying, writing about them. But all of the rest of us should know about it, too.

Of course, we can wander the Internet. We can visit the National Oceanic and Atmospheric Administration, which, in 2007 set up a new Web site (www.drought.gov) to help encourage drought coverage. We can drop in at blogs like RealClimate.org and ClimateProgress.org, which

make a habit of keeping up with, or ahead of, such stories, or even, for instance, the Georgia Drought Web site of the University of Georgia's College of Agricultural and Environmental Sciences. But, believe me, even when you get to some of these sites, you may find yourself in an unknown landscape with no obvious water holes in view and no guides to lead you to them.

In the meantime, there may be no trail of tears out of Atlanta; there may even be enough rain in the city's near future for all any of us know. But it's clear enough that, globally—and possibly nationally—tragedy awaits. It's time to call in the media first team to take a glimpse or two over the precipice as the world turns and bakes and burns...and to ask these questions: How bad is it, really, and what can we do?

33

Chapter 3

THE CRISIS AND SOLUTIONS: A CONVERSATION WITH PETER GLEICK

By Roger Stone

It is hard to overstate the severity of the freshwater problems that surround us: over-consumption, contamination, unjust distribution, and the dangers of commodification. We face the likelihood of worsening water conditions if human population grows and we fail to improve our water policies, practices, and attitudes. One of the world's leading experts on our water crisis, Dr. Peter H. Gleick, a MacArthur fellow and the founder of the Pacific Institute for Studies in Development, Environment, and Security in Oakland, California, has been studying the connections between water and human health, globalization, and climate change for 20 years. Gleick tells us how we managed to get ourselves into this mess, and what we can do to get out.

Roger Stone: In your book *Water in Crisis*, published in 1993, you said that water was going to be a major challenge for the world in the coming century. Well, here we are well into that century. Are things now better or worse than you thought they would be?

Peter Gleick: I do think there is a water crisis. There are still more than a billion people who don't have access to safe drinking water

A Mexican woman skirts a Jaguey water hole near San Marcos Tlacoyalco, Mexico. The Tehuacan Valley southeast of Mexico City has long experienced severe water shortages.

and 2.5 billion people or so without access to adequate sanitation. Two million people a year die of water-related diseases that are preventable, curable, unnecessary. And that, by itself–what I describe as a failure to meet basic human needs for water–is a crisis. Sometimes the word is overused, but not, in my opinion, in this case.

RS: So what's the better news?

PG: The good news is that, in part because of the nature of the water crisis, in part because of how bad it has gotten in parts of the world, there's growing attention to water by the public, by politicians, by scientists, by academics. And that's leading to new efforts to use water more efficiently, to think about incorporating ecosystems into water planning and management. There are many good examples of political cooperation over water. All around the world we're seeing bits and pieces of what, if taken altogether, is a sustainable strategy of what I call a "soft path to water."

RS: Are industrial users becoming interested in the soft path?

PG: Yes. At the Pacific Institute we spend a lot of time looking at water-efficiency potential across the board. In the 1920s, it took 200 tons of water to make a ton of steel. Today, the best steel plants in the world use 2 or 3 tons of water to make a ton of steel. That's a 99 percent re-

WHAT IS THE "SOFT PATH" FOR WATER?

In the last century, most water managers focused on finding and developing new supplies of water by building large, centralized infrastructure, such as dams, aqueducts, and centralized treatment facilities. While this approach—the "hard path" —brought many benefits, it left much of the world with critical unresolved water challenges, including billions of people without basic safe water and sanitation, and significant ecological devastation. Now in the 21st century, it is time for new thinking and new approaches to global and local water problems—it is time for a "soft path" for water.

The "soft path," as described by Peter Gleick and colleagues at the Pacific Institute, is a comprehensive approach to water management, planning, and use. The soft path can be distinguished from the traditional, hard path to water in six main ways:

1 Ensures water for human needs.
The soft path directs governments, companies, and individuals to meet the water needs of people and businesses, instead of just supplying water. People want clean clothes or to be able to produce goods and services—they do not care how much water is used and may not care if water is used at all.

2 Ensures water for ecological needs.
The soft path recognizes that the health of our natural world and the activities that depend on it (like swimming, water purification, ecological habitat, and tourism) are important to water users and people in general. Often times, by not returning enough water to the natural world, the hard path harms humans and other ecological users downstream.

3 Matches the quality of water with its use.
The soft path advances water systems that supply different qualities of water for different uses. For instance, storm runoff, graywater, and reclaimed wastewater, although not of the highest quality, are well-suited for landscape irrigation or for certain industrial purposes.

4 Matches the scale of the infrastructure to the scale of the need.
The soft path for water recognizes that investing in decentralized infrastructure can be just as cost-effective as investing in large, centralized facilities. There is nothing inherently better about providing irrigation water from a massive reservoir instead of using decentralized rainwater capture and storage.

5 Includes public participation in decisions over water.
The soft path requires water agency or company personnel to interact closely with water users and to engage community groups in water management. The hard path, governed by an engineering mentality, is accustomed to meeting generic needs.

6 Uses smart economics.
The soft path recognizes the public and economic aspects of water and uses the power of water economics to encourage the equitable distribution and efficient use of water.

Source: Pacific Institute, Oakland, California: www.pacinst.org

duction. In general, the drumbeat from industry used to be, "Oh, we can't comply with these environmental regulations, they're too expensive." But the reality has turned out to be that they made these industries more efficient and made the environment cleaner. Everybody benefited. The steel industry would have died a slow, horrible death in the United States. Instead, it was fundamentally restructured.

Other smart, innovative industries get it, and they get it early, and they reduce their environmental footprints, in every aspect—energy, environment, water, toxics—and it's to their credit that they do so. They don't want to get in trouble with their consumers. They don't want to have people badgering them to measure their water footprint. They want to get ahead of the problem.

RS: Global warming in many respects is making matters worse in the water world. What sort of response can we expect?

PG: It's sometimes a little depressing to look back and see how little progress we have made in getting water managers to understand the true risks of climate change. I do think the debate about climate change itself is over. The next step is integrating that understanding into changes in the way we manage water. It is still happening very slowly—too slowly, in my opinion. But it is happening. We are, especially in the western United States, coming to the realization that tomorrow's climate is going to be different

from yesterday's climate and that we're going to have to manage our complex water system for that new reality.

RS: What about money issues?

PG: It takes less money to meet basic human needs for water than the economic cost of not meeting those needs—in terms of health, lost work days, lost education opportunities for small girls and young women in the developing world. The faster we understand that, the less we'll complain about how much is involved.

People are willing to pay for water that meets their needs, and I think that's key to a lot of this. I also believe that the economic models we've used in the past—the role of the World Bank and the big international funding agencies—are not going to get us to the solutions we need. In particular, while there is a need for some big, expensive infrastructure, there's also a desperate need for much smaller-scale investments: at the village level, on the individual level, at the community level. The World Bank is very good at spending a billion dollars in one place, but they're not good at spending a million dollars in a thousand places—or a thousand dollars in a million places. That requires a new model of financing and one that the World Bank and organizations like [it] are not capable of addressing.

RS: How about technology? Drip irrigation and the other refinements of agricultural watering have come online. To what degree do those kinds of techno-fixes represent a solution to the problem?

PG: Just as education is important, just as regulatory policies are important, just as proper economics is important, there's a critical role for technology. If someone were to come to me and say (and they do all the time), "I've got the technology that's going to solve our water problems," that's not the right way to think about the

---

FACT

In the 1920s, it took 200 tons of water to make a ton of steel. Today, the best steel plants in the world use 2 or 3 tons of water to make a ton of steel.

problem. Because this isn't just a technological problem. But equally, if someone says, "Technology has no role to play," I don't think that's right either. And so the question is: What's the right role for technology? I think technology for water is going to be a little different in the coming years than it has been in the past when we focused on large-scale central models.

We've done a lot of work here at the Pacific Institute on water-use efficiency, by which we mean learning how to do what we want to do with less water. How to grow more food with less water, how to produce semiconductors with less water, how to have a healthy lifestyle while using less water, while using water more efficiently. And I think the potential for that is enormous.

RS: In reorganizing the bureaucracies to cope with all this: What do we need?

PG: I would make two points. The first being that, it's obvious, of course, the institutions we have today have not solved our water problems. But the second point is that doesn't necessarily mean we need new institutions. It certainly suggests that we need, at minimum, better-run institutions.

But it is also possible that we in the U.S. need to fundamentally rethink the way we manage water. We should be managing water at the watershed level, rather than the state level. Or we should be managing it for local resources rather than relying on federal subsidies and federal policies. There are certain things we have to do at the federal level and certain things we have to do at the local level. And we haven't been very good about figuring out which is which.

RS: Much is made of interpretations that position water as a commodity rather than a human right. What is your view?

PG: I do think that water is a human right. The challenge is how do we implement that right, what does it really mean? Water is also an economic good, and figuring out how to balance these things in ways that protect humans and ecosystems is going to be a challenge. It's going to be a leading challenge.

RS: What about managing political conflict? Is there a need for a new world body to arbitrate water disputes?

PG: There's a long history of conflict going back 5,000 years. And as water becomes more scarce in some places, or if the demand for water goes up, the risk of political conflict and violence over water will grow. The places that concern me most are, as you might imagine, already water scarce: the Middle East, the Persian Gulf, parts of Asia, the southwestern United States. Where water is already tight, where supplies are scarce or demand high compared to water availability, political tensions are high.

Most disputes over water are subnational, local often, and they're under the jurisdiction of local courts, local laws, local water rights, local water allocations. There has been some discussion about some sort of water tribunal at the international level for shared water. And that might have some value. But the best way to reduce conflicts over shared water resources is by a bilateral or multilateral treaty with the parties involved.

FACT

More than 1 billion people don't have access to safe drinking water and 2.5 billion people do not have access to adequate sanitation. Two million people a year die of water-related diseases that are preventable and curable.

A woman in Kenya collects rainwater from the roof into a clean barrel and saves many hours of time previously spent going to a well.

The U.S. and Mexico signed a treaty on the Colorado River. The U.S. and Canada signed a treaty about the Great Lakes. Nile River riparian nations are working hard to come up with a treaty acceptable to all of them. That's the only real way to get a comprehensive agreement. I don't think a new world body would necessarily help that.

RS: Every three years there's this thing called the World Water Forum that takes place somewhere, and thousands of people go. In your writings you've been somewhat critical of those forums. Is there any way to get them to be more productive?

PG: There's value to some of these meetings and no value to some of them. The value, of course, is that they provide an enormous opportunity for networking and information exchange. There's been an effort in the last few years to have these massive meetings be also ministerial meetings, where you force some ministerial agreement or statement. And those have always been very wishy-washy, they've never been binding. I think if you're going to have ministerial level gatherings about water, have them separately from these big public events. Get the diplomats in a room and lock them in, and make them discuss and come to an agreement about something, and have these bigger meetings be scientific exchanges of information, social networking, community development. I think that's what's most effective.

RS: In regards to water privatization, your books propose a set of principles to

guide the relationship between public- and private-sector water managers. Do you see evidence of those principles being picked up and adopted, or is it too soon?

PG: Yes, we do see evidence of that. There's enormous public opposition to privatization. The public is very concerned about it. The public is very concerned about private control of water resources, about the transparency of private water providers. And so, increasingly, as privatization has been proposed, there's been push-back, there's been opposition. So balancing the public and private aspects of water is also going to be part of the challenge in the coming years. And my feeling is that, unless some of the principles that we put forward are adopted–of public transparency, government oversight and regulation, of public participation and decision making about rates and design and systems operation–then public opposition can stop privatization. So it makes sense in my mind for the private companies to try and do this properly, or they're not going to get a chance to do it at all.

RS: So overall, what's most urgently needed?

PG: We can't do it all, but we don't have to. But what we really need to do is the things that are the most effective and the most efficient and the quickest. I very firmly believe that there are sustainable solutions to dealing with the complex set of challenges to fix in the water area. There are lots of smart people working on the problem. There are lots of innovative ideas and practices being tested. I think the real question is, how fast will the transition to what I call a "soft path for water" occur, and how much suffering will have to happen before we are well along on that path.

Kids swimming in a polluted harbor in India.

WATER

PRIVATIZATION HAS BECOME THE WORD OF THE 21ST CENTURY. AS GOVERNMENT LOOSENS ITS HOLD ON THE REMAINS OF OUR SHARED RESOURCES, PRIVATE INTEREST GOBBLES UP WHAT ONCE BELONGED IN THE PUBLIC TRUST.

AT GREAT PERIL TO HUMANITY AND NATURE, THE WATER FROM RIVERS, LAKES, STREAMS, AND AQUIFERS IS BEING SOLD FOR PROFIT. SEVERAL DECADES AGO, FEW WOULD HAVE THOUGHT THAT SMALL RURAL COMMUNITIES WOULD BE BATTLING HUGE MULTINATIONAL CORPORATIONS FOR THE RIGHT TO CONTROL THEIR OWN DRINKING WATER. FEW WOULD HAVE ALSO THOUGHT THAT MUNICIPAL GOVERNMENTS WOULD HAND OVER CONTROL OF THEIR MOST VITAL RESOURCE TO FOR-PROFIT COMPANIES HOPING TO MAKE A BUCK.

INC.

UNFORTUNATELY, THIS IS BECOMING THE PATTERN, FROM THE GLOBAL NORTH TO THE GLOBAL SOUTH. AND AS A HANDFUL OF BIG BUSINESSES MOVE IN FOR CONTROL OF DRINKING WATER, MORE ARE SIPHONING FRESHWATER FOR UNSUSTAINABLE AGRIBUSINESS, AND OTHERS ARE DIVERTING RIVERS FOR DEVASTATING BIG DAM CONSTRUCTION.

BUT AS THESE LARGE CORPORATIONS PUSH FORWARD WITH PRIVATIZATION, COMMUNITIES ARE PUSHING BACK—FIGHTING FOR CONTROL OF THEIR RESOURCES AND FINDING LOCAL SOLUTIONS TO THE WATER CRISIS.

WATER is NOT A
PRIVATE
COMMODITY
Bechtel: STOP
EXTORTING Bolivian Poeple!

Chapter 4

THE NEW CORPORATE THREAT TO OUR WATER

By Alan Snitow and Deborah Kaufman

A bridge collapses in Minneapolis.

A city is destroyed when levees break.

A burst steam pipe shuts part of Manhattan.

A quarter of the country loses power when the grid goes down in Ohio.

The crisis of American infrastructure has long been predicted, but in recent years, particularly under the Bush administration, government negligence towards basic public assets has become endemic. The squandering of a budget surplus and the refusal to raise taxes even for essential government services was intended to "starve the beast" of government. Right-wing ideologues argued that this would not only force government cutbacks, but also fuel a private sector takeover of public services from parks and traffic lights to water and schools. They were right.

By 2007, a fire sale was well underway. The city of Chicago had leased its major highway and Indiana its toll road. Private companies were managing major ports and bidding for control of local water systems across the country. Promising big profits from infrastructure, major financial institutions from Wall Street's Goldman Sachs to Australia's Macquarie Bank accumulated billions of dollars from investors and even union pension funds to buy public assets. Government jobs were also up for sale. For the first time in American history, the federal government employed more contract workers than regular employees. Not even the military was exempt with Blackwater's hired guns wreaking havoc in Iraq.

This radical shift to the private sector could become one of history's largest transfers of ownership, control, and wealth from the public trust to the private till. But more is at stake. The concept of democracy itself is being challenged by multinational corporations that see Americans not as citizens, but merely as customers. They don't see government as something of, by, and for the people, but as a market to be entered for profit.

And it is a huge market. About 85 percent of Americans receive their water from public utility departments, making water infrastructure, worth trillions of dollars, a prime target for privatization. To drive their agenda, water industry lobbyists have consistently opposed federal aid for public water agencies, hoping that federal cutbacks would drive market expansion. So far, the strategy has worked. In 1978, just before the Reagan-era starvation diet began, federal funding covered 78 percent of the cost for new water infrastructure. By 2007, it covered just 3 percent. In the 20 years ahead, local and state governments,

A street protest at the Bechtel Headquarters in San Francisco organized because of the role Bechtel played in privatizing a formerly public water system in Cochabamba, Bolivia.

Alan Snitow and Deborah Kaufman

ratepayers, and taxpayers will have to come up with well over half a trillion dollars to purify drinking water and treat sewage.

As a result, local and state governments are desperately trying to figure out how to pay these bills without huge, and politically unpopular rate increases that would constitute a regressive tax on poor and working people. An increasing number of mayors and governors, Republicans and Democrats, are turning to the industry's designated solution: privatization.

When it comes to water, the multinationals may have met their match. Providing clean, accessible, affordable water is not only the most basic of all government services, but throughout history, control of water has defined the power structure of societies. If we lose control of our water, what do we as citizens really control through our votes, and what does democracy mean?

The danger is that most citizens don't even know there's a problem. Water systems are mostly underground and out of sight. Most of us don't think about our water until the tap runs dry or we flush and it doesn't go away. That indifference could cost us dearly, but privatization is not yet destiny.

A citizens' water revolt has been slowly spreading across the United States as private water companies come to towns and cities. The revolt is not made up of "the usual suspects"; it has no focused ideology, and it's not the stuff of major headlines. It often starts as a "not-in-my-backyard" movement to defend the character of a community or to assert a desire for local control. But quickly, almost spontaneously, the revolt expands its horizons to encompass issues of global economic justice, and its constituency grows to include people across lines of party, class, and race.

In Lee, Massachusetts, the revolt was against potential water plant layoffs. In Felton, Califor-nia, it was about rate increases and local control. In Atlanta, it was broken pipes and sewage lines. In other communities, it was the fear of corruption, cover-ups, and complicity between politicians and giant corporations.

An epicenter of this nascent movement has been Stockton, California, population, 250,000, in the heart of the state's agricultural San Joaquin Valley. A citizens' group in Stockton took on not only the mayor and city council, but also some of the world's largest private water corporations in a preview of the corporate water wars to come.

When private water companies case a city as a potential privatization target, one of the things they look for is a "champion" in city government, someone who will take the lead in selling off the city's water services. In Stockton, they found their champion in Mayor Gary Podesto, a former "big box" grocery store owner, who wanted to expand development, reinvigorate downtown, and streamline city services. In his view, "it's time that Stockton city government treat its citizens as customers."

Privatizing the city's water department seemed like just the place to begin. "Departments like this don't compete for profits," said Podesto. "They have no incentive to improve." Sentiments like this are commonplace in the United States, but water services are different than other commodities: there is no marketplace competition. Citizens have no choice about whether to have water or not. There is only one set of pipes in town.

But Mayor Podesto had other reasons to privatize. Stockton, like other cities, was under pressure from state and federal environmental agencies to modernize its sewage plant to reduce San Joaquin River pollution. This was an expensive project, and the mayor thought that a private company could do it cheaper, if not better.

Podesto also had a more personal reason:

a vision for the future of his city. An avid baseball fan and player since childhood, he had always wanted to bring a minor league baseball team to Stockton, and privatization might have been just the ticket. All along, critics suspected that he wanted to build his field of dreams using utility funds that would otherwise be reserved for water infrastructure. Podesto wasn't shy about pushing hard to realize his dream. On his desk was a mounted baseball. Embossed across the stitching: "Sometimes you just have to play hardball."

In 2002, Podesto sought bids from private water companies to take over the city's water department. The winner of the bidding war was a consortium of two multinational giants: OMI, the water division of Colorado-based CH2M-Hill, one of the largest engineering firms in the United States, and London's water company, Thames Water, which was itself a subsidiary of German energy powerhouse Rheinisch-Westfälisches Elektrizitätswerk Aktiengesellschaft (RWE). For OMI and RWE/Thames, Stockton was a plum—a well-run, in-the-black municipal utility at the center of California's fierce water politics. For them, this was an opportunity to show California, and the country, what a private utility could do. It would be the largest water privatization deal in the western United States, a 20-year, $600 million contract.

All along, Podesto insisted that he was not privatizing the city's water department at all. "Don't use that word 'privatization,'" he warned. Nowadays, the growth market is in long-term contracts for private companies to manage and operate city-owned urban water systems like the one in Stockton. The lingo for these deals is a masterpiece of public relations: "public-private partnerships," suggesting a relationship of equality rather than subservience.

In the case of long-term "partnerships," cities lose the capacity to run their own water systems. In that case, corporate control becomes the de facto reality no matter what terminology is used.

In Stockton, the privatization deal seemed in the bag, but Mayor Podesto and the water giants were in for a surprise.

Water's Dirty History

Although hidden out of sight and scent, even pipes have a history. In the nineteenth century, water ownership and management in the United States was largely in private hands. Historian Norris Hundley, author of *The Great Thirst*, has written about a chaotic period in the late

> **"The country's clean water infrastructure can be thought of almost as a circulatory system. Rather than the blood that keeps our bodies alive, our local utilities pump the water that keeps our societies functional. Pipes act as arteries, carrying the fresh water to be used by people and businesses, then as veins, carrying dirty water away. Wastewater treatment facilities serve as the kidneys and liver, cleaning impurities and waste. Like, the circulatory system, water infrastructure is largely out of sight; like the circulatory system, it is largely out of mind until it breaks down."**
>
> —Food and Water Watch

Alan Snitow and Deborah Kaufman

nineteenth century when "entrepreneurs promised clean, bountiful, reasonably priced water supplies" in return for a chance to make a profit. "These dream deals soon became nightmares of diversion facilities ripped out by floods, wooden pipes leaking more water than they carried, mud holes pitting the streets, pollution exceeding anything witnessed in the past, and an escalating fire threat."

In 19th century New York, for example, the city's private water provider, the Manhattan Company, was actually a front to win public subsidies. Company founder Aaron Burr then diverted the money to establish a bank to compete with the Bank of New York, which was controlled by his archenemy, Alexander Hamilton, who Burr later killed in a duel!

It took the devastating cholera epidemic in 1832 and the Great Fire of 1835, so huge it was seen as far away as Philadelphia, to push the devastated commercial center of the United States into taking its water future into its own hands. Although Burr's Manhattan Company was a disaster as a water company, it survived as a bank, becoming Chase Manhattan, buying out Hamilton's old Bank of New York, and finally becoming JP Morgan Chase. The company's logo, however, remains the same: a cross section of a 19th century wooden water pipe.

The story was similar in cities across the United States and Canada. As populations grew, private water companies did not have the resources or expertise to meet the need. Citizens demanded and eventually won modern public water systems, financed through bonds, operated by reliable engineers and experts, and accountable to local governments. The nation built a dazzling system of community waterworks that provided clean, reasonably priced water and sewer systems that still rank among the best in the world.

But in recent years, the federal disinvestment in water services has sparked a new era of privatization with contemporary players repeating promises made by 19th century entrepreneurs. The world's largest private water companies have quickly entered the American market: Suez and Veolia from France and Germany's RWE/Thames. Few Americans have heard of them, but the "Big Three" have dominated the global water business and are among the world's largest corporations. Together they control subsidiaries in more than one hundred countries.

Relying on hegemonic free market ideology rather than research, neither government officials nor the media bothered to check the shaky record of these multinationals in cities around the world. Suez and Veolia have had a reputation for influence peddling in France right into the presidential palace, and Suez's first foray in the United States was in Atlanta, which threw the company out after four years of brown water, low water pressure, and general incompetence.

The companies directly involved in the Stockton deal have also had their share of controversy. OMI was charged with falsifying water quality reports in several small U.S. cities. RWE/Thames had been named "worst polluter" in Britain several years running. That inspired London's rowing crews to organize Rowers Against Thames Sewage (RATS) and a widely publicized "Thames Turd Race" in which rowers in gas masks towed ten-foot-long inflatable "feces" to company headquarters, demanding that the company clean up river pollution.

How to Privatize a U.S. City

If Stockton Mayor Podesto had doubts about OMI and RWE/Thames, he didn't let on,

The Federal Government's Failure to Fund Clean Water

From 1991 to 2007 in Billions of Dollars (b)

Federal Grants   2007 Inflation-Adjusted Federal Grants

Since 1991, the federal government has cut 66 percent of the money to the Clean Water State Revolving Fund that helps communities keep their water clean.

saying only that Suez's failures in Atlanta would come back to haunt them in the American market. In his view, privatization promised efficiencies of scale, competitive cost cutting, lower water rates, and a business culture that would favor real estate development.

Economies of scale are one of the industry's biggest selling points, but critics have questioned the significance of size for a local service like water. A study of England's private water industry did not find significant benefits from economies of scale, a conclusion later confirmed by none other than RWE/Thames's then CEO Henry Roels. "It's a very local business," in which a global water company "just doesn't have outstanding advantages."

The argument for marketplace competition loses all traction in a monopoly service like water, but water companies still contend the profit motive gives them an incentive to cut costs. However, such efficiencies must come from somewhere, usually from service cutbacks, staff layoffs, and failures to invest in preventive maintenance. In Indianapolis, customer complaints nearly tripled in the first year of Veolia's contract. In Urbana, the mayor demanded public control of an RWE subsidiary because of nonfunctioning fire hydrants. In Milwaukee, Suez subsidiary United Water discharged untreated sewage into Lake Michigan after the company shut down pumps to reduce its electricity bill.

As for rates, studies from across the country reveal that private water systems charge more–often much more–than public systems right next door. But private water operations make their biggest profits by expanding their service areas

Alan Snitow and Deborah Kaufman

as cities grow. The industry's business culture makes it a natural ally of developers against citizens' groups trying to limit growth, preserve agricultural land, or establish greenbelts.

All these political and business considerations make it easy to forget that even when water is public, it is not really *our* water at all. It is the planet's circulation and life force. Climate change expresses itself through water or the lack of it. Droughts are a spreading problem across the United States, making conservation of water a high priority. However, private water companies want customers to use *more* water, not less, in order to maximize profit for their shareholders.

Stockton Fights Back

It's not always easy to define the spark that ignites local rebellion and transforms it into a national movement. In Stockton, the spark was the growing distrust between citizens and their local government. The Concerned Citizens Coalition of Stockton ("the coalition") had formed in 2001 to monitor and challenge what its members called Mayor Podesto's "political-control machine." For the next six years, fighting water privatization would become its defining cause.

The coalition was a congenial group of like-minded, mostly middle-class Stocktonians

"Fix it in your constitution that no corporation, no body of men, no capital can get possession and right to your waters. Hold the waters in the hands of the people."

–John Wesley Powell, 1890 North Dakota Constitutional Convention

that included locally based environmental groups, unions, churches, the NAACP, and police and firefighter organizations. It was chaired by Sylvia Kothe, a popular long-time leader of the local League of Women Voters whose grandparents were Christian missionaries in Brazil. She prided herself on her honesty and on the coalition's commitment to taking the "high road" in politics.

Many coalition members were Stockton natives who felt they were defending American ideals of citizenship and democracy. "I'm *not* a community activist," said orthodontist Dale Stocking. "I'm an involved *citizen.*" Others in the group included a stock analyst, a barista, the owner of a party store, an engineer, and several employees of the city's water department, including Michael McDonald, the head of maintenance at the sewer plant. The coalition also received support from Public Citizen, the national consumer group, which later spun off its water division to create a separate organization: Food and Water Watch.

The citizens' coalition was unified by the conviction that Mayor Podesto was out to railroad the privatization plan through the city council without a thorough public hearing and a citywide vote. Members had a visceral sense that democracy itself was being hijacked by the mayor's machinations, and their research showed that the award-winning utility could be fixed without privatization.

One of the coalition's overriding concerns was transparency. In public systems, major decisions must be made in public so that citizens can be involved at every stage. Getting information from—much less auditing—a private company based in another state or another country is much more difficult, if not impossible.

For Podesto, coalition members and their ilk were classic meddlers. He publicly dismissed them as "the butcher, the baker, and the candlestick maker."

"They want to write the contract," he complained. "If you want to be in that position, run for city council and sit up here."

Coalition members tenaciously confronted Mayor Podesto and his allies at every step. When it appeared the mayor still wouldn't listen, they gathered 18,000 signatures to put an initiative on the ballot to require a citywide vote before privatization could take place.

For their part, OMI and Thames also had a lot at stake. If they could succeed in Stockton, they had big plans, "We look forward to working with each other throughout the globe," said OMI president Don Evans. The companies would also be well-placed to influence water and development issues affecting California's 35 million people and the world's fifth-largest economy.

The Long Fight

Increasingly embattled, Mayor Podesto recognized that the coalition's initiative to require a citywide vote was a poison pill for privatization. He wasn't about to be outmaneuvered. In early 2003, less than two weeks before the initiative went to the voters, he put the proposed OMI/ Thames contract on the city council agenda in an effort to derail the coalition.

Hundreds of people came out to protest the mayor's city council vote that would preempt the upcoming voters' decision. They jammed the wide neoclassical colonnade of city hall, union members from the sewage treatment plant leading the way.

As the meeting began, the crowd poured inside city hall, overflowing the council chambers into the hallway and filling the downstairs lobby. Inside the chambers, speakers, the vast majority of them against privatization, addressed the council for two electrifying hours.

The details of the privatization deal itself had become secondary. Everyone at this meeting was debating the rights of citizens, the value of the ballot, the meaning of representative democracy, and the human right to water. Coalition chair Sylvia Kothe voiced the crux of the coalition's objections to Podesto's authoritarian style. "It is clear that the decision to privatize has been made covertly without a public vote."

OMI president Don Evans responded to those fears, "You have the absolute commitment of our company, and you have the commitment of Thames Water to deliver this contract effectively," he told the council, concluding that this was not just the promise of a faceless corporation "but my personal commitment to you."

The city council was deeply divided, but old hands were certain that Mayor Podesto would not have called the meeting if he didn't have the votes. In the end, it was Podesto himself who cast the deciding vote in a 4 to 3 decision to approve the contract.

Michael McDonald, an African American whose mother had been a civil rights activist, took the vote as a personal blow. "People have fought and died for the right to vote on these issues," he said, "And I for one will never give up my right to vote." He predicted that the companies would abandon Stockton within five years once they had completed the most profitable construction parts of the contract.

Days later, Stocktonians voted overwhelmingly to approve the coalition's initiative, but their votes had been made moot by the earlier city council action. The initiative was not retroactive.

The coalition responded with a guerilla campaign against the privatization on two fronts. The city council resolution to approve the contract had included a unilateral declaration to exempt the decision from a California law requiring environmental-impact reports on major water projects. The coalition's lawyers believed the exemption was illegal. Joined by the Sierra Club and League of Women Voters, they filed suit to stop privatization.

Coalition members also decided to go back to the voters, gathering signatures once again, this time for a citywide referendum to overturn the city council decision. They had just 30 days to collect 10,000 signatures, a huge challenge for people with families, full-time jobs, and small businesses.

OMI and RWE/Thames also mobilized, showing how multinationals' financial, legal, lobbying, and public relations muscle can torque a local political process. The two companies gave the antireferendum campaign $60,000, an enormous sum for Stockton.

Meanwhile, the coalition's Sunday morning pancake-breakfast fund-raisers barely made a dent in underwriting the coalition's legal and initiative campaign costs. Everything rode on getting the needed signatures, but volunteer efforts dwindled dangerously. With the campaign in jeopardy, a no-nonsense aide to the local state assemblywoman brought in professional signature gatherers to increase the total. They helped bring the number of signatures above the required ten thousand, but not by much.

A few days later, a headline in the *Stockton Record* said it all: "Privatization Foes Dealt Setback." The signature-gathering effort was shy by just a few hundred signatures. There would be no referendum.

With that threat out of the way, Podesto and OMI/Thames moved quickly to implement the contract. On July 31, 2003, water department employees turned in their city badges for ones with the OMI/Thames logo. Veteran sewage plant supervisor Michael McDonald was not among them. All along he had promised he would never work for a private company. On his last day, his coworkers held a going-away barbeque in his honor. Grown men and women wept as they hugged him goodbye. Thus began the turnover of experienced staff that characterizes so many private takeovers.

Meanwhile, the coalition's legal challenge went before superior court judge Robert McNatt, whose record indicated that it would be a hard sell. However, in October 2003, McNatt shocked observers by throwing out privatization and giving the city 180 days to unravel the deal. McNatt wrote that the city's unilateral self-exemption from environmental law was "an abuse of discretion" and added, "Common sense dictates that methods of operation will differ between a government and the private sector based on (at a minimum) the profit motive…There will always be situations in which profits versus environment considerations will militate a decision [which] negatively impacts the public."

The city and OMI/Thames announced they would appeal. The coalition had won, but it was to be only the first round of a long and costly odyssey through the courts. Every month that passed allowed OMI/Thames to tighten its control of the water department. "I never thought we'd be in court this long," said coalition activist Stocking more than two years later.

Keeping the Pressure On

The coalition didn't leave the battle solely up to its lawyers. Each year of private control, the group issued damning report cards on OMI/Thames' performance. Written by coalition members Bill and Susan Loyko and Dale Stocking, the reports were signed "BBC Consultants"—

WE NEED A FEDERAL TRUST FUND FOR CLEAN WATER

The United States has a public trust fund for highways, for harbor maintenance, for cleaning up oil spills, for botanical gardens, and for restoring wildlife habitat. We need one for water. Here's some reasons why:

- The majority of states are facing current and projected wastewater infrastructure needs far out of line with available funding. California faces the worst deficit, with five-year projected needs of $10.5 billion, 210 times its projected 2008 federal funding.

- Federal support for state and community wastewater projects through the Clean Water State Revolving Fund has declined from a high of approximately $2 billion in 1991 to slightly more than $1 billion in 2007—a 66 percent drop when adjusted for inflation.

- As a proportion of overall wastewater infrastructure spending, federal support accounted for 78 percent of funding in 1978 but makes up just 3 percent today.

- Combined sewer overflows from failing and insufficient infrastructure wreak environmental havoc on a massive scale: between 23,000 and 75,000 occur each year, spilling out 1.26

trillion gallons of untreated sewage and incurring $50.6 billion in cleanup costs.

- Nearly half of all evaluated waterways did not meet federal water quality standards in the most recently released EPA assessment.

- An overwhelming 83 percent of Americans would support legislation to create a clean water trust fund to keep the clean water they see as a right for future generations.

Find out more by visiting www.foodandwaterwatch.org/water/trust-fund

an inside joke, "BBC" standing for butcher, baker, and candlestick maker.

The reports were in-depth, technical, and damning. Mayor Podesto had claimed that rates would rise only 7 percent over the 20-year life of the contract, but the coalition analysis showed an 8.5 percent increase in just the first three years. In addition, leakage doubled, maintenance backlogs skyrocketed, and staff turnover was constant, even on the management level, where there were two general managers and four operations managers in the first two years.

Some residents of Stockton also noticed a difference when they sniffed the air. Michael McDonald's mother lived not far from the sewage plant, and she and her neighbors complained about increasing olfactory offenses. Workers at the plant told McDonald that OMI/Thames cut back on odor-control chemicals to save approximately $40,000 a month.

Although that is the most odoriferous example of OMI/Thames' management style, it was hardly the most serious. On the Friday before a hot summer weekend in 2006, the wastewater-treatment plant spilled eight million gallons of sewage into the San Joaquin River, contaminating a mile-long stretch where people go swimming. It took 10 hours for managers to notice the problem and another three days to notify the public about the health danger. The city and the company blamed one another for the delay, a confusion of authority not unusual in public-private partnerships.

But the most serious problem detailed in the coalition report cards was that OMI/Thames was saving money by not doing preventive maintenance. OMI/Thames general manager Gary

Opposite page: Protesters, including "Water Consciousness" contributors Wenonah Hauter, Tony Clarke, and Maude Barlow, from "Water for the People Network" hold bottles containing coins during a rally to stop the privatization of water during the World Trade Organization (WTO) Ministerial Conferences at Hong Kong in 2005. Above: Michael McDonald, the head of maintenance at the Stockton sewer plant, attends a coalition organizing meeting.

Nuss acknowledged the policy when he told city officials, "Permission is not required from the city should OMI/Thames choose to operate a piece of equipment in a run-to-fail mode." Independent investigators also confirmed complaints about the lack of transparency, concluding that it was difficult to assess the condition of equipment because "maintenance records are incomplete."

The maintenance failures even threatened the entire operation at the sewage treatment plant. In particular, OMI/Thames failed to maintain the grit system, which removes equipment-damaging sand from the sewage as it enters the treatment plant.

Even the construction projects–supposedly the biggest cost-saving from privatization–were called into question with reports of leaks in one system and delays in bringing major projects online.

"What struck us," said Bill Loyko, "was the fact that everything we said they were doing wrong, they *were* doing wrong. It's scary that common people could figure that out and the city couldn't."

Tenacity's Reward

In the end, Gary Podesto made good on his dream to bring minor league baseball to downtown Stockton. However, a scathing grand jury report condemned large cost overruns on

Alan Snitow and Deborah Kaufman

the stadium project, and in another report titled *Pillaging the Public Trust*, a former city finance commissioner concluded the city had inappropriately drained $36 million from water and sewer accounts to pay for the mayor's dream.

Forced to retire because of term limits, Podesto ran for the state senate in 2004. Republican governor Arnold Schwarzenegger made his election a top priority, and the $10 million battle became the most expensive state legislative race in U.S. history. During the campaign, Podesto's opponent, a critic of privatization, reminded voters of Podesto's maneuvers to prevent a public vote on the issue. In the end, people clearly had had enough of Podesto's high-handed style. He lost not only the campaign, but he failed to win a majority even in his own county.

In late 2006, the courts finally reaffirmed the coalition's position that the city had violated California environmental law, and in the spring of 2007, Stockton's new city council–dissatisfied with OMI/Thames' performance–voted not to appeal. The city and OMI/Thames agreed not to criticize one another in public–a "nondisparagement" clause–and set March 1, 2008, for Stockton to resume full control of its water system. It turned out to be an exact fulfillment of Michael McDonald's prediction that OMI/Thames would

"The concept of democracy itself is being challenged by multinational corporations that see Americans not as citizens, but merely as customers. They don't see government as something of, by, and for the people, but as a market for profit."

abandon ship once profitable construction projects were completed.

Coalition activist Dale Stocking put it bluntly: "This is another nail in the concept that the private industry model is better than the public model in delivering essential services." At a celebratory dinner, members of the victorious Concerned Citizens Coalition toasted each other and vowed to remain guardians of water as a public trust.

Nevertheless, the city faced all kinds of problems taking back its water system from the private consortium. The water department remained understaffed with a huge backlog of maintenance. Some of the construction projects were of questionable quality, and McDonald estimated it would take millions of dollars to fix the system. Where would the money come from?

In December, 2007, coalition chair Sylvia Kothe and Wenonah Hauter of Food and Water Watch wrote an op-ed in the *Stockton Record* calling upon Congress to end the beggaring of local water infrastructure. They proposed the creation of a federal trust fund specifically for water services. Such dedicated revenue streams already exist for highways and airports, and polls indicate enormous bipartisan public support for the idea. Republican pollster Frank Luntz told a House subcommittee that 86 percent of the people he polled support a water trust fund. "I have been a professional pollster for almost twenty years," Luntz testified, "and I can tell you from personal experience that such an overwhelming consensus about the role of Washington does not happen often–but it exists here."

There is one more ironic twist in the Stockton water war, a twist that reveals how water battles can suddenly change the political landscape and create new alliances. Gary Podesto's successor as mayor was apparently so fed up by the water privatization experience that just days before the March 1 takeback deadline, he made a radical proposal of his own. He called for the city to take over its electric power utility from the private Pacific Gas and Electric Company. That probably won't happen soon, but public power may some day join public water as the anchors of Stockton's future.

Reverberations

The events in Stockton were followed by activists around the country and quickly reverberated throughout the private water industry as well.

RWE/Thames cited growing "public resistance to privatization schemes" in its decision to get out of the water business. In leaked minutes of a company executive board meeting in Essen, Germany, then CEO Henry Roels complained that the water business required too much long-term investment in plant and equipment and offered little hope of the quick profits once anticipated. He concluded that his earlier belief that privatization would quintuple in the United States by 2010 was wrong and "there could no longer be any talk of globalization of the water market."

But there was an ominous note in the RWE minutes. An unidentified board member cited a Goldman Sachs prediction that the "water business would become the oil business of the decade from 2020 to 2030." And Roels predicted that pension funds and global financial institutions would soon take up the promise of making a bundle from water privatization.

And so, a new stage of water privatization wars beckons as Goldman Sachs, Macquarie Bank, huge pension funds, and billionaire investors hop on the infrastructure bandwagon. And indeed, RWE sold London's Thames Water to Macquarie in 2006 and still hopes to spin off its U.S. water division in spite of growing citizen demands for local control.

The battle against water privatization is morphing once again. This time, the players looking to take over local water supplies will be the largest and most powerful financial institutions the world has ever known. But they will be squaring off against local groups that have now coalesced into a national movement for a democratic and sustainable water future. The unanswered question is whether these 21st century water wars are merely a last stand against an inevitable corporatized future, or the beginnings of a far-reaching revolt to reclaim citizenship, reassert democracy, and redefine how we interact with our environment.

Alan Snitow and Deborah Kaufman

Chapter 5

THINKING OUTSIDE THE BOTTLE

By Kelle Louaillier

Bart Sipriano lived on his own land—a modest ranch at the end of a dead-end road in East Texas. City water pipes didn't make their way out that far, but Sipriano had his own source—a 100-year-old well that provided all the water he and his wife needed for drinking, cleaning, and cooking.

At least that's how it used to be.

Four days after Nestlé began its pumping operation for an Ozarka brand bottled water plant next door, Sipriano awoke to an unwelcome surprise: there was nothing but a drip when he turned on the faucet. Later, peering down his well shaft, he found that his well had been sucked dry.

"I'd been here 20 years, and I never had any problems until Ozarka came out here," he told a reporter with the *Dallas Observer*.

Sipriano sued Nestlé to restore his well, but the Texas State Supreme court ruled in the corporation's favor, thanks in part to Texas' industry-friendly water laws.[1]

Today, Sipriano is one of the thousands whose livelihood has been upset by the recent bottled water boom that has targeted rural communities'

Workers stock shelves with bottled water in Sydney.

spring water, profited from municipal tap water, and launched ad campaigns that have undermined people's trust in public water systems.

But his actions challenging the corporate control of water 10 years ago have been a wake-up call for communities across the country. Now there are more resources for communities hoping to fight privatization as citizen groups are banning together, telling their stories, and sharing information. Groups in Michigan, Maine, California, and elsewhere are also linking up with national and international nonprofits to help fend off multinational corporations.

Thirty years ago, few could have foreseen the rapid growth of this boutique industry into a $100 billion international juggernaut[2] that is threatening public control over humanity's most vital resource. As in much of the industrialized world, strong public water systems have been a cornerstone of national prosperity in the United States. These systems have generally been managed by local governments that are accountable to the public through the democratic process. This has helped assure access to safe and healthy drinking water for almost all Americans regardless of their means.[3]

It was unthinkable just three decades ago that a person would pay a $1.50 for what they could have free at a water fountain or for virtually nothing at the tap. Drinking water, simply, was a public trust and a basic human right.

But, as Sipriano's experience exemplifies, times have changed.

Today the bottled water industry is a $15 billion business in the United States alone[4] and its growth has come at a significant environmental and social cost. Currently, three out of four Americans drink bottled water, and one out of five Americans drink only bottled water.[5]

The growth of the market has come at the expense of communities from California to Texas to Maine.[6] It has also come at a great expense to the public's confidence in municipal water supplies, which continue to be highly reliable and more regulated than bottled water.

As the bottled water industry has grown, the political will to adequately fund public water systems has diminished. The gap between what these systems need and the capital available to them is more than $22 billion and growing.[7] And perhaps the biggest challenge to public water systems has been the fact that cities are now spending millions in taxpayer dollars on contracts with bottled water corporations for a resource that they could provide themselves in a more economically and environmentally friendly manner.[8]

The industry has achieved significant inroads, but it hasn't been easy.

Jeff Caso, a former senior vice president with Nestlé, was quoted in *AdAge* in 2003 as saying, "We sell water…so we have to be clever."[9] But, in reality, the industry needs to be not just clever, but well-endowed. It has taken tens of millions of dollars in flashy advertising to open up the market.[10] And to create this market, the industry's largest players, Nestlé, Coke, and Pepsi needed to imply, somehow, that their product was better than what you could get from the tap.

So far, their ad money has paid off. A recent survey in Philadelphia found that 20 percent of residents refuse to drink tap water, even though there doesn't appear to be any problem with the water itself. The water department has had no health-based violations in at least 10 years.[11] In a Conference of Mayors taste test, the water even ranked 12th among 93 cities.[12]

Unfortunately, attitudes like those in Philadelphia are all too common.

But, the tide is turning. Transnationals may have money to spend on advertising, but they underestimated the lengths that communities will go to in order to keep their water under public control. They also didn't bank on a huge public outcry in response to the truths about bottled water.

With a combination of education and advocacy, consumers are pulling back the curtain on the bottled water industry. A diverse coalition of public officials, restaurants, faith communities, student groups, and national organizations are "thinking outside the bottle" in an effort to preserve our common values about water for the benefit of generations to come.

More cities and states are moving to limit bottled water waste and require better labeling, and are canceling contracts with bottled water distributors. These actions are happening in large part because of a rapidly growing national movement to opt for tap over bottled water.[13]

But even as public pressure grows, bottled water industry executives are pushing back. In an effort to ensure business growth, they are engineering new niche markets such as infused water and vigorously attaching their products to environmental and social causes in "bluewashing" efforts that are as transparent as the water they are pushing.[14]

And most importantly, in order to keep the profits rolling in, they need access to as much

WHICH COUNTRIES ARE LEADERS IN THE GLOBAL BOTTLED WATER MARKET?

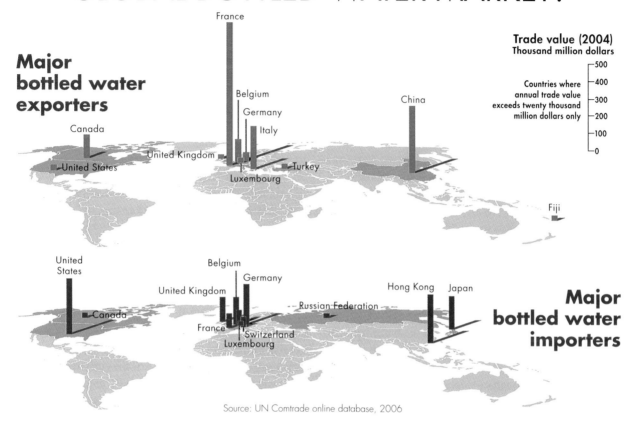

Source: UN Comtrade online database, 2006

cheap water as possible. They have two tactics: target rural communities to mine their spring water and use public water systems. The first tactic is the one that Nestlé has worked hard to perfect.

Nestlé: Mining Rural America

In the decade since Nestlé moved in next door to Bart Sipriano, the transnational has built or proposed spring sites or bottling plants in dozens more rural communities across North America, making the corporation the largest water bottler on the continent.[15]

While Nestlé is the largest player in the industry, it is by no means alone. Hundreds of corporations, large and small, are moving to control water formerly held in the public trust.

Why the current rush to profit from water?

Well, for one, water is being given to these corporations practically free, allowing for quick returns and enormous profit margins. The giveaway is caused by a host of problems, from outdated lawmaking (that could not have foreseen the commodification of water) to good old-fashioned backroom politicking.

Nowhere is this more apparent than in the current struggle between the citizens of McCloud, California, and Nestlé.

The economically rebounding former logging town is nestled in the foothills of the Cascades in the shadow of Mount Shasta. The poet Joaquin Miller once described the peak that marks McCloud's place on the map as, "Lonely as God, and white as a winter moon."

What better an image to put on the label of a water bottle? That's what Danone, Coke, and other bottlers must have thought.

Three plants have been built around Mount Shasta since 1990, but it was not until 2003 that Nestlé's designs on the McCloud watershed began to take shape. At a public meeting that year, the board governing McCloud's water services approved a 50-year deal under which the corporation agreed to pay the city between $300,000 and $400,000 a year to house a million-square-foot bottling facility.[16]

A sweet deal for a town on the mend, right?

Locals didn't think so. The contract had been negotiated behind closed doors with the local water utility and made available to the public just days before the meetings. Requests for longer public review and debate were denied.[17]

What's more, it was revealed that the agreement had the corporation paying just 1/64 of a cent per gallon, which they would then resell at an average price of more than $1 per gallon. The agreement was set to lock in these bargain prices for the next 50 years, with an automatic 50-year extension.[18]

All of a sudden the math wasn't adding up for residents. They knew that the plan meant a significant impact on health, safety, and local traffic flow, with an estimated 200 to 300 diesel trucks servicing the plant per day.[19]

Judging from the experience of nearby communities, they also could not count on the plant to provide needed jobs. While Nestlé promised 240 new jobs, locals knew better. Other area plants had employed far fewer laborers and had tended to hire out-of-town help.[20]

To add salt to the wound, Nestlé had not even bothered to perform a required environmental review. Citizen groups raised a series of concerns about potential habitat destruction, a decline in the water levels of lakes and streams, and depletion of groundwater wells.[21]

As one citizen group put it, "Nestlé Waters North America has a documented history of draining and letting the community ask questions later."[22]

Locals began bracing for the inevitability of this outcome, believing their town officials had been manipulated and rushed into approving an unfavorable contract before the public had the chance to weigh in.

Nestlé's public relations shop conceded to the *Sacramento News and Review* that the corporation had already put $1.5 million into sealing the deal, with an undisclosed chunk of that going to PR and lobbying.[23]

"People need to wake up and see the contract doesn't give them anything," said Sid Johnson, a ranch caretaker and McCloud resident. "We've got a foreign corporation coming in to buy our water supply for peanuts."[24]

Another local group, Concerned McCloud Citizens, has taken the corporation to court and is continuing to fight the proposal. Their efforts may be paying off. In the spring of 2008, Nestlé announced it was drastically scaling back its plans for the bottling plant and would review its contract with the town.

If the demand for bottled water continues to grow at the current rate, Nestlé and others will likely need to find many more water sources like

McCloud in the coming decades. And if history is any indication, they will look first to regions that are struggling economically and are politically vulnerable.

As is the case with so many extractive industries, the bulk of the profits will be made elsewhere, while local communities are left to deal with the externalized costs. For some, like those in McCloud, it is still possible to prevent a potentially devastating corporate water grab. For others, like Sipriano, the damage has already been done.

Coke and Pepsi Take On the Tap

While Nestlé has focused on mining rural water sources, Pepsi and Coke have taken a different approach. In the early 1980s, Pepsi developed a clever marketing device to challenge Coke's share of the soft drink market—a blind taste test called the Pepsi Challenge.[25]

Twenty years later the two leaders of the soft drink market are still squaring off—this time over their bottled water brands Dasani (Coke) and Aquafina (Pepsi). And just as each is working to corner the growing market, consumers are poking holes in the advertising used to make these brands the most popular bottled water in North America.

Stealing a page from the Pepsi Challenge, consumers across the country have been setting up card tables, dixie cups, and blindfolds to perform their own Tap Water Challenges. Passersby take a sip of Dasani, Aquafina, and tap water, and are asked if they can tell the difference.

What is most surprising about the results is that for the amount each corporation spends talking about enhanced taste and special filtering, the majority of test participants can't tell the difference. Straw polls conducted by news organizations have found similar results. In a November 2007 poll by CBS News in Chicago, two-thirds of the participants preferred tap to the bottled brand names or couldn't tell which was which.[26]

One reason for this might be that up to 40 percent of bottled water, including Aquafina and Dasani, in fact comes from the same source as tap water[27]–the same source, interestingly enough, that these corporations have cast doubts upon in order to build a market for their brands.

In a 2007 poll conducted by the University of Arkansas, researchers found that young people were overwhelmingly choosing bottled water over tap water, because they felt it was somehow cleaner.[28] To figure out how such an impression was formed, one needs to look no further than bottled water labels.

In order to market water back to consumers at hundreds, even thousands, of times the cost,[29] Coke and Pepsi have attempted to differentiate their brands both from each other and good, old-fashioned tap water.

Dasani labels claim its "crisp, fresh taste" is a result of a "state-of-the-art purification system." It is labeled simply as "purified water," with no reference to its municipal source.[30]

Aquafina claims, "All bottled waters are not the same. Aquafina's state-of-the-art HydRO-7 purification system consistently removes substances most other bottled waters leave in."[31]

Like Dasani, Aquafina promises "purified drinking water" and the words "pure water" appear three times on its label.[32] Unlike Dasani, Aquafina employs an image of snow-capped peaks, suggesting the source may be somewhere other than a city's water system.

These marketing strategies seem like an indictment of public water. After all, why would consumers buy something for $1.50 when they could have virtually the same thing for next to nothing? What does the emphasis on "state-of-the-art purification" imply about the adequacy of tap water treatment? Why have these corporations been so reluctant to tell consumers that their product comes from city water systems?

Coke, for one, does not believe its marketing of bottled water is at all misleading and responds to consumer concerns about Dasani by stating, "Bottled water is not produced by our system to usurp the need for potable water in public water systems."[33]

But the marketing tells a different story.

These corporations offer minimal proof that all this "advanced" processing actually results in a product that is better than tap. Consumer groups have demanded they fully disclose the health and safety information of their products, but the corporations have refused.

Why?

Much of the answer may lie in how differently bottled and tap water are regulated. Both are evaluated using similar standards, but tap water is tested far more frequently and has more independent oversight by state and federal environmental authorities (like the U.S. Environmental Protection Agency and the Department of Environmental Protection). Lacking adequate capacity to regulate bottled water through the U.S. Food and Drug Administration, the government relies on bottled water corporations to police themselves,[34] which in some cases has resulted in bottled water contaminations that were concealed for weeks before the public was ever warned.[35]

Most importantly, public water systems are required to make health and safety information

TOP FIVE MYTHS ABOUT BOTTLED WATER

Myths	Realities
Bottling plants are beneficial for communities	• Groundwater levels have dropped by as much as 40 feet in Mehdiganj, India, home to a Coca-Cola bottling facility • In Gandhre, India, Coke has drawn water for its factory operations that could have otherwise served 75,000 villagers a day
Bottled water tastes better	• A November 2007 poll by CBS News in Chicago found that two-thirds of the participants preferred tap to the bottled brand names or couldn't tell which was which
Bottled water is inexpensive	• Bottled water costs hundreds or thousands of times more than tap water
Bottled water is cleaner and safer than tap water	• The Food and Drug Administration regulates only 30 to 40 percent of bottled water sold across state lines • Plastic bottles can leach chemicals into the water • A 1999 survey of more than 1,000 spring and publicly sourced bottled water brands found that some violated state standards on bacterial contamination, and others were found to contain harmful chemicals such as arsenic
Bottled water doesn't negatively impact the environment	• U.S. plastic bottle production requires more than 17 million barrels of oil, enough to fuel 1 million cars • About 86 percent of the empty plastic water bottles in the United States are not recycled

available to the public. Bottled water corporations are not, though you'd think it'd be in their interest to do so. Especially since their marketing relies on distinguishing what's in the bottle from what's in the tap.

Are these corporations hiding something about the quality of their water? Are they cutting corners when it comes to purification? Are they covering up for the fact that their product is no different and sometimes might be of lower quality than tap water.

There are reasons for consumers to be concerned. For example, in 2004 Coke was forced to recall more than half a million Dasani bottles in the United Kingdom after finding samples that contained higher than permitted levels of the chemical bromate. As it turns out, Coke's "state-of-the-art" purification systems can in fact cause this chemical to form.

In a 1999 survey of more than 1,000 spring and publicly sourced bottled water brands, the Natural Resources Defense Council came up with some disturbing results. While most brands were safe, some violated state standards on bacterial contamination, and others were found to contain harmful chemicals such as arsenic.[36]

These water safety lapses raise an even bigger question: Who are we allowing to control this essential resource and why?

In India, Coke has made immense profits at a tremendous human cost as a result of pumping groundwater to make everything from soda to Dasani.

Not far from the holiest of Hindu cities, along the Ganges River, is the village of Mehdiganj. And though water is the daily object of worship along this great Indian river, in this nearby village, it is a source of despair.[37]

Mehdiganj's latest neighbor is one of Coke's more than 60 bottling facilities in India,[38] and villagers are convinced that the plant is pulling water needed for irrigation, causing crops to suffer and wells to run dry.

"Water is central to our livelihood," Nandlal Master, a local schoolteacher told the *Atlanta Journal-Constitution*. "Water levels are down everywhere. We want Coke to go away."[39]

Coke dismisses community concerns, even as groundwater levels surrounding Mehdiganj have receded, in some cases by as much as 40 feet.[40] Coke's regional spokespeople point to agriculture and weather cycles as the problem for India's water woes. Coke has also effectively used the prospect of jobs and investment to pit those in desperate need of a paycheck against those who have seen their livelihoods dry up. In Mehdiganj, for example, unemployment is as high as 65 percent.[41]

But while Coke is finger-pointing and using economic misfortune to make its case for privatizing local water resources, communities like Mehdiganj are paying a dire long-term price.

Elsewhere in India, in Gandhre village, Coke has drawn water for its factory operations that could have otherwise served 75,000 villagers a day.[42] In Plachimada, Coke has extracted hundreds of thousands of gallons of clean water through electric pumps, resulting in the desiccation of hundreds of wells. Its actions have forced residents to travel great distances to access water in a country already strapped for water—the United Nations in 2005 ranked India 130 among 180 countries in terms of water availability.[43]

And when the news in the international press got ugly about Coke's practices, the "blue-washing" started. In February of 2005, Coke's vice president for environment and water resources gave remarks at the Global Water Futures Workshop at Sandia National Laboratory touting the corporation's new water conservation efforts.[44]

A tap water challenge taste test. In nation-wide tests, two-thirds of participants prefer tap to bottled water or can't tell the difference.

The following year, the World Water Forum was scheduled to convene in Mexico City. Since its inception, the forum had been a means for advancing global water policies favorable to transnational bottling and water services corporations, under the guise of high-minded and inclusive rhetoric about solving the looming water crisis. Involving United Nations agencies and industry-friendly NGOs, the forum had endeavored to position itself as the authoritative international gathering on water management and policy.[45]

Following in Nestlé's footsteps, Coke seized on the opportunity to become an event sponsor.

Protesters in the streets outside the forum were quick to point out just how inappropriate Coke's sponsorship was. In a forum supposedly aimed at addressing the world water crisis, the lead sponsor was responsible for using more than 283 billion liters of water a year and selling much of it for profit. It was like Exxon-Mobil sponsoring a global conference to examine the health effects of climate change.[46]

And if the forum's sponsorship didn't give Coke enough bang for its PR buck, in June 2007, Coke entered a partnership with another WWF—the World Wildlife Fund—to the tune of $20 million, to fund watershed protection programs in seven global watersheds.[47] For WWF such a partnership was nothing new. It had, in the past, taken money from tobacco corporations to fund its environmental causes. It also continues to

Kelle Louaillier

JOIN THE BOTTLED WATER BOYCOTT

Here's how to take part in the campaign against bottled water:

Individual Action

Thousands are visiting www.ThinkOutside TheBottle.org and related Web sites to educate themselves about the harm of bottled water, taking actions that include pledging to choose tap over bottled water. People are increasingly using reusable water bottles and cutting bottled water out of their personal budgets.

Community Action

Members of faith communities, student groups, local organizations, and social clubs are using resources from Think Outside the Bottle to organize workshops, pledge drives, and visibility events.

Source: Corporate Accountability International

Campus Action

Students are calling on administrators to cut spending on bottled water, get rid of bottled water vending machines, and fix drinking fountains.

City/Regional Action

Mayors and local officials from New York City to San Francisco are responding to community actions by halting city spending on bottled water, committing increased resources to city water systems, and/or launching citywide education efforts to restore confidence in the tap, such as Salt Lake City's Knock Out the Bottle campaign.

National Action

A groundswell is beginning that calls for a national commitment to better fund public water systems and to keep water resources under public control.

maintain a board with close ties to many of the world's most polluting industries. Such partnerships have allowed corporations like Coke to project a green public image while avoiding their obligation to directly address the problems they have created.

But no amount of public relations can change reality. The United Nations estimates that two-thirds of the world population, 5 billion people, will lack access to enough clean drinking water by 2025.[48]

Coke and its competitors sometimes argue that bottled water is the one source of clean, safe, and reliable drinking water for many communities in the developing world, where the global crisis is most rife. But wouldn't it be a better investment to build local public water systems that can stand the test of time than to ask locals to buy bottled water indefinitely?

U.S. Cities Join the Backlash

In 2003, California Assembly member Ellen Corbett (D-San Leandro) introduced a bill in the state legislature requiring bottled water to meet some of the same labeling and water quality standards as tap water.[49]

The bill garnered little media attention and invited the ire of a Nestlé subsidiary and a host of surrogates for major bottlers, namely the International Bottled Water Association.[50] It never made it to the governor's desk.

But by 2007, the public climate had shifted considerably. Assembly member Corbett's bill was signed into law by California's Republican governor, Arnold Schwarzenegger, with California's major papers favorably editorializing or covering its passage.[51]

At the signing ceremony, advocates reminisced about the bill's humble beginnings. "When we first introduced this bill in 2003, it was an uphill battle, and everyone said it was 'a solution in search of a problem,'" said Jennifer Clary of Clean Water Action. "No one was saying that this time."[52]

Earlier in the year, California also began a domino effect among national mayors. San Francisco's Gavin Newsom became one of the first prominent mayors to cancel a city's bottled water contracts. "All of this waste and pollution is generated by a product that by objective standards is often inferior to the quality of San Francisco's pristine tap water," Newsom wrote in a two-page executive order.[53]

In raw economic terms, San Francisco would save $500,000 a year after cutting its own bottled water contracts.

"There's no rational reason for people to buy it," Jared Blumenfeld, the city's environmental director, told the *San Francisco Chronicle*.[54] Only around 20 percent of plastic drinking bottles are recycled in the United States, and water bottles are among the 40 billion plastic bottles that end up in the waste stream each year, costing cities over $70 million to clean up.

But although Newsom's decision saved the city money and won praise from San Francisco's eco-minded voting public, the industry shills were quick to paint him as the villain. After appearing on NBC News to discuss his decision, one industry friendly blogger tagged Newsom an "anti-bottled water jihadist."[55] Newsom was unfazed and took his campaign one step further. Partnering with the progressive mayors of Salt Lake City and Minneapolis, he took the bottled water fight to the U.S. Conference of Mayors—a forum where bottlers like Coke are on the Business Council as dues-paying members[56]—and won.

Mayors Rocky Anderson of Salt Lake City, R.T. Rybak of Minneapolis, and Newsom got a resolution passed calling for renewed investment and support for public water systems.[57] The resolution also called for the U.S. Conference of Mayors to look at the impact of plastic water bottles on the municipal waste stream.[58]

The industry found itself on the defensive, struggling to address the new political will to challenge the bottled water industry. As more and more cities cancelled contracts and got behind the spirit of the mayors' resolution, the bottled water industry began testing out some new talking points.

The trade groups representing major bottlers also came up with a scheme to respond to the three mayors' concerns about plastic water bottle waste. They began trumpeting their dedication to recycling programs, but at the same time, these same trade associations were working across the country to oppose "bottle bills" that would have placed a small deposit on plastic bottles in order to help deal with the more than 4 billion pounds of plastic bottles that usually wind up in landfills.[59]

The players behind the industry's public relations machine were the American Beverage Association (Coke and Pepsi's voice in the media and halls of government) and the International Bottled Water Association (Nestlé's surrogate).

Undaunted, however, by these powerful industry trade groups, mayors sensed growing public support. Months after the U.S. Conference of Mayors passed its resolution, mayors nationwide took another step, pledging renewed support for public water systems and to opt for tap over bottled water.

Boston's mayor, Thomas Menino, took the lead by calling his city's water "Boston Ale" and committing to look into the city's spending on bottled water.[60]

Soon after, cities across the country began making similar commitments, with a valiant effort by the state government of Illinois to cancel all of its bottled water contracts.[61]

Think Outside the Bottle

From outward appearances, these actions by city governments may appear to come from the top down. But the fact is, for years citizen groups have been fighting for accountability from the bottled water industry and at last, the groundswell has begun.

Groups across the country, which were challenging Nestlé's abuses in their communities, began sharing stories and resources, and Coke's abuses in India gained the attention of activists across the world.

Corporate Accountability International and its members, student volunteers, and allies, including the Ottawa, Canada-based Polaris Institute, the Women's International League for Peace and Freedom, and the Alliance for Democracy, began talking to people about the dangers of bottled water at campuses and community forums across the country. The group's environmental and religious allies began outreach in churches, synagogues, and homes.

As the grassroots campaign blanketed the country, lead groups took their demands straight to the corporations. After just over a year of grassroots pressure and months of dialogue, Pepsi came around. In July of 2007, Pepsi announced that its Aquafina brand would spell out "public water source" on its labels. The news appeared on major television networks and newspapers.

It was a victory that could be credited to the power of grassroots action and education. But the success will also require a long-term commitment by thousands of dedicated citizens. In the coming months, Pepsi is expected to follow through on its commitments, but Coke still stubbornly refuses to answer to its consumers about Dasani's source—even to the potential detriment of its brand image.[62]

Continuing to take water "back" from the bottlers will be no small task. In the same way

Mount Shasta looms over a street in McCloud, California, where Nestlé hopes to mine water.

that water has been parceled out among bottlers, it can be reclaimed by communities and officials. With continued involvement in these efforts, we can stop water bottlers from targeting economically disadvantaged rural communities. And we can also fend off the attack in cities on our democratic control of what, only three decades ago, was considered a basic human right.

When we "think outside the bottle" we take on more than the bottled water industry—we help make sure water systems remain under public control and continue to serve and strengthen our communities for generations to come.

Community Groups Take on Nestlé

Defending Water for Life in Maine is a project of the Alliance for Democracy and is involved with the fight against a Poland Spring/Nestlé bottling plant in Fryeburg, Maine. Learn more about their work at DefendingWaterInMaine.org.

Michigan Citizens for Water Conservation is working to protect Michigan's water, including Mecosta County where they have been fighting Perrier/Nestlé since 2000. Learn more about their work at SaveMIWater.org.

McCloud Watershed Council in Northern California has been fighting the sale of its water to Nestlé in 2003. Learn more about their work at McCloudWatershedCouncil.org.

Chapter 6

AGRICULTURE'S BIG THIRST: HOW TO CHANGE THE WAY WE GROW OUR FOOD

By Wenonah Hauter

You know things have gotten bad when a reservoir that is used to quench the masses of Beijing instead yields corn stalks. On a recent trip to Beijing, as I was traveling north of the city to visit peasant farmers, I gazed out the window of the bus to glimpse the Miyun reservoir–a body of water that is a main source of drinking water for Beijing's 17 million residents. But instead of lapping waves on the shores, there were rows of corn. The water was gone.

Unfortunately, this may become a more common sight as the world's water runs short and we struggle to feed our growing numbers. Already agriculture drinks more than twice as much water as all other uses combined. Watering and washing by more than six billion people and all global industrial water consumption pale in comparison to watering crops and livestock.

What we eat and how our food is grown is key to our global water crisis. Your hamburger or cup of coffee or cotton shirt or salad all have a water footprint that is largely determined by an industrial agriculture model. But this model is one that we have the power to change, if we can harness the political will.

How the "Green Revolution" Began

Agricultural water use often is wasteful, and intensive agrochemical application and factory-farmed livestock only add to water pollution. It irrigates crops inefficiently because much of the water evaporates or runs off the land. It guzzles surface and underground water to satiate the thirst of millions of livestock animals crammed together into confined animal feeding operations and to refine corn and other crops into biofuels such as ethanol.

The industrial agriculture model also relies on a toxic cocktail of petroleum-based fertilizers, pesticides, and herbicides that run off the land and seep through the soil to pollute water above and below ground. Overall, industrial agriculture's use of water is a self-perpetuating cycle of overuse, waste, and pollution. Unfortunately, most of us are a part of that cycle, too.

Once industrial agriculture became entrenched in the United States and Europe, transnational agribusiness used its political power to promote it overseas. In the 1950s, the industrial

Irrigation in Tulelake, California. When the salmon population crashed a few years ago on the Klamath River in Northern California, many people blamed the farmers taking water for irrigation in the Upper Klamath Basin in places like Tulelake.

Wenonah Hauter

model of farming, including thirsty seed varieties and large irrigation projects, was exported to the developing world and became known as the "Green Revolution."

The water that farmers use, as well as the fertilizers and pesticides they apply, primarily benefits transnational agribusiness corporations that control commodity crop and animal farming. Most farmers employ these industrial agriculture techniques to bring enough crops to market to make a living. A handful of agribusinesses sell the seeds, buy the harvests, and slaughter the livestock. Farmers are essentially forced to use water-intensive and agrochemical-dependent methods to sell their farm products.

Too often, the blame is placed on farmers for driving this speeding train known as global industrial agriculture. This is not the case. Transnational agribusiness corporations run the show. Many U.S. farmers effectively have no choice but to grow huge quantities of commodity grain and oilseed crops, such as wheat, rice, corn, and soybeans, for human food, animal feed, and the production of biofuels on thousands of acres.

The farmers who lack the land, equipment, and other inputs that would allow them to remain viable by growing and raising a huge volume of crops and animals, or who don't live near enough to a city full of people with disposable income who will buy their niche grains, fruits, vegetables, and animal products directly, often have to get out of farming. The result is fewer farmers growing a limited variety of commodity crops on thousands of acres of depleted and dying soils amidst polluted watersheds.

The Irrigation Dilemma

Irrigating crops accounts for more than 65 to 70 percent of world water use.[1,2] The usual methods of flooding crops or sprinkling them from overhead wastefully deplete surface and underground water sources. Once on the fields, much of that water is lost to evaporation. Salt residues can build up to the point where high salinity levels degrade soil fertility.[3]

Every year, thirty trillion gallons of water irrigate U.S. cropland.[4] In the 18 U.S. states that are dependent on irrigation, about 70 percent of the stream and river water has been depleted.[5] And in the U.S. western and southern regions, about 60 percent of irrigation water is from surface sources. The rest comes from underground water, which rain replaces at less than a 0.1 percent annual rate.[6]

Corn, a major commodity crop that transnational agribusiness demands for use in livestock feed and food processing (think corn oil and high fructose corn syrup to sweeten soda), provides a snapshot of industrial agriculture's hoggish ways with water. In the United States, about 500,000 gallons of water are poured into the ground on each acre of corn annually.[7] That pencils out to about 75 gallons to get just one pound of corn, an unsustainable level of water use.

Virtual Water: Using Food to Export Peoples' Water

Most people think of water in its real, physical form. But the concept of "virtual water" also plays a role in agriculture's negative effects on the world water crisis. When a state or country imports a ton of wheat, corn, or other grain, it also effectively is importing the water from the place it was grown.

Some argue that it makes sense for a water-rich country to pour its water into food for export to drier places, but consumers might not fully appreciate that when their nation exports water-fed, water-rich crops, they effectively are just selling their water. Moreover, virtual water exporting countries might be water rich on the whole but not in the areas where the export crops are grown. For example, iceberg lettuce, which is 99 percent water, is grown in Arizona for distribution across the United States, which amounts to taking Arizona's scarce water reserves and sending them somewhere else.

Halfway around the world in Africa, the tragedy of the virtual water trade is in full swing. Save for various large lakes and rivers, Kenya does not have an abundance of water. Nonetheless, transnational horticultural conglomerates have taken advantage of the country's water-rich areas, such as Lake Naivasha and the Ngiro River, to grow flowers, strawberries, and other thirsty crops for export to the water-wealthy United Kingdom and other destinations in the European Union. Over decades, this industrial horticulture has diminished and, with the use of fertilizers and pesticides, polluted those limited water resources.

Factory Farm Faucets

But crops are not all that are sucking up copious amounts of water. So do factory farm livestock operations, also known as concentrated animal feeding operations (CAFOs), which cram together thousands or tens of thousands of hogs, chickens, or cows.

In 1950, some 2.1 million U.S. farmers sold hogs, averaging about 31 hogs per farm. By 1999, only 98,460 hog farms remained.[8] By 2004, this number had dwindled to 65,000.[9] Today's facilities now average thousands of hogs per operation and have spread throughout rural areas in the United States.

Thousands of animals crowded together in hot conditions drink a lot of water. One hog raised in factory farm conditions requires about five gallons of water daily.[10] Industrial dairies can use more than 150 gallons of water per cow per day.[11] Slaking the thirst of livestock raised in CAFOs is draining the water table in rural America. For example, crop production and animal factory farms are depleting the Ogallala aquifer, which provides water from America's High Plains to the Southwest, 160 percent faster than it can recharge, prompting analysts to predict that it will be spent in a few decades.[12]

In one county in eastern New Mexico, a state that relies heavily on the Ogallala, water levels have dropped more than 20 feet, due in large part to industrial dairy CAFOs. In 1999, before many large dairy CAFOs had even moved to the area, state officials estimated that concentrated pumping would deplete water from the most productive areas of the basin as early as 2010.[13] The 355,000 dairy cows in New Mexico could completely exhaust portions of this stressed aquifer in just a few years.[14]

Thirsty factory animal farms have expanded worldwide, into Central Europe, the former Soviet Union, Brazil, Mexico, India, China, and the Philippines. Industrial feedlots provide for 43 percent of the world's beef, and more than half of the world's pork and poultry comes from factory farms.[15]

Fertilizer, Manure, and Pesticide Pollution

While water drawn from wells and reservoirs to irrigate crops and water livestock depletes water resources, the agrochemical runoff and factory farm manure spills pollute downstream water supplies and aquifers. Agriculture is the leading pollution source for America's impaired rivers and lakes and a major cause of water impairment for the country's estuaries.[16]

Wenonah Hauter

Studies show that over the last 40 years, the use of synthetic fertilizer has increased by seven times. Most of the petrochemical-based fertilizers are composed of nitrogen and phosphorus. Often the fertilizers are overapplied, or the crops can't absorb all of the nitrogen, so the nutrients either run off the land or seep through the soil into water sources. Nitrogen pollution is considered to be one of the biggest sources of water pollution in lakes, rivers, and other surface waters.[17]

The excess nitrogen in the water can lead to a process called eutrophication, which causes algae and aquatic plants to grow out of control. The microbes that live on decomposing algae blooms also suck all the oxygen out of the water, resulting in the death of fish, shellfish, and other organisms. In the United States, there is a dead zone the size of New Jersey where the Mississippi River drains into the Gulf of Mexico. Much of this nitrogen pollution comes from upstream industrial commodity farms in the Dakotas, Kansas, Missouri, Iowa, and Illinois.[18] Other regions, like Vermont's Missisquoi National Wildlife Refuge and Maryland's Chesapeake Bay, have experienced similar problems.

Poultry, hog, and cattle factory farms spill millions of gallons of manure and other waste into waterways. The waste they produce cannot be properly managed, because it emits toxic chemicals that cause hazardous water and air pollution. People working in these animal factories or those living nearby often suffer from negative health effects.

One chicken farm in Maryland produces 2 million pounds of manure each year alone, which is as much as a city of 25,000 people.[19] This waste runs off into streams and rivers, polluting the watershed.

Industrialized hog production has a similar record. Over the course of the past two decades,

An aerial view of the irrigated region of the lower Murray-Darling river complex north of Adelaide, Australia. Irrigation turned this dry, desolate area into fertile farm country, although the Murray-Darling has been threatened by recent droughts.

hundreds of millions of gallons of swine manure and toxic chemicals from factory farm lagoons in North Carolina have spilled into waterways. The result has been contaminated drinking water, millions of dead fish, and damaged ecosystems that have still not recovered.

Additionally, public officials have been forced to close thousands of acres of fishing and recreational sites.

Dairy factories are also the source of major water pollution problems. They produce large amounts of liquid waste that ends up in local waterways. As dairies have become extremely large, they have started moving to the arid West, to states such as California, Texas, Idaho, and New Mexico, where the region's meager water resources are being polluted.

In addition to fertilizers and manure pollution, pesticides have contaminated surface and underground water in the United States and around the world. The 992 million pounds of pesticides used in U.S. farming have polluted most of the country's streams and rivers with carcinogenic chemicals.[20]

Pesticide residues also have contaminated America's underground water, which is the source of 50 percent of America's drinking water. Studies carried out since the 1970s have shown the presence of more than 139 different types of pesticide residue in groundwater, often in U.S. corn and soybean growing regions.[21]

And the problem has gone global, with nearly 5 billion pounds of pesticide used worldwide—pesticide use has increased 26-fold in the last 50 years.[22]

The Corn Ethanol Conundrum

Industrial agriculture is poised to gulp even more water as fields are converted into fueling stations to produce biofuel crops. Current technology relies on conventional commodity crops in the developed world, primarily corn and soybeans, and tropical energy crops in the developing world, mostly sugar cane and oil palm. These crops are refined into ethanol, which can be used to supplement or replace gasoline or diesel as a transportation fuel.

Rising energy prices and increased concern about global warming and the impact of fossil fuel consumption on the climate have created a buzz about ethanol from Manhattan investment houses in New York City to Manhattan, Kansas, coffee shops to plantations in the developing world. Everyone is eagerly pursuing the ethanol gold rush.

The basic building blocks of ethanol—the biofuel crop itself—rely on the same water-intensive agriculture as any crop grown for food or livestock feed. Cultivating corn for ethanol refinery uses industrial irrigation methods and depends upon the liberal application of herbicides and pesticides. This production contributes to polluted soil erosion that taints the potability of aquifers and eutrophication of waterways. But biofuel production multiplies the consumption of water beyond what would be used, wasted, and polluted for a food crop.

Ethanol refineries lubricate the metamorphosis of dry corn into transportation fuel with large gushers of water. It takes about four gallons of water to produce a single gallon of ethanol from corn.[23]

Wenonah Hauter

In 2007, there were 135 ethanol refineries producing 7.4 billion gallons of ethanol in the United States, mostly concentrated in the Midwest Corn Belt, which is already straining to fulfill current water demand by farmers, feedlots, factories, and families. Surging demand for biofuel stocks can also bring more land into agricultural production.

In the developed world, increased demand for agricultural acreage can bring less tenable and sustainable land into active crop production and create perverse incentives to eliminate land set aside for conservation, wildlife habitat, or open space.

In the developing world, the potential biofuel windfall encourages large agricultural landowners to bring even more land into production. Deforestation of virgin tropical forests has enabled the expansion of sugar cane plantations in Brazil and palm oil plantations in Southeast Asia. In Malaysia, the development of palm oil plantations has been responsible for 87 percent of deforestation between 1985 and 2000.[24] Eliminating environmental conservation lands in developed countries and clear-cutting tropical forests in developing countries only hastens agrochemical runoff and soil erosion, further squandering water resources and exacerbating ground and surface water pollution.

Exporting Unsustainable Agriculture to the Developing World

The industrial agriculture model that relied on high-input application of agrochemicals,

A field of mustard greens in the Three Parallel Rivers area of Yunnan, China.

monocropping, and the use of extensive irrigation that began in the United States was quickly exported to the developing world. The international financial institutions like the World Bank worked cooperatively with Western philanthropists to pressure and cajole governments, landowners, and farmers in the developing world to adopt the intensive, chemical-dependent agriculture model that had found a foothold in the American Midwest.

This model of agriculture, which became a major profit center for agribusiness, transformed the relationship many people had with the land, with their food, and with their water. Instead of providing sustenance for local families and communities, agriculture was driven to produce bulk commodities for export to large cities and to the international markets. Overreliance on industrial irrigation and application of agrochemicals has drained and polluted water resources in the developing world.

Today, agriculture consumes 85 percent of the water used in developing countries, primarily for irrigation.[25] Between the 1960s and 2000, irrigated farmland in the developing world doubled to 772,000 square miles.[26] Wasteful irrigation projects have exacerbated water scarcity in the developing world and overpumping has degraded agricultural land. These industrial agriculture techniques have increased water pollution, clogged drinking water reservoirs with silt, and contributed to deforestation and loss of biodiversity.[27]

The Green Revolution was the vehicle for exporting new technologies (primarily agrochemicals and new seed varieties) to the developing world. It began in 1943 with the Rockefeller Foundation sending scientists to Mexico to develop higher-yielding varieties of wheat, maize, and other crops, and expanded into pressuring the adoption of petrochemical fertilizers, pesticides,

and large-scale irrigation projects throughout the developing world.

The high-yield, water-hogging seed varieties replaced drought-resistant local crop varieties, such as millet, sorghum, chickpeas, lentils, and other pulses. This resulted in the drawdown of aquifers in water-scarce regions. By the 1980s and 1990s, agricultural projects in the developing world began to focus on building export capacity for commodities wealthy European and American consumers and agribusinesses found highly desirable. Cash crops were emphasized over food production—a major shift from the famine-fighting promises of the Green Revolution's earliest proponents.[28]

The demand for large-scale, intensive agriculture increased water consumption and in many tropical areas brought more land into production through deforestation. In Brazil, decades of deforestation to cultivate monoculture soybeans and to graze cattle has not only reduced water supplies but has reduced rainfall because of climate change. Paulo Moutinho, research coordinator for the Amazon Institute of Environmental Studies, has said that "deforestation could eventually change Brazil's—and Earth's—climate, reducing rainfall and the supply of water for irrigation."[29]

Harnessing the Political Will

We have the technical know-how to solve the problems caused by industrial agriculture, but the political will for solving these problems is missing. Earth-friendly solutions include agricultural practices such as recapturing water, low tillage techniques, use of drought-tolerant grain varieties, rotational cropping, and other new sustainable technologies.

For example, in Israel's Negev Desert, farmers are recycling irrigation water. This involves

Wenonah Hauter

A farmer sprays pesticides onto fruit trees in the Po Delta, Italy. Over seven tons of pesticides end up in the Po every year, affecting groundwater and contaminating hundreds of wells.

collecting water in a bath under the soil and then pumping it out into the field again. The practice allows farmers to save water and reduce their fertilizer use because the water is recycled.[30]

The low-tillage mantra is beginning to pick up steam in Asia. Farmers in India are moving to zero tillage and raised beds, which reduce soil depletion and erosion, save water charges, and allow for more cropping.

Around the world peasant farmers are leaving behind the water-guzzling hybrid grain varieties of the Green Revolution and returning to traditional, drought-tolerant grains, such as millet.

A recent study from the University of Michigan found that organic agriculture can produce more than enough food to feed the world: "In addition to equal or greater yields than conventional industrial agriculture, the authors found that those yields could be accomplished using existing quantities of organic fertilizers, without putting more farmland into production," they reported.[31] Less land in production, less irrigation, and fewer fertilizers and pesticides mean more water and cleaner, safer water.

Perhaps the best hope for sustainable agriculture in many parts of the world is agroecology, which emphasizes a food production system based on biodiversity and sustainability. Some experts view it as the next step beyond organic in environmentally friendly food production.

HOW WE CAN GROW FOOD SUSTAINABLY

Rebalance the agricultural market. The United States government should begin to actually enforce antitrust laws put in place in the early 1900s to protect farmers, workers, and all citizens against the monopolistic and oligopolistic power and vagaries of corporations.

Buy local to save water. Consumers should use their food purchases to address the water crisis. As much as possible, they should buy food products grown organically and locally (or regionally). Eating low on the food chain—less meat and dairy products—saves water.

Rethink U.S. agriculture policy. We need to completely revamp farm policy to put farmers, consumers, and the environment first—before the economic interest of agribusiness. Farm policy should encourage and reward local and sustainable agriculture.

Change the policies of the international finance institutions. It is time for a new model of development that puts feeding people first and relies on traditional agriculture practices that are appropriate for the local ecology. Programs promoted by the World Bank, the International Monetary Fund and other international aid agencies rely on high-yield varieties of crops requiring imported irrigation pumps, diesel, fertilizers, and pesticides that leads to wasted water and massive pollution.

Rethink international trade policy. International free trade agreements promote an unsustainable, export-oriented agricultural model that benefits agribusinesses while farmers, consumers, and the environment lose out. U.S. trade negotiators should abandon efforts to conclude the Doha Round agreement at the WTO, which would dramatically accelerate the devastating effects of industrialized agriculture.

Support the concept of food sovereignty. In February 2007, at an international gathering in Sélingué, Mali, called the Forum for Food Sovereignty, more than 500 delegates from 80 countries met to discuss how to create a sustainable global food system. The assembly's Declaration of Nyéléni lays out an agenda that addresses agriculture's role in causing the world water crisis and provides food security for people around the world.

There is hope that we can ensure a sustainable relationship between agriculture and water, but the change must come at multiple levels.

If we are to feed future generations, our long-term goal must be to create a food system based on sustainable, diversified family farms that are providing food locally and regionally.

We must do the political work that is necessary to create this vision for the future, or we will end up, like China, with thirsty fields of corn where there was once a water-rich lake. Change starts with us—with making the personal choices that help support local and regional food systems.

Wenonah Hauter

Chapter 7

THE AGE OF CONSEQUENCES: A SHORT HISTORY OF DAMS

by Jacques Leslie

By every standard, China's Three Gorges Dam is monumental. It is not just the world's largest dam, but by some measures the world's largest manmade structure, and the reservoir forming behind it will become the world's largest manmade creation.

It does not aspire to elegance: it juts rigidly across a bend in the Yangtze River like a provocation, an advertisement for the use of brute force to subdue nature. Yet it is on its way toward becoming an international embarrassment even before all its turbines are installed, probably in 2009. The dam has already broken records for its width (nearly one and a half miles across), reservoir size (nearly 400 miles long), hydropower capacity (a prodigious 18,200 megawatts), cost (between $25 billion and $40 billion), people it displaces (at least 1.6 million), and communities it floods (13 cities, 140 towns, 1,350 villages).

Three Gorges is no anomaly, for dams are the ultimate expression of the majestic, deluded spirit of the fading Industrial Age. They were constructed on a seductive, impossible premise–conquering nature–and, for a few generations at least, seemed to live up to expectations. Dam

A woman looks at dam construction on the Nam Ha near Luang Nam Tha, Laos. Built by the Chinese, the dam has almost never had enough water to generate any power.

builders oozed with civic pride, and a grateful public looked on dams as beneficent providers of electricity, irrigated water, and flood control. Now, however, the Age of Consequences has arrived, and it is becoming increasingly clear that dams' benefits are temporary, while the damage they inflict on societies and landscapes approaches permanence.

Take the environmental impacts. Though the Three Gorges reservoir is still 75 feet below its projected full capacity, the dam is already causing massive damage. First, the reservoir is turning into a cesspool. Hundreds of factories, mines, and waste dumps were inundated as the reservoir filled; now their effluents are combining with others from continuing dumping of untreated sewage into the Yangtze River to create a festering mire. Polluted river water surrounds upstream ports, and sewage is backing up into tributaries, causing toxic algae blooms.

The rising reservoir has also set off landslides in the notoriously unstable cliffs that border it. In March 2007, a group of hydraulic engineers and environmentalists reported that more than 4,700 landslides had already taken place and warned that their continuing threat requires preventive actions or evacuation of an additional thousand localities. Eight months later, the government acknowledged that it must relocate as

Jacques Leslie

many as 2 million or more people threatened by landslides.

The creation of the vast reservoir has even changed the local climate, increasing rainfall and fog and lowering temperatures.

The problems extend all the way down the Yangtze to its mouth and beyond. Saltwater has moved up the river as the flow of freshwater has declined, and tidal wetlands near the mouth are quickly deteriorating because the naturally silty river brings them less than half the amount of sediment than before the dam's construction. Within two months after the reservoir began to fill, scientists detected a massive decline in the plankton that forms the bottom of the food chain in the East China Sea. By one projection, fish catches in the East China Sea, one of the world's biggest fisheries, will decline by a million tons a year as a result.

An oceanographer at Florida State University has even predicted that the decrease in freshwater entering the Pacific Ocean because of dams on the Yangtze and Yellow Rivers will cause an increase in speed and temperature of ocean currents that "will most likely cause a warming of the atmosphere over Japan."

Compare these adverse consequences against the dam's presumed benefits. China has suffered grievously from floods, most recently in 1998, when a Yangtze flood killed 3,000 people

"Now, the Age of Consequences has arrived, and it is becoming increasingly clear that dams' benefits are temporary, while the damage they inflict on societies and landscapes approaches permanence."

and left 14 million people homeless, and Three Gorges is intended to provide the antidote in the form of flood control. Yet even in this respect it is likely to disappoint, for the reservoir's flood control capacity is only one twentieth of the annual flow of the Yangtze's upper reaches and thus will have little hope of warding off a huge spate.

More likely, the dam won't prevent downstream floods, while increasing upstream floods as sediment accumulates in the reservoir. Further, to maximize the dam's flood control potential, officials would have to keep the reservoir's water level low during the flood season, which would cut into hydropower production, the dam's other major benefit. At its peak, Three Gorges will meet nearly one ninth of China's electricity needs, but its production will gradually decline as the reservoir fills with sediment.

No matter what, Three Gorges' impact will be vast. And the same is true for dams across the globe. The world's biggest manmade structures, they exist on more than 60 percent of the world's 200-plus major river systems, and their reservoirs collectively blot out a terrain larger than California. They have shifted so much weight that geophysicists believe they've slightly altered the speed of the earth's rotation, the tilt of its axis, and the shape of its gravitational field.

Dams are so plentiful that merely counting them accurately has proved impossible. It is believed that the world possesses between 50,000 and 54,000 large dams, but even the higher figure may underestimate China's contribution, currently pegged at the already-astounding number of 22,000. For smaller dams, the numbers descend into guesswork. In the United States, for example, an inventory managed by the Army Corps of Engineers places the total of significant dams at 79,777, while the sum of dams compiled by individual states—with varying criteria for included dams, ranging in height minimums from 20 to 35 feet—amounts to more than 99,000. Even that figure is probably low, since it includes suspiciously small counts from several states. In addition, state officials are constantly discovering previously uncounted dams during routine inspection trips. And if the definition of dams is broadened to include the smallest ones, the estimates run as high as several million.

From the inception of the modern dam era, ushered in by Hoover Dam in 1935, advocates viewed dams as passkeys to the modern world. When the Bonneville Power Administration hired Woody Guthrie to produce musical celebrations of dams' contributions to society, he responded with 26 songs. One of them, "Roll On, Columbia," so epitomized conventional beliefs about dams that in 1987 the Washington state legislature named it the "state folk song":

> *...Your power is turning our darkness to dawn*
> *So roll on, Columbia, roll on....*
> *And on up the river is Grand Coulee Dam*
> *The mightiest thing ever built by a man*
> *To run the great factories and water the land*
> *So roll on, Columbia, roll on.*

True enough, energy from Hoover, Grand Coulee, and other early hydroelectric dams transformed the American West, enabling the growth of such cities as Los Angeles, San Diego, and Phoenix, and facilitating the Allied victory in World War II by powering the factories that built American warplanes and ships. Even now, dams' turbines generate one fifth of the world's electricity supply, and the water they store makes possible as much as a sixth of the earth's food production.

It took decades before the realization set in that this bounty was accompanied by a vast ar-

Impacts of dams

DOWNSTREAM IMPACTS
disrupts water and sediment flow; reduces biodiversity; causes suffering in communities from poor water quality, lower crop production, and decreased fish populations.

DAM
blocks fish migration; disrupts water and sediment flow; poses safety hazard as structures age.

RESERVOIR
displaces communities; floods and fragments ecosystems; increases water-born diseases; triggers earthquakes.

ROTTING VEGETATION
releases greenhouse gases contributing to global warming; degrades water quality.

ray of unintended consequences. Only then did the wisdom of environmentalist Aldo Leopold, writing presciently in 1933, gain traction: "We build storage reservoirs or power dams to store water, and mortgage our irrigated valleys and our industries to pay for them, but every year they store a little less water and a little more mud. Reclamation, which should be for all time, thus becomes in part the source of a merely temporary prosperity."

The prosperity has long been evident, but so, increasingly, is its transience, for dams have lifetimes as surely as any natural thing. On average, the sediment trapped in reservoirs reduces their storage capacity by 1 percent a year, and has filled more than half the capacity of some reservoirs within a decade. In China, where most soil erodes easily, the reservoirs fill up at a rate of 2.3 percent a year. One dam on the silty Yellow River, the Yangouxia, lost almost one third of its storage capacity even before it began operating.

The breadth of damage that dams inflict is stunning. A study of a single dam in the tiny southern African country of Lesotho identified 20,000 environmental consequences as a result of altering its river's flow. Dams fragment the riverine ecosystem, isolating upstream and downstream animal populations, and, by preventing all but the largest floods, cut off the river from its floodplain. As a result, animals victimized by

---

FACT

A study of a single dam in the tiny southern African country of Lesotho identified 20,000 environmental consequences as a result of altering its river's flow.

---

dams include not just the river's native fish, but a broad range that relies on a watered floodplain as far from the river as several miles.

Reservoirs change river temperatures dramatically. Deep reservoir water is usually colder in summer and warmer in winter than river water, while surface reservoir water is warmer throughout the year. For 240 miles below Glen Canyon Dam on the Colorado, the water is too cold for native fish to reproduce. Thanks to the introduction of better adapted non-native fish, in little more than half a century, a foreign fish population has essentially replaced the Colorado's native one.

A reservoir traps not just sediment but nutrients. Algae thrive on the nutrients, and end up consuming the reservoir's oxygen. The water turns acidic, which makes it more erosive. It emerges from the dam "hungry," more energetic after shedding its sediment load, ready to capture new sediment from the river bed and bank. As it scours the downstream river, the bed deepens, losing its gravel habitats for spawning fish and the tiny invertebrates they feed on.

Within nine years after Hoover Dam was sealed, hungry water took 89,000 acre feet of material from the first 87-mile stretch of downstream riverbed. In some places, the riverbed dropped by more than thirteen feet and sometimes took floodplain water tables down with it.

"A dammed river," Wallace Stegner wrote, "is not only stoppered like a bathtub, but it is turned on and off like a tap." Instead of varying with snowmelt and rainfall, its flow is regulated to meet the requirements of power generation and human recreation. Most fluctuations reflect electricity demand: the river level changes hour by hour, and is lower on Sundays and holidays. These quick shifts intensify erosion, eventually washing away river-bank trees, shrubs, and grasses as well as riverine nesting areas. Riverside

Construction of the Three Gorges Dam in China. The project has been plagued by corruption, technological problems, human rights violations, resettlement difficulties, and profound environmental impacts.

creatures lose needed food and shelter.

In many areas, water piped from reservoirs slowly poisons the land with salt. Salinity has affected one fifth of the world's agricultural land; each year it forces farmers to abandon one million hectares and becomes a factor on an additional two million hectares. Even using high-quality water, a farmer applying the unremarkable sum of 10,000 tons of water a year to a single hectare strews two to five tons of salt across that plot. It's precisely the process by which ancient Mesopotamia turned into the barren desert of contemporary southern Iraq. Salt problems are severe in China, India, Pakistan, Central Asia, and the Colorado River basin and San Joaquin Valley of the American West. Human use of the Colorado has approximately doubled its salinity, resulting in the death of aquatic organisms in the lower river and corroded pipes in Los Angeles, San Diego, and Phoenix.

The changes in the water's composition are registered all the way to the river's mouth and beyond. Without its customary allotment of sediment, the coastline is subject to erosion. By one estimate, dams have reduced by four-fifths the sediment reaching the Southern California coast, causing once wide beaches to disappear and cliffs to fall into the ocean.

Estuaries, where riverine freshwater mixes with ocean saltwater, are crucial in the development of plankton, which support a huge abundance of marine life. Deprived of large portions

Jacques Leslie

of freshwater and nutrients, the estuaries decline, and with them the fisheries.

Migrating fish such as salmon and steelhead trout find their paths obstructed, both as juveniles swimming downstream to mature and as adults going upstream to spawn. For this reason, the Columbia River, where 2 million fish returned annually to spawn just before the dam era began, hosted half that number at the turn of the 21st century, and most remaining stocks in the upper Columbia are in danger of extinction. Only by multiplying all these effects by the number of the world's river basins studded with dams can their full environmental impact be appreciated.

Who Benefits?

The most obvious beneficiaries of dams are politicians, bureaucrats, and builders, all of whom reap benefit from the dams' huge price tags. Think of the towering political leaders of the 20th century—Roosevelt, Stalin, Mao, Nehru. They all loved dams. Dams provide jobs and generous portions of money to constituents, some of whom don't mind donating a portion back to the politicians. Bureaucrats like dams because that's where the action is: the expense of dams insures power to its overseers. The constituents include dam builders, road builders, engineers, electricians, carpenters, cooks, plus every sort of professional that boom towns attract, from developers to prostitutes.

Dams' attraction to farmers is obvious. Supported by funding from central governments and international agencies, farmers rarely pay more than 20 percent of the real cost of irrigated water. The subsidies distort the farmers' economic outlook: instead of planting crops that match the hydrology of their fields, they take advantage of abundant cheap water to plant crops that guzzle water, even if the crops bring a low return.

Who Loses?

The biggest losers are people displaced by dams. They're usually minorities, often uneducated and powerless, and therefore hard to count or sometimes even notice, particularly by a government's ruling elite.

In India, 40 percent of people displaced by dams are tribal people, who represent only 6 percent of the country's population. Generations of indigenous people often have inhabited the same land, which is desirable to them precisely because a river runs through it. If the government bothers to relocate them, it's usually to inferior land, where they're resented by settled residents. Rates of illness and death usually increase after relocation.

The World Commission on Dams, which conducted the most thorough study ever done of dams' social and environmental impacts, concluded that dams have displaced between 40 million and 80 million people. As startling as that sum is, it omits a larger group, the floodplain residents living downstream from dams whose livelihoods are jeopardized by the sudden loss of fish, plants, herbs, or nutrient-bearing floods that enrich their fields—their number is in the low hundreds of millions.

On top of all this, dams are dangerous. The weight of reservoir water often triggers earthquakes—the most powerful one, a magnitude 6.3 tremor in western India in 1967, killed about 180 people, injured 1,500, and leveled a village, leaving thousands of inhabitants homeless.

Occasionally, too, dams fall down—Chinese dams are notorious for collapsing. Thousands were built with little or no engineering expertise in mass campaigns during the Great Leap Forward and Cultural Revolution, and became known for their "bean curd construction." Chinese anti-dam activists have reported that by

An opponent of the San Roque dam in the Philippines, a project that violated the Indigenous Peoples' Rights Act of 1997.

1981, some 3,200 dams—3.7 percent of all Chinese dams—collapsed.

The most lethal episode occurred in August 1975, when a typhoon triggered the failure of as many as 62 dams in Henan, inundating a vast swath of densely populated villages for up to two weeks. Chinese authorities successfully suppressed news coverage of the catastrophe until two decades later, when the New York–based Human Rights Watch published an account. It estimated that 85,000 people were drowned, and another 145,000 people died in the ensuing famine and epidemics.

But dam collapses are not just a Chinese phenomenon. In 1963, accelerating seismic activity that was probably caused by the filling of the reservoir behind what was then the world's fourth-highest dam, the 856-feet-tall Vaiont in the Italian Alps, unloosed a huge landslide into the reservoir. That produced a monstrous wave that towered over the dam by 360 feet and reached the downstream town of Langarone in two minutes, drowning 2,600 people.

Dams' massiveness and lethality make them tempting military targets, a prospect that has grown more foreboding in an era of skyscraper assaults and suicide bombings. Yet in the world's most bomb-plagued country, Iraq, explosives may not even be necessary to bring down the nation's biggest dam, called the Mosul—the U.S. Army Corps of Engineers labeled it "the most dangerous dam in the world" in September 2006.

HISTORY OF GLOBAL DAM DEVELOPMENT

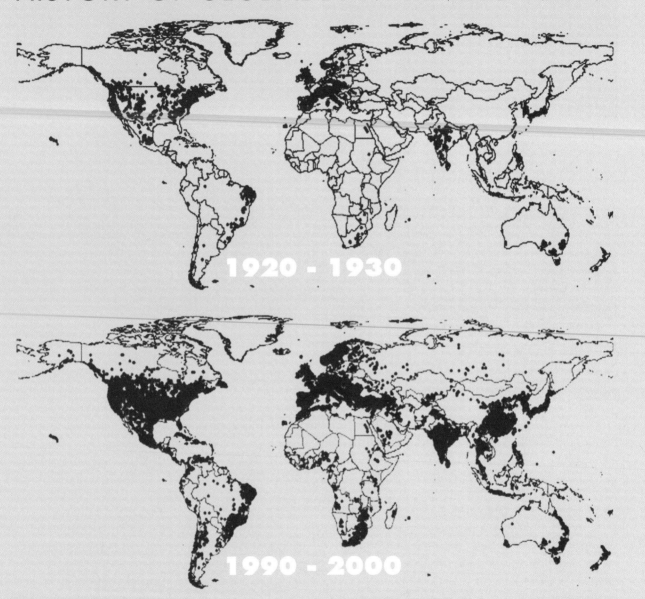

1920 - 1930

1990 - 2000

The rate at which large dams are built has declined from around 1,000 a year from the 1950s to the mid-1970s, to around 260 a year during the early 1990s. Today, it is estimated there are over 50,000 large dams worldwide, with the most being built in China, Turkey, Brazil, and India.

Source: Nature Conservancy

U.S. ambassador to Iraq Ryan Crocker and Lt. Gen. David Petraeus, commander of American troops in Iraq, have warned that the dam's collapse could result in the submergence of the city of Mosul and its nearly 2 million inhabitants in a 65-foot-high wave. The structure suffers from the most ominous of dam engineering problems: an unstable foundation. Built during Saddam Hussein's rule in the 1980s, the dam sits on porous, water-soluble soil, which has repeatedly given way to huge cavities. An October 2007 report by the U.S. Office of the Special Inspector General for Iraq Reconstruction revealed that the United States has spent $27 million trying to fix the problem without making headway.

The United States has its own dam safety problems. In March 2005, the American Society of Civil Engineers awarded the United States' dam infrastructure a "D," a grade that is still justified three years later. For starters, the nation's dam stock is rapidly aging. Most dams need major repairs between 25 and 50 years after they're built, and most U.S. dams are at least 25 years old; some were built more than a century ago. As dams age, their danger increases. This is not just a matter of advancing decrepitude, but "hazard creep"—the tendency of developers to build directly downstream from dams, in the path of floods that would follow dam failures. The result is that even though Americans now build few dams, more and more dams threaten humans with loss of life.

Chiefly for this reason, the number of U.S. dams identified in one estimate as capable of causing death and needing rehabilitation more than doubled between 1999 and 2006, from more than 500 to nearly 1,400. The civil engineers' report placed the number of unsafe dams much higher, at more than 3,500.

Unlike waterways and sanitation facilities, a majority of dams—56 percent of inventoried dams in the United States—are privately owned, which is one reason dams are among the country's most dangerous pieces of infrastructure. Many private owners can't afford the cost of repairing aging dams; some owners go so far as to resist paying by tying up official repair demands in court or, in one instance, by campaigning to weaken state dam safety laws.

Climate change will make dams more dangerous, as increases in precipitation volume undermine the flood assumptions that underlie dam designs. Consider that in October 2005 and May 2006, two strong but hardly cataclysmic New England rain storms caused the overtopping or breaching of more than 400 dams in three states; a much fiercer storm would compromise far more dams, exacerbating flooding and potentially endangering thousands of people.

Who Foots the Bill?

The many controversies that dams have generated have reduced the World Bank, once the world's leading dam financier, to a virtual bystander in international dam construction. At the peak of its efforts, from 1970 to 1985, it supported an average of 26 dams a year. But as awareness of dam's social and environmental impacts grew, resistance to the projects spread, to such an extent that the bank supported only four dams a year over the following decade.

Midway through the 1990s, choking on its frustration, the bank reluctantly embraced a proposal by dam opponents to create an independent commission that would assess dams' performance and set down rules for future construction. The bank hoped that if anti-dam groups were represented on the commission, they would have no grounds for protest after agreeing to reasonable rules for building dams. The bank made one provision—that the commission assess not just the bank's dams but all large dams—in an apparent attempt to divert attention from the bank's many problem-ridden dams.

The bank then joined forces with the World Conservation Union (IUCN), a Geneva-based quasi-official nonprofit, to create what became known as the World Commission on Dams. To insure balance, its 12 commissioners were drawn equally from three categories —"pro-dam," "mixed," and "anti-dam." Among them were Göran Lindahl, president of ABB Ltd., then the world's largest supplier of hydropower generators, and Medha Patkar, an anti-dam firebrand whose protests against a huge dam project on India's Narmada River repeatedly involved courting her own death.

"Truce called in battle of the dams," said a 1997 *Financial Times* headline over a story about the commission's creation. Dam stakeholders were skeptical that such a diverse group could reach consensus, but as time went on, the commissioners developed rapport, and found a way to work towards a common objective. As late as September 1999, 14 months before the commission issued its final report, World Bank senior water advisor John Briscoe lauded its "absolutely extraordinary process" and declared, "We have every confidence" that it will deliver "very good advice." Bank officials even spoke confidently of using the World Commission on Dams' approach to launch another commission on oil, gas, and mining.

As it turned out, the commission's advice was notably sharp-edged. It said large dams showed a "marked tendency" toward schedule delays and cost overruns, that irrigation dams typically neither produced the expected volume of water nor recovered their costs, that environmental impacts were "more negative than posi-tive" and in many cases "led to irreversible loss of species and ecosystems," and that their construction had "led to the impoverishment and suffering of millions."

The commission even challenged the conventional assumption that dams provide "clean" energy; on the contrary, it said, dam reservoirs, particularly shallow tropical ones, emit greenhouse gases released by vegetation rotting in reservoirs and carbon inflows from watersheds. In hopes of heading off future tragedies before they occur, the commission listed 26 recommendations to guide future dam construction. Some, such as examining cheaper and less destructive options before deciding on a dam, were commonsensical, while others, such as obtaining the consent of affected indigenous people, were matters of social justice.

The bank responded by turning its back on its own creation, taking 13 months to issue a response rejecting the commission's recommendations, and instead touting the far less ambitious policies it already had in place. Briscoe charged that anti-dam activists "hijacked" the commission process, and the bank announced a new "high reward/high-risk" policy of renewed support for large dams. Its first fruit was approval in March 2005 of a loan for Laos's Nam Theun 2 Dam.

But if the bank expected that it would

FACT

Dams have shifted so much weight that geophysicists believe they've slightly altered the speed of the earth's rotation, the tilt of its axis, and the shape of its gravitational field.

The Itaipú hydroelectric power plant is one of the largest in the world and was built on the Paraná River between Brazil and Paraguay. Its construction drowned the planet's greatest waterfall—the "Seven Falls of Guaíra"—a series of 18 waterfalls more than double the flow of Niagara Falls and 12 times the flow over Victoria Falls.

resume its central role in dam building, it was mistaken. On the one hand, the World Commission on Dams report has not suffered the fate of most commission reports: to fade quickly into oblivion. Seven years since its unveiling, few institutions have embraced all the report's recommendations, but it has become a standard, a compilation of best practices, against which less rigorous approaches are measured. Unheeded but not forgotten, it hovers over dam projects as an admonition to dam builders in the name of human decency and environmental sanity.

At the same time, China's government-owned Exim Bank has supplanted the World Bank as the world's leading financier of international dams. For the world's remaining undammed rivers, this is a foreboding development. Whereas the World Bank adhered to modest social and environmental standards, Chinese projects embrace no standards at all. China's dam projects seem straightforwardly designed to provide a form of recompense for the natural resources that China imports from the host countries. In addition, some of the projects provide hydropower for Chinese overseas investments in mines, factories, and oil exploration.

International Rivers, a Berkeley, California-based nonprofit that monitors trends in dam construction, has counted 47 recent dam projects in Africa and Asia with Chinese involvement, and more are planned. Many have provided support for outcast regimes in such countries as Burma and Sudan. Thus, with a loan of $520 million,

Jacques Leslie

Migrants from the areas near the Three Gorges dam reservoir arrive in Hefei, Anhui Province, China in 2004. Over 1.5 million have been displaced from around it, and 40-80 million people have been displaced by dams worldwide.

China Exim Bank has become the main funder of the highly controversial Merowe Dam on the Nile River in Sudan. The dam will forcibly displace about 50,000 people and has already resulted in the shooting deaths by security forces of four villagers who resisted the project.

What's the Alternative?

Most of the desirable alternatives to dams involve cheaper, lower-tech, decentralized approaches that respect natural processes instead of trying to conquer them. The cheapest may be the most widely overlooked: conservation.

To a degree, water conservation can be achieved with honest pricing. If, for example, California farmers were charged the true delivery cost of the water that irrigates their fields, they'd quickly stop growing water-guzzling crops. Instead, Arnold Schwarzenegger, the self-proclaimed environmentalist governor, has proposed the construction of two new dams to meet water demand in coming decades, and a coalition of California leaders is promoting bonds to finance them. Yet according to a study by the respected Pacific Institute, California could meet water demand through 2025 while cutting water use by 20 percent simply by adapting sensible conservation measures. Among them are replacing lawns with low-water gardens and requiring home appliances to meet water-efficiency standards.

THE ALTERNATIVE TO DAMS

The World Commission on Dams found major problems with water-supply and irrigation dams. Seventy percent of water-supply dams did not meet their targets, and half of large-scale irrigation projects underperformed.
The WCD report included numerous suggestions for alternatives to dams for water supply, including the following:

Irrigation and Agriculture Sector
- Improve performance and productivity of existing systems
- Use alternative supply-side measures that incorporate rain-fed, local, small-scale, and traditional water management and harvesting systems, including groundwater recharge methods

Water Supply Sector
- Revitalize existing sources
- Introduce appropriate pricing strategies
- Encourage fair and sustainable water marketing and transfers, recycling, and reuse
- Employ local strategies such as rainwater harvesting

Source: World Commission on Dams

Throughout the world, municipal water systems are notorious for poor maintenance; in the world's largest cities, water lost to leaks ranges from 40 to 60 percent. Investing in repairs is less glamorous than dam building, but it is far more cost-effective. Even without price reforms, agriculture, which uses 70 percent of water devoted to human uses worldwide, is a fertile realm for conservation. For instance, the replacement of flood irrigation by drip systems can double water efficiency.

As water has grown scarce, many cultures have been surprised to discover the benefits of reviving traditional water harvesting techniques. In the Indian state of Rajasthan, the building of communal ponds has recharged depleted aquifers and revived dried-up streams; in the Middle East, officials are discovering that ancient self-regulating aqueducts called *qanats* can be reliable sources of water.

In the energy sector, conservation also makes sense. By one estimate, it could cut U.S. consumption by as much as 50 percent, reducing the need for reliance on hydropower. In addition, in some countries, electricity lost between power stations and customers' meters amounts to 40 percent or higher. Where conservation and effective maintenance don't deliver sufficient savings, new energy technologies—including solar, wind, wave and tidal, geothermal, and fuel cells—all show potential and would benefit from more investment in research. Even in flood control, a cheap, infinitely simple alternative to dams exists: stop building on floodplains.

In the end, of course, nature will reassert itself. Some dams will crumble into the basins from which they rose, while others may still be intact but no longer storing water, which instead runs over or through or around them. They'll be relics of the 20th century—reminders of an ancient time when humans believed they could conquer nature and found themselves conquered instead.

Jacques Leslie

WATER

IN ORDER TO HELP ADDRESS THE WATER CRISIS, WE NEED A NEW WAY OF THINKING AND TALKING ABOUT THE PLACES WE CALL HOME. WE EACH LIVE IN A WATERSHED AND WE NEED A LITERACY OF PLACE THAT HELPS US UNDERSTAND HOW WE ARE CONNECTED TO THAT WATERSHED AND THE GLOBAL WATER CYCLE THAT SUSTAINS LIFE ON OUR PLANET.

SOLUTIONS

WE CAN BEGIN BY ASKING SEVERAL QUESTIONS: HOW MUCH WATER DO WE USE? WHERE DOES IT COME FROM? WHERE DOES IT GO? HOW CAN WE LEARN MORE ABOUT OUR OWN WATERSHEDS? WHAT CAN WE DO TO PROTECT AND RESTORE THE WATER AROUND OUR HOMES?

INVESTIGATIONS INTO OUR WATER LITERACY CAN LEAD US TO A MORE HOLISTIC UNDERSTANDING OF THE POSSIBLE SOLUTIONS TO THE WATER CRISIS. WE CAN LEARN FROM NEW TECHNOLOGY AND DESIGN; FROM NATURE ITSELF; FROM THOSE AROUND US, INCLUDING TRADITIONAL AND INDIGENOUS CULTURES; AND FROM OTHER COMMUNITIES THAT ARE WORKING TOWARD LIVING IN BALANCE WITH OUR WORLD'S RESOURCES.

Chapter 8

WATERSHED LITERACY: RESTORING COMMUNITY AND NATURE

by Brock Dolman

Watershed, catchment, drainage, basin, cuenca: by any name they function the same, and everyone on the planet lives in one, sailors on the sea alone excepted. Watersheds at all scales are uniquely evolved geomorphic, hydrological, and biological entities that provide all members of the community a benchmark for judging the wisdom of our past, present, and future land and water use practices.

At the most basic level, a watershed encompasses all of the land surface that collects and drains water down to a single exit point. The continual cycle of erosive water flowing over uplifting and weathering land has sculpted all landscapes into distinct cradlelike entities known as watersheds. Everything we do for work, play, school, shopping, farming, recreation, and so on occurs in a watershed somewhere.

Watersheds can be as large as the Mississippi basin, the fourth-largest in the world, which drains 41 percent of the lower 48 U.S. states into the Gulf of Mexico. Or watersheds can be as small as all the land in your neighborhood that flows from your yard, roof, driveway, and streets to the storm drain and out to your local creek, lake, and

Though most of the Clinch River runs through private land, it still has some of the finest undeveloped riverfront in the Appalachians, including this stretch in Virginia.

eventually the ocean.

If you want to envision a watershed, bring your hands together and cup them, creating a vessel. Imagine the rim of your hands being a water-parting divide with thumb and fingertips as ridgeline spires. Fingers become the mountain slopes, palms the hills and floodplains. Each wrinkle and crease a watercourse conveying flow to the riparian ecotone of adpressed hands, spilling forth towards the mouth of articulated wrists. We all hold the watershed in our hands, and in turn, we are all held by the watershed.

The History of "Watershed"

The word "watershed" has many different meanings and intentions. In its most literal sense, watershed refers to the parting of waters, the actual ridge dividing drainages. In 1852, Charles Darwin referred to the "Line of Watershed dividing inland streams from those on the coast," the Continental Divide of North America being a primary example. In 1878, Thomas Henry Huxley invoked watershed as a landscape entity or catchment basin, stating it is "all that part of a river basin from which rain is collected, and from which therefore the river is fed." This definition encapsulates the basic physical definition of a watershed in common parlance today.

Our challenge is to move beyond a static, hydrologic definition towards a dynamic understanding of the wholeness of watersheds and how they literally underlie all human endeavors. Watersheds at all scales are evolved, living entities that topographically define community. The health of your watershed depends on collaborative relations between neighbors in your shared basin, so ensuring a healthy "basin of relations" is paramount.

In the world of watershed thinking exists the phrase "We all live downstream," implying a deep sense of interconnection between how the behavior of one person can impact the quality of life for someone downstream.

The exciting art and science behind thinking like a watershed nurtures our hearts and sparks our imaginations. I emphasize *heart* here because as a global society, the quality we most urgently need is an open heart, a humility that allows us to perceive the Earth's watersheds not as human commodities but as living communities. In light of recent events and global climate trends, the current commodity-based path seriously threatens the continuance of our own and all species. Solar power functionally fuels all life and watershed processes, but it will take *soul-ar* power to regenerate and restore healthy watersheds.

Watersheds in the Mind

Soular-powered watershed regeneration rests in the hands and hearts of each one of us: the power to restore ourselves by restoring our relations with our home basins. This challenge before us begs our collective capacity to think like a watershed, striving to understand the wisdom of watershed consciousness.

Again, like all watersheds that begin in the headwaters, so must we begin our restoration process in the most critical of all headwaters—the very water in our own heads! Thus watershed restoration begins with *restoryation*. What is the story you believe? Is our planet a community or a commodity? Are you on the path of dead oil or living water?

To begin with, we need to learn to read the place that we are in. Ecological illiteracy is the single greatest global epidemic we face as a human species today. Effective watershed regeneration and restoryation must be based in watershed literacy—a literacy of home, a literacy of place.

How do we bring to bear the scientific and professional capacity to convey this information in a manner that pragmatically supports an increasing proficiency of watershed management at all levels of society? The pedagogy of place-based learning is critically dependent on the clarity of being actually able to describe where you are.

We need to learn to speak of and teach about place in terms that are inclusive to the idea that we are a part of place and not apart from place. Speak with elders in your community about what the river used to look like after a rain storm or where there used to be big trees or good fishing and hunting. Make a public map of your watershed and engage the community in adding to it points of historical interest or rare resources or issues of concern and pollution. Interview local farmers or public servants on their memories of place and concerns about the future of your watershed. Take guided walks with native plant or wildlife experts, or simply explore places in your watershed you are drawn to, from the ridgeline down to the river mouth.

In what ways can we support a literal sense of embodiment with our watershed? In many ways the body mirrors our watershed. We can imagine the branching patterns of waterways as a macro expression of the same branching patterns of our lungs, capillaries, and neural pathways. Wetlands provide a similar environmental service for watershed health as our livers and kidneys. Soil and skin are both thin and proportionately cover the most surface area. Like our bodies, the life of the watershed is by volume mostly water–in the soil and vegetation such as in our flesh and living tissues. We are actually walking watersheds.

A Watershed Moment

"Watershed" is continually used in reference to a significant event. Lodged deep within our collective psyche is a subconscious recognition of the profound meaning each distinctive drainage basin holds: new creatures, new places, new experiences, a new face of divinity awaits. A certain excitement of impending discovery, an archetypal intrigue, arises as you pass into a new "watershed."

Watershed as metaphor brings awareness to a critical transition or point of demarcation, as, for instance, "they reached a watershed in the peace negotiations." What does it imply to "reach a watershed"? How does this resonate with the feelings of awe and apprehension at cresting a ridge and gazing down into a new, unknown, and promise-filled "basin of relation"?

The figurative watershed moments in one's life are often where a certain clarity is achieved, marked perhaps by a rite of passage fulfilled or by the unexpected reappraisal of deeply held beliefs.

In Aldo Leopold's *A Sand County Almanac*, he describes a personal "watershed" moment after shooting a wolf in the Gila Wilderness in 1922: "We reached the old wolf in time

How Big Are Watersheds?

● Watersheds can be as large as the Mississippi basin, the fourth-largest in the world, which drains 41 percent of the lower 48 U.S. states into the Gulf of Mexico

● Watersheds can be as small as all the land in your neighborhood that flows from your yard, roof, driveway, and streets to the storm drain and out to your local creek, lake, and eventually the ocean

What is a Watershed?

Literally:
A watershed refers to the parting of waters, the actual ridge dividing drainages

Technically:
A watershed encompasses all of the land surface that collects and drains water down to a single exit point

Metaphorically:
Watershed as metaphor brings awareness to a critical transition or point of demarcation, as, for instance, "they reached a watershed in the peace negotiations"

to watch a fierce green fire dying in her eyes. I realized then, and have known ever since, that there was something new to me in those eyes, something known only to her and to the mountain. I was young then and full of trigger itch; I thought that because fewer wolves meant more deer, then no wolves meant a hunter's paradise. But after seeing the green fire die, I sensed that neither the wolf nor the mountain agreed with such a view."

In this watershed moment, Leopold witnesses an interconnectivity that comes to fruition later in life when he writes about the idea of "thinking like a mountain"—an understanding of the relationship among wolves, healthy deer herds, and forested mountain watersheds.

These literal watershed moments allow us to observe the many ways in which water weaves together all living things into a dynamic whole.

The Threatened Health of Our Watersheds

Our watersheds today are vastly different than just centuries ago. The earliest descriptions of North America by Europeans evoke a vision of snow-capped peaks, forested ridges, wooded slopes, rolling prairies, flood plains, riparian jungles, beaver wetlands, and river mouth estuaries brimming with wildlife. It was an ecstatically pervious world that cleansed and cycled and savored its own water to the benefit of unfathomable biodiversity.

Let us dive into that vision for a moment: rain falling at 30 mph is slowed and sweetened by outstretched leaves; these in turn drip nutrient-laden tea from the canopy to the forest floor. Infused with humus capable of absorbing 10 times its own weight in water, this protective sponge spreads the life-giving liquid over soil shot through with nutrient-grabbing mycorrhizae, the fungal threads connecting all the rooted plants. These vegetated landscapes of yore seeded and combed the aqueous clouds, rehumidifed the downwind air, buffered their own climates, and passed on the surplus to recharge groundwater aquifers that sustained the flow of springs, creeks, and rivers.

Now imagine this hydrological wonderland after some centuries of development based on dessication: Wholesale clearing of forests and draining of wetlands have hardened rivers and streams, the upland capillaries and aquatic arteries of the landscape. Clear-cut logging, mining, overgrazing, plow agriculture, housing, commercial development, road building, and parking lots have all damaged watersheds, making them extremely impervious.

This is where we stand today, with a major challenge ahead of us to restore our water systems, for the sake of our own survival and that of the world around us. Astute ecosystem managers clearly recognize that watershed-scale restoration begins with addressing issues that affect the headwaters of any watershed. To seriously take on this survival challenge, we must first and foremost mitigate the cerebral imperviousness of our own internal "headwaters"—to change the way we think about the natural world and our place in it.

Therefore, it becomes clear that the work of the day to restore ecosystem function must begin with functional restoryation of our collective ego system. Forming collaborative interpersonal and working social relationships between all people who share a watershed rests at the center of our potential for success or failure.

A waterfall in Silver Falls State Park, Oregon.

The wrong way to landscape. Rain, runoff, and topsoil are quickly drained off the landscape to the street where the sediment-laden water contributes to downstream flooding and contamination.

The right way to landscape. Rain, runoff, leaf drop, and topsoil are harvested and utilized with the landscape contributing to flood control and enhanced water quality.

We Face a Future of Thirst

Some will argue that water has never limited human growth and development, that humans have tenaciously applied their technological ingenuity to move water great distances and pump it from deep below the surface to fuel burgeoning growth. It has been said, "Simply bring the water, and the people will come." In the past few centuries, however, this command-control-and-conveyance attitude towards water has begun to show signs of deepening failure.

Our societal addiction to the combustion of carbon-based fossil fuels for energy is now unequivocally understood to cause global climate change due to excessive accumulation of "greenhouse" gases in the atmosphere. These gases thicken the atmosphere's capacity to retain solar energy, leading to an increase in the planet's average surface temperatures. Solid, liquid, and gaseous phase changes by water are the thermal mechanisms through which the planet primarily attempts to regulate its human-induced "fever." Water is manifesting some of the most dramatic expressions of this climate change, with melting polar ice and glaciers, rising sea levels, coastal inundation, ocean acidification, warmer tropical water and air temperatures, slowing of the Gulf Stream, stronger hurricanes, and increased floods and droughts.

Peak Water

As we confront the burgeoning reality of "peak oil"—the knowledge that we are now approaching the halfway point of global petroleum production capacity—we also see a new crisis appearing on the horizon: "peak water," which has deep implications for "peak food," and consequently, "peak population." Responding in a timely manner to this triangle of energy, water, and food interdependence is one of our challenges. The difference between peak oil and peak water is that, while the total amount of water and oil on the planet is finite, water, unlike oil, cycles infinitely through our lives and watersheds.

Watershed by watershed, functional sustainability will be exemplified by our ability to sustain the integrity and resilience of the water cycle. As the Titanic of cheap energy sinks below the surface, a prudent option would be to perceive our watersheds as living lifeboats and to use the principles of "conservation hydrology" to batten down the hatches. It is incumbent upon us to realize that together we can each work to ensure that all watershed lifeboats float together as a regional raft of resilient stability.

Moving from a "Dehydration Model" to a "Rehydration Model"

There are tools, like conservation hydrology, that we can use to begin to restore our watershed and our thinking.

Conservation hydrology utilizes the disciplines of ecology, population biology, biogeography, economics, anthropology, philosophy, and history to guide community-based watershed literacy, planning, and action. It advocates that human development decisions must move from a "dehydration model" to a "rehydration model."

To achieve this goal we must retrofit existing development patterns with new ones based on the principles below. Therefore, much like the discussion of our carbon footprint (i.e., the relative relationship of our lifestyle and how it impacts the planet via our consumption of carbon), we can also invoke this same process of inquiry and evaluation to the idea of our water footprint.

Developing a consciousness that appreciates water as the ultimate resource is critical. Thank-fully, the federal Clean Water Act now recognizes the "pave, pipe, and pollute paradigm" of past decades as disastrously flawed and hydro-illiterate. These outmoded engineering practices captured, concentrated, and conveyed water away from a site as quickly as possible. The old *drain-age* is now being replaced by a new *retain-age*, the key to a healthy watershed.

Balancing Our Water Budget

Our new way of looking at watersheds is a lot like managing money. For a moment, consider water in budgetary terms. Successful businesses must account for income and expenses in order to ensure profitability. Yet how many cities or counties actually have balanced income and expense budgets for their water resources?

In simple fiscal terms, most municipalities are operating deeply in the "red," with ecologically and socially damaging hydrological deficits. Typically, the demand or expense side of their water budgets far exceeds their income streams. Impervious surfaces, such as roads, parking lots, and compacted fields, impede water's ability to make deposits that could recharge groundwater savings accounts.

Ever-increasing reliance on overdrafted groundwater accounts will leave our grandchildren with unrecoverable and undrinkable debts as many of the world's watersheds verge on hydrological bankruptcy. Unlike corporations and people, our watersheds cannot file for Chapter 11 and then just reorganize. Direct deposits of freshly distilled rain and snow are the annual allowance, the only real renewable income source on Earth.

Expenditure of our groundwater trust reserves should be limited to the annual earned interest income of infiltration, with the principal left untapped. All life-forms are shareholders with a fixed interest in ensuring that our watershed economies remain viable and continue to operate in the "blue.

Four Rs of Conservation Hydrology

Here's how that budget actually breaks down. The four "Rs" of a water budget are equivalent to income, deposit, savings, and expense. We want the water balance of our watersheds to run in the blue and not in the red. We want to insure that our liquid assets continually produce a high quality return on investment back into our watershed.

Receive=Income. Watersheds receive water only as snowfall, rainfall, and fogfall. Annual precipitation is the only true source of income to resupply our community's water budget allowance.

Global climate changes are predicted to dramatically alter the frequency, intensity, and type of precipitation events that watersheds can expect to receive. Thus, conservation hydrology advocates the adaptive management of watershed lands to optimize rehydration. Practices such as eco-forestry, holistic rangeland management, organic no-till agriculture, urban forestry, stormwater management with bioswales and rainwater harvesting are but a few examples of land-use practices that can be designed to help rehydrate our watersheds. We must implement and enforce these types of land-use patterns that enhance the receptive capacity of our watersheds in times of excess and in times of scarcity.

Recharge=Deposit. Recharge processes are critical for the water cycle to annually refresh itself via the deposit slip called infiltration. The capacity to make water deposits depends on the watershed's recharge potential. Precipitation received by our watershed must percolate and be absorbed, or else there is no replenishment of our water savings account.

Recharge potential and functions are impaired by the hardening and paving over of natural recharge areas, the disconnection of rivers from their floodplains, the deforestation of native vegetation, and the draining of wetlands. Therefore, to increase recharge, we must limit impervious surfaces and the wholesale conversion of native vegetation.

We must implement stormwater techniques designed to "slow it, spread it, and sink it" so that water seeps back, as a deposit, into the Earth. We must protect open space in known groundwater recharge areas. If site conditions and/or soils are not conducive to recharge, then we install proper biofiltration structures, such as rain gardens or bioswales, to help clean all surface waters prior to their discharge from the site as they are redeposited into rivers, wetlands, lakes, estuaries, and oceans.

Retain=Savings. The retention of recharged precipitation is a savings account asset. The storage of water is often the most challenging aspect of water supply management. Conservation hydrology strategies should appropriately slow water down, increasing the residence time of water storage in our watersheds. This will optimize the amount of water available.

We must avoid overdrafting our watersheds. Water should never be extracted from storage in amounts greater than what is annually received and recharged. All sources of water must not be polluted by development, wastewater systems, agricultural runoff, or industrial effluent.

To protect our water savings, we must develop water budgets for all watersheds to ensure that extractions of water do not exceed inputs of water. We must implement groundwater and surface water management programs. We must ensure that surface and groundwater quantity and quality protection programs are funded, monitored, and enforced.

A rainstorm in north central Arizona is typical on most warm summer afternoons in the area.

And we must continually defend the legally established public ownership of water as a public trust resource and resist the privatization of water.

Release=Expense. The planet utilizes many ways to release its signature element naturally to the ocean, land, and atmosphere in a process known as the water cycle. Through seasonally melting glaciers, groundwater springs, and seeps, water is returned to creeks and rivers. Solar evaporation and the evapotranspiration of plants help to form clouds and feed the cycle anew. The infinite nature of this cycle is to continually flow and be in flux as the expense of one stage produces income for the next.

Human development practices (creating impervious surfaces, channeling stormwater, etc.) tend to increase the rate and volume of stormwater's return to the ocean via excessive runoff and heightened flood discharges. This directly reduces the landscape's ability to retain water and diminishes the amount of water available for later release during the dry season, when it is most needed.

Therefore the implementation of watershed-scale conservation hydrology practices must be designed to protect reception, amplify recharge, and thus optimize retention. These are the critical steps that can ensure optimal amounts of water will be available for future release.

Watershed issues provide us with many avenues to become involved. Some solutions are small and only require making different choices as an individual or family. These can be done

Brock Dolman

today in your home or yard by using low-flow appliances, creating a stormwater harvesting rain garden, focusing on the use of drought-tolerant native plants, and installing a rainwater cistern for all irrigation and a graywater system to irrigate a home orchard. Other solutions are more complex, requiring behavioral changes in neighborhoods, communities, or cities, with broad-based participation over some years. Ideas like forming a community watershed group, or implementing habitat restoration projects, or creating watershed literacy curriculum for your local schools are projects that require more group collaboration and planning.

In order to catalyze changes in water security for future generations, we must implement a whole class of democratic opportunities for social policy change at all levels of government. Changes are necessary at the personal, public, and political levels.

On the personal level, practicing water conservation by reducing our demands for water is one of our most powerful acts, individually and collectively. Water conservation has a cascade of positive effects and can influence the overall quantity and quality of available freshwater.

Every gallon of water you choose not to use equals one gallon not taken from your river or aquifer. It means the system does not need that gallon's worth of electricity to pump it nor the chemicals to make it potable. It means that one gallon is not being degraded into "waste" water, which would require additional electricity to pump again, treat, and dispose of in our environment. Choosing not to use water saves water quantity and improves quality. It saves energy and money. It helps reduce demands on our watersheds. And it helps to mitigate climate change-induced water stresses by reducing the collective water footprint of humankind.

On the public level, we are perched on the tipping point of a "watershed moment." From the global scale to the local scale, we are faced with a multitude of issues and decisions that will determine the future world our children will inherit and how to ensure that our watersheds remain healthy in perpetuity.

Viewing your watershed as a shared "basin of relations" allows you and your neighbors to truly define the boundaries of your community and organize around meaningful issues of true and lasting local social security. Each process, like every watershed and its associated community, is unique. Oftentimes you will find that certain local, city, county, state, and federal jurisdictions are ready and waiting to collaborate with these efforts. In the absence of support from the local community, it is often impossible to achieve measurable objectives and resource management goals, especially in areas where the majority of the land is in private ownership.

And politically, when you consider the importance of water, it is essential to involve yourself in the politics of water resources. Do you know the members of your local, city, county, or regional water board? Of your irrigation district, planning commission, board of supervisors, or city council? How about your state and federal legislators? How do they make decisions? Have you ever thought about running for a local office yourself?

Sustainable Water Policies

Ultimately, lasting change will have to occur via the arenas of politics and democratic decision making. "We the People" are responsible for sane water policies and laws through our legislative, executive, and judicial branches. Metaphorically, you could conceive of these three branches as expressions of social watersheds. At the confluence of these three watersheds, the health of the "mainstream" is only as good as the health of each contributing watershed branch. It is our collective responsibility to make sure each branch of our democratic structure crafts adequate, supportive conditions to care for our collective water resources.

The choice is ours whether to move forward to face the challenges head on or not. We do not lack the prescient clarion call of the future or the opportunity to observe the highly degraded state of our watersheds after only a few hundred years of so-called civilized occupation. We do not lack any amount of information or practical knowledge on how to implement regenerative watershed practices.

So, what will it take to motivate us to move in the direction of mitigation and adaptation on behalf of future generations? The ecological literacy of seeing the world through the lens of our watersheds offers communities a realistic scale for feedback that is pragmatic and inspirational.

In ancient Greece, the mathematician and inventor Archimedes purportedly stated: "Give me a place to stand and a lever long enough, and I will move the world." Several thousand years later, his wise insight offers us a perfect challenge to social movement organizing: Are you willing to take a stand for your watershed community? Where strategically will you place yourselves and insert your lever against what fulcrum? If you wish to move your watershed world in the direction of resiliency, how many people can you convince to pull on the lever with you? Can you leverage the community willpower to pull on the oars of your watershed lifeboat in a coordinated manner as if your lives depended on it? It is time not just to ask the hard questions but to find the answers, because all of our lives and those of future generations do depend on it.

HOW TO HELP PROTECT YOUR WATERSHED

Household Actions

- Use low-flow appliances and fixtures
- Create a stormwater harvesting rain garden
- Focus on the use of drought-tolerant native plants
- Install a rainwater or graywater system for all irrigation

Community Actions

- Form a community watershed group
- Implement habitat restoration projects
- Create watershed literacy curriculum for your local schools

Chapter 9

ACEQUIAS: A MODEL FOR LOCAL GOVERNANCE OF WATER

By Paula Garcia and Miguel Santistevan

Throughout most of human history, water has been viewed as a gift of creation and an element that nurtures all life. Many cultures and belief systems regard water as sacred and incorporate water into ritual and ceremony. In regions around the world, indigenous and land-based peoples have maintained a relationship to water that embodies both the spiritual and the material. Where communities retain a connection to ancestral places and lands, decisions about the use and sharing of water are often guided by a spiritual consciousness.

From a cultural perspective, water is inextricably linked to community, land, celebrations, ritual, food traditions, and all living things that depend upon it for survival. In contrast to this integral view, water is also viewed as an element apart from the rest of creation, subject to usurpation and control.

As an element separated from the whole, water is treated as an object to be owned and potentially exploited. What is increasingly referred to as a global water crisis is really a complex mosaic of local struggles against management regimes that do not value all the spiritual, cultural, and ecological dimensions of water. What these local struggles all share is the same goal of striving to defend water as a common good.

One such example is in New Mexico and Southern Colorado, where historic, land-based communities are continuing a lineage of water-sharing traditions that are thousands of years old.

Water Scarcity and Commodification in the Southwest

In the southwestern United States, the landscape tells of the finite nature of water. Unlike areas of the country with more rainfall, human settlements were historically constrained by the availability of water. In the 20th century, growth of cities in this arid land was enabled by appropriations of water through dams, pipelines, and the large-scale and irreversible tapping of ancient aquifers. Sunbelt cities (Phoenix, Las Vegas, and Los Angeles) and their suburbs dominate the annual lists of the fastest-growing cities in the country. As population growth reaches unprecedented levels, previous strategies to acquire water are no longer viable. Climate change further compounds water scarcity and the uncertainties surrounding future water supplies in the Southwest.

Given that there are no new supplies of water, the region must deal with the reality of an extremely limited and increasingly variable water

An acequia runs through Candaleria Farm in Albuquerque, New Mexico.

Paula Garcia and Miguel Santistevan

What Are Acequias?

- The word "acequia" is of Arabic origin, meaning "quencher of thirst" or "bearer of water"

- They are a communal irrigation system with intricate water-sharing customs that still exist in the Southwest United States

- Acequias are part of an ancient legacy with roots extending back thousands of years to the arid-land peoples of present-day India, the Middle East, and the Americas

- By the time of their establishment in New Mexico, acequias were a synthesis of Moorish influences and adaptations learned from Mesoamerica and the Native Americans of the Southwest

- Their system of water distribution is made possible by communal labor and participation

- The fundamental principle underlying the acequia system of water management is *equidad* (equity)

- The right to use water is attributed to individual families but is contingent upon contribution of cooperative labor

- Because of their resiliency as "water democracies" acequias have earned recognition in the global water movement and they offer some insights for other communities facing chronic water shortages

supply. Not only is water finite but also fully allocated to a range of uses—agricultural, municipal, and industrial. The right to use water, known as a water right, can be owned by an individual or an entity and is considered a property right in the water rights doctrine of the western United States.

Because all water rights are owned and appropriated to some use, any new use of water requires that a water right be passed from an existing use through a transaction known as a water transfer—such as drying up agricultural land in order to increase pumping of a municipal well. When a water right is transferred, the place and purpose of use changes by discontinuing an existing use and commencing a new use. Depending on the situation, water transfers may or may not involve the physical movement of water with pipelines or other types of conveyance.

Because water rights can be bought and sold by individuals as well as corporate or governmental entities, a water market has emerged that is driven by the demand to move water rights from existing uses to new uses. The legal framework that defines water as private property and the economic forces that drive water transfers are resulting in the commodification of water in the Southwest.

Water: Economic Commodity or Shared Resource?

As urban areas explode with population growth, the water market is often viewed as the silver bullet to address water scarcity. Market proponents argue that water should be transferred to uses with the greatest "economic value." Already, market-driven water transfers have resulted in a rural to urban movement of water that is devastating and often eliminating rural communities. Such rural-to-urban water transfers illustrate the axiom often quoted in the West: "Water flows uphill to money." All economic development decisions hinge on the availability of water rights, and, therefore, the transfer of water rights tends to be toward those entities in positions of economic power.

One of the most important issues regarding water is how decisions about water transfers will occur and who will decide. Will decisions to address water shortages be made through an open and democratic process? Or will allocation of water occur through an unfettered water market? The debate occurring in the western United States reflects the global struggle over whether water should be treated as an economic commodity or as a common good.

Leaders in the global movement who are challenging the commodification of water believe in the basic principles of democracy, equity, and sustainability. What is also needed is a working model that embodies these principles. The southwestern United States is home to a centuries-old institution in which these principles are embodied in community traditions that are very much alive–acequias. Acequias are communal irrigation systems that continue to operate in regions of the Southwest that were settled before American occupation. They are uniquely adapted to the arid climate of the Southwest. Each one has intricate water-sharing customs to ensure everyone gets some water in times of shortage.

The History of Acequias

Acequias are part of an ancient legacy of water civilizations. Their roots extend back thousands of years to the arid-land peoples of present-day India, the Middle East, and the Americas.

In contrast to the water rights doctrine of the western United States in which water rights are treated as a commodity, acequias were established within a worldview in which water was treated as a community resource. Although legal regimes have changed from Spanish to Mexican to American, acequias in New Mexico have continued to operate under the same principles and customs for over 400 years. They are a living testament to the resiliency of local water governance.

Acequias made their way to the Southwest via Mexico, Spain, and North Africa. By the time of their establishment in New Mexico, acequias were a synthesis of Moorish influences and adaptations learned from Mesoamerica and the Native Americans of the Southwest, who themselves had developed sophisticated water harvesting and distribution techniques. The development of acequias in Mexico and the Southwest was shaped by influences from the Iberian Peninsula as well as agricultural techniques and adaptations learned from the indigenous peoples of the Americas. The result was a highly localized and unique system of water management and a polyculture of diverse crops from Europe, Asia, Africa, and the Americas.

The word "acequia" is of Arabic origin, meaning "quencher of thirst" or "bearer of water." Defining an acequia requires both a physical and sociocultural description. From a physical standpoint, an acequia is defined as a system that diverts water from a common source (a river, stream, or spring) and moves water by gravity flow through earthen canals spreading snowmelt and runoff from the upper watershed throughout the valleys of irrigable land via an intricate network of waterways.

This system of water distribution is made possible by communal labor and participation. The social dimension of the acequia is the community of families that rely upon the acequia for

Paula Garcia and Miguel Santistevan

A History of Water Use in the Southwest

Pre-1598 Native peoples for thousands of years practiced both dryland and irrigated agriculture, using sophisticated water harvesting techniques and irrigation.

1598 First acequia constructed in upper Rio Grande. Acequias were the first community structures, other than churches, constructed in the Spanish- and Mexican-era settlements.

1848 War between the United States and Mexico ended with the signing of the Treaty of Guadalupe Hidalgo.

1851 First New Mexico territorial laws enacted, codifying existing acequia customary laws of participatory democracy and water sharing customs.

1907 Territorial water code enacted. Adopted the prior appropriation doctrine, private ownership and transferability of water rights, and jurisdiction of state engineer over water rights administration. Opened the door for the commodification of water.

1960s State of New Mexico filed adjudication suits to determine amount, priority dates, and private ownership of water rights on several stream basins with acequias.

1980s Acequias organized into watershed-based regional associations for united defense in adjudication suits.

1990s Acequias formed statewide New Mexico Acequia Association and mobilized against precedent-setting water transfers and state legislation promoting the commodification of water.

2000s Launched campaign to build consensus around principles of democratic decisions over water transfers at the acequia level. Passed legislation recognizing acequia authority to exercise democratic decisions over water transfers.

Source: New Mexico Acequia Association

water and collectively manage, maintain, and govern the system. Acequias evolved as communal systems in which the right to use water from the acequia was tied to fulfilling certain responsibilities, such as contributing labor to clean the acequia every spring.

For example, every spring, *parciantes* (irrigators) from each acequia are required to provide *peones* (workers) for the annual *saca* (cleaning or taking out) of the acequia. Depending on the number of families served by the acequia, anywhere from 10 to 100 *peones* will meet at a designated location with their shovels and other tools at the crack of dawn to fulfill their communal duty.

Acequias also embody a spiritual dimension that is expressed in local culture. The sacredness of water is expressed in religious ceremonies and processions that sanctify the acequias and agricultural land at certain times of the year, such as saints' days and periods of extreme water scarcity and drought.

The fundamental principle underlying the acequia system of water management is *equidad* (equity). This system, which we refer to as the *repartimiento* or *reparto* (sharing), refers to the beliefs and cultural practices of water sharing in times of shortage. Each acequia has a unique set of customs and traditions that guide the sharing of water within the acequia and between acequias that share a stream system. Historically, water scarcity was an ever-present challenge. Over time, acequia communities evolved unique customs of distributing water based on the fundamental principle that water was essential to life and that it had to be shared for the common

Local food economies are tied to the acequia system.

good. It is the day-to-day embodiment of the belief that water is life.

Intricate water-sharing customs depend on water availability during the seasons, the climate and crops of a given locale, and even the personalities that shape communities. While customs are based in fundamental principles of sharing, they are highly variable and require a depth of indigenous knowledge that can be acquired only through generational connections to a place.

In addition to water-sharing customs and cooperative work, a defining characteristic of acequias is their democratic governance. For hundreds of years in New Mexico, acequias have been self-governed. The *parciantes* who have water rights from the acequia are able to elect one from among them to be a *mayordomo*, or caretaker. The *mayordomo* is usually a person who has learned through generational teachings the ways of the water.

One of the most important virtues of a *mayordomo* is to have the ability and patience to work with people and guide the use of water to uphold the principles of sharing and equity. He or she walks the acequia to ensure that irrigators adhere to the agreed upon system of distributing or sharing water. In addition to the *mayordomo*, acequia *parciantes* elect a three-member *comisión* (commission) that is entrusted with enacting and implementing the bylaws that govern the acequia.

Paula Garcia and Miguel Santistevan

Within this cultural context, water is communal. The right to use water is attributed to individual families but is contingent upon contribution of cooperative labor. A water right, or *derecho*, is also conditioned by the limitations of nature. The extent of water available to a community (and therefore to the individual families who share the water) is limited by what nature provides through runoff. Water is therefore parceled out to the irrigators as fractions of a whole and in units of time that may be days, hours, or minutes, depending on the extent of the scarcity in a given year.

Lastly, the water is inextricably tied to the land. According to the fundamental principles underlying acequia governance, a water right is not an individual property right that is transferable by severing it from the land. This principle continues as a cultural belief and customary practice. However, during the 20th century, this customary view came into direct conflict with a new legal regime, which defines water as a transferable property right, severable from the land and from the community.

New Mexico's Acequias Are Threatened

Even after northern Mexico was ceded to the United States, acequias remained intact, because the water rights intertwined with them were attached to irrigated land. It wasn't until 1907 that a territorial water code was enacted that delineated water rights as private property rights that were severable from the land.

However, pressure against acequias didn't begin to mount until the 1980s and 1990s, when real estate developers sought to acquire water rights from acequias. The only recourse

Why It Matters Who Controls Our Water

Before 1907, each acequia community controlled its own water rights. That changed when the New Mexico state engineer was put in charge instead, opening the door for the commodification of water. Here's a breakdown of the changes that took place:

Acequia Water Governance
- Water is attached to the land
- Water rights determined locally
- Decisions are made by local, community-elected leaders
- Water law is guided by *repartimiento*—equity, flexibility, indigenous knowledge

Management by State Engineer
- Water rights can be bought and sold like property
- Forfeiture of water rights by state
- Decisions are made by a centralized bureaucracy
- Water law is guided by priority administration—strict, static, technical knowledge

Source: New Mexico Acequia Association

for acequias was to object to water transfers through administrative proceedings and legal appeals. Rather than having a role as decision makers regarding the water rights of their own communities, acequia community leaders had been relegated to being objectors (legally defined as protestants) in hearings before the state engineer.

During this time, the leaders realized that they would need to adopt new strategies to challenge the economic and political forces threatening the acequias' survival. Because acequias were most vulnerable to forces in the water market, they realized that acequias would need a unified voice to serve as a political force to defend their continued existence. This was the basis for the formation of the New Mexico

The growing market for selling water rights in New Mexico threatens the acequia system and local control of water.

Acequia Association.

During the 1990s, the commodification of water was unleashed as government and developers became more aware that any plans for new growth hinged on the availability of water rights. All water was appropriated so that any new use of water had to come at the expense of existing and likely historical/agricultural uses of water. A pattern was established. Cities and developers would apply to the state engineer to transfer water rights, and in turn, acequias, other agricultural communities, concerned citizens, and an occasional environmental group, would file protests.

By the early 2000s, developers and industry representatives looking to easily acquire water rights were seeking changes in state law to expedite water markets. They introduced legislation to "facilitate the movement of water from low value to high value uses" by limiting opportunities for water transfer protests.

Paula Garcia and Miguel Santistevan

Because of their experience in filing water transfer protests, acequias became some of the leading opponents to such policies and were instrumental in blocking legislation intended to expedite water markets.

By 2003, the New Mexico Acequia Association pursued a legislative strategy aimed at renewing and strengthening acequia governance in order to retain local ownership and control of water rights. This was based upon an ancient value system but also upon recognition of the immense challenges regarding water scarcity. The objective was to recommunalize water and democratize the water transfer process.

Acequias and supporters in the legislative leadership successfully amended state laws to recognize the power of acequias, through their local commissions, to approve or disapprove water transfers and to allow acequias to make internal reallocations of water to avoid "use it or lose it" provisions in state law. This was a historic affirmation of the role of acequias as vital community institutions. In regaining some measure of control over the movement of water, acequias had altered the relations of power in their respective communities. Since any decisions about development depend upon the availability of water, acequias now have a greater role in achieving self-determination of their communities.

In long-term visions, protecting water as a common good is only a critical first step. Rebuilding local food systems is another goal that will require not just defending land and water but also creating food economies that honor local traditions and provide a socially just livelihood for land-based people. Being more intentional about passing on land-based culture to youth and instilling a love of the land is another aspiration embedded in the acequia grassroots movement.

Connections to the Global Water Movement

Because of their resiliency as "water democracies" that incorporate the values of equity, sustainability, and community, acequias have earned recognition in the global water movement, and they offer some insights for other communities facing chronic water shortages.

Principles of equity need to be grounded in culture but also codified through systems of participatory local governance. Local democratic decision making and indigenous knowledge enable acequias to accommodate community needs while adapting to changing conditions in water availability. Very importantly, cooperative work and ritual provide the glue for community customs that require frequent practice in order to be perpetuated.

These attributes, which contribute to acequia resiliency, can also be incorporated into other contexts and systems of water governance. However, even in communities with these characteristics and strengths, the threats to water are daunting. Commodification of water is a pervasive and divisive trend that can unravel community cohesiveness. Not only acequias but all communities face the specter that water can be manipulated for profit. It is essential that public policy, from the very local to the global, explicitly defines water as a common good and a human right. Overcoming the political and economic forces driving the commodification of water will require strategic collective action and mobilization to defend water. In addition to countering commodification of water, other interrelated needs are to protect and restore the cleanliness of water and to prevent the irreversible mining of our groundwater.

A challenge for the future is to proactively address rural-urban tensions surrounding water.

An acequia runs through a meadow in Northern New Mexico.

The greatest creativity and good faith will be needed to meet our moral imperative to ensure water for all, while also protecting the natural systems intertwined with water and the fundamental need to sustain and regenerate local food systems. An essential ingredient to that process will be to put social justice at the forefront, since the inequities surrounding water are often grounded in historic injustices affecting indigenous peoples, the working poor, and traditional, small-scale farmers.

It is a defining moment in human history in which people around the world are taking action to defend water with mass mobilizations and community-based strategies to retain local owner-ship and decision-making control of water. Like the acequia movement in New Mexico, these movements are integral to other struggles for land rights, human rights, and basic human dignity.

Regardless of the place or context, acknowledging the finite nature of water is crucial. Strategies to address water scarcity should be grounded in local culture and governance, and those strategies should be defined and led by communities with the greatest stake in defending water as a life-giving resource. The refrain that "water is life" is universal and held by peoples throughout the world. Building upon that principle and transforming institutions to reflect it is one of the greatest challenges facing humanity. If recent grassroots struggles are any indication, we have reason to be hopeful. And with acequias, we have a model from which all of us can learn.

Paula Garcia and Miguel Santistevan

Chapter 10

CAN WE CONSERVE OUR WAY OUT OF THIS?

By Christina Roessler

Those who do not know history are doomed to repeat it.

—Edmund Burke

In February 2008, a *New York Times* headline read, "Lake Mead Could Be Within a Few Years of Going Dry, Study Finds." It was grim news for two of the fastest-growing cities in the country. Lake Mead, fed by the Colorado River, provides up to 90 percent of the water for Las Vegas, and Phoenix gets close to 40 percent of its water from the Colorado.

Of course, this desert area is no stranger to water shortages, but the current condition of the Colorado River, which has seven states gulping from it, could be devastating for the region. It is difficult to imagine these days what kind of catastrophe that could spell. You have to go back a long way to find the last major drought in the Southwest that actually sent people packing.

The period from about 1200 to 1300 AD is considered the golden age of the Ancestral Pueblo culture, an ancient civilization of farmers and potters whose ancestors had been living in the Four Corners region of the Southwest for close to 1,000 years. Settlements at that time were increasing in number and size, as evidenced by the magnificent cliff dwellings in Mesa Verde, including the elaborate 150-room Cliff Palace. Agriculture was flourishing; the population was growing.

Then, suddenly, this seemingly stable society collapsed. Mesa Verde and other communities on the Colorado Plateau were abandoned forever. What happened? Tree ring records indicate that the collapse of the Ancestral Pueblo culture coincided with a particularly prolonged period of drought, giving rise to the speculation that a "Great Drought" drove people from the region.

There were other climatological changes as well, including warmer, wetter winters and cooler, drier summers that disrupted the growing seasons and impacted traditional agriculture. Some areas experienced sharp drops in water table levels.

Sound familiar? This history seems especially relevant today as the Southwestern United States and many other parts of the globe are facing extended periods of drought, increasing temperatures, and dwindling water supplies. The Ancestral Pueblos didn't have the advantage of tree ring studies and climate models, but their rapid decline is still a cautionary tale. The ques-

A fountain at Caesars Palace in Las Vegas shows water profligacy while there is a water war going on between the City of Las Vegas and the ranchers of rural Nevada.

121

tion for us in the 21st century is, can we do better? What will it take for our desert communities and ecosystems to survive?

The Recent Past to Today

The American West, and particularly the Southwest, has been going through a seemingly unstoppable period of population growth for the last several decades. The combined population of the seven Colorado River Compact states—Arizona, California, Colorado, Nevada, New Mexico, Utah, and Wyoming—has grown from just over 21 million people in 1960 to over 48 million people in 2006. Sunny weather, warm temperatures, and lovely landscapes have drawn people from other parts of the country and fed the booming development of the region. At one time the 10 biggest cities in the United States were all located within 500 miles of the Canadian border. Now, seven of the top 10 are in the Sunbelt.

Most of this growth took place during an unusually long, wet period in the history of the West. Rainfall in many parts of the Southwest in the years between 1975 and 2000 were at some of the highest levels the region has seen in 2,000 years, according to tree ring studies.

The West experienced an earlier exceptionally wet period during the 1920s, at the time the Colorado River Compact apportioned Colorado River water to its seven member states. Unfortunately, this means that the allotment of water to these states is based on a calculation of flow in the river that was unusually high in historical terms. The Colorado River—the lifeblood of the region, supplying water for 30 million people in seven states and Mexico—is overallocated in terms of the flow volume we can expect in the future.

In fact, it turns out that the 20th century as a whole was water rich, even by North American standards. We got accustomed to abundance, and abundance became "normal." Now, not even a full decade into the 21st century, we're beginning to recognize that the 20th century was abnormally wet. What we consider drought is largely a return to more typical patterns of precipitation.

Bad as all this sounds, things are almost certainly going to get worse. Climatologists predict that global warming is only going to make the American Southwest hotter and dryer, with precipitation far lower than what we have come to expect. Communities are beginning to recognize that they need to plan for a more water-scarce future. Most of the existing surface water is overallocated. Many communities hoping to augment their water supplies with groundwater are discovering that overpumping is already a problem, and water tables in many aquifers have fallen dangerously low.

What we really need are inclusive process-

The Colorado River Compact

- The Colorado River provides water for 30 million people in seven states and Mexico
- The Colorado River Compact of 1922 apportioned water to Arizona, California, Colorado, Nevada, New Mexico, Utah and Wyoming
- Population in the seven states has grown from 21 million in 1960 to over 48 million in 2006
- The Colorado River irrigates 4 million acres of farmland

A look at the Colorado River, crossing from west to east about 75 miles south of where the Glen Canyon Dam forms Lake Powell at Page, Arizona.

es to figure out regional approaches for equitably sharing diminishing water supplies. While necessity may finally get us there, for now rural and urban communities are often pitted against each other as more and more water is required by growing urban centers. Rural communities are justifiably prickly as they are increasingly pressured to make what they consider their water available for transfer to big cities.

And the biggest elephant of all is agriculture, which globally accounts for about 70 percent of water use. Agriculture in the West, and particularly in California, accounts for a significant amount of the food that makes its way to tables all over the United States, as well as to other countries. Yet, as we know, growing this food requires massive inputs of water in order to make the desert bloom. The Colorado River alone helps irrigate 4 million acres of farmland.

Agricultural and urban users alike are going to have to face the fact that, as water becomes scarcer, all of us are going to have to adjust to using less. Changing agricultural practices is a monumental undertaking and is absolutely necessary, but it is not the only culprit. Individuals and families can make a tremendous difference by lowering their water consumption. This will require both becoming more water efficient and changing our notion of how much is enough.

Where Do We Go from Here?

As water supplies diminish, we're facing a fundamental supply and demand issue that has to be addressed. Many cities intent on growth are exploring ways to increase supply. However, many of the supply-side solutions are both risky and expensive.

Desalination, for example, poses many challenges. It remains an energy-intensive way to produce freshwater, raising concerns both about cost and the degree to which facilities contribute to climate disruption. There are questions about how to safely dispose of the concentrated salt brine and also about the impacts of the facilities on fragile coastal ecosystems. For these and other reasons California, an obvious place to locate facilities, has been slow to approve the many proposed desalination projects.

Cities are also looking at ways to transfer water from one place to another. Many of these projects involve multibillion-dollar pipeline systems that are extremely energy-intensive because of the need to move water long distances and have severe environmental impacts. Fast-growing Washington County in southwestern Utah is proposing to build a 158-mile pipeline to bring Lake Powell water to its towns. In Colorado, an entrepreneur is proposing a 400-mile transmountain diversion to bring water from the Flaming Gorge Reservoir on the Utah-Wyoming border to Colorado's Front Range.

The reality is that our water supplies are limited and to a great degree overextended. We need to focus less on costly, energy-intensive ways to increase supply and instead concentrate far more on the demand side of the equation. Finally, there is some good news. It turns out that most cities have tremendous water conservation potential. By reducing demand per person, cities can serve more people with the same amount of water, thus eliminating the need for new water supplies. And for the most part, conservation is both less expensive and better for the environment than supply-side alternatives.

Conserving Our Way into the Future

By global standards, U.S. residents use a great deal of water per person per day—an estimated 151 gallons actually. The United States and Canada top the consumption list worldwide. By comparison, people in the United Kingdom use about 31 gallons per person per day, and in developing countries like Ethiopia, that number goes all the way down to 3 gallons.

Partly this is because we turn on the tap and water comes out, clean and cheap. It's just so easy to use more than we really need.

But because issues of water scarcity are not new to people living in the West and Southwest, many cities have robust programs that demonstrate that water conservation combined with water efficiency—using enough but not too much—can extend water supplies far more than most people would imagine. These cities can help us see what we are doing wrong and right when it comes to dealing with issues of supply and demand, and the question of how much water is enough.

Las Vegas: The Lush of the Southwest

A good way to take the measure of an area's water culture is to drive around. As you travel through the Las Vegas Valley, it's hard to conceive of a place with a more schizophrenic attitude towards water. On the Strip the message is one of water abundance. Streets are lined with massive palm trees; blocks are punctuated with impressive water displays; people relax outside in 100-degree heat, thanks to overhead misters that cool the air. It's easy to forget that water here is a scarce and precious resource.

Drive off the Strip and things get a bit more confusing. In many parts of the valley, desert landscaping is the norm, in keeping with the arid climate—Las Vegas gets about four inches of rain a year. But other areas in the valley are resplendent with emerald green golf courses, gushing fountains, and waterfalls. Raise your eyes a bit,

and just above the tops of the palm trees, the landscape is dry as dust.

From the standpoint of demand, Las Vegans have historically used a lot of water per person. In 1994, single-family residences used 264 gallons of water per person per day. The water profligacy of those days is gone, partially due to the 1992 National Energy Policy Act, which requires the use of water efficient fixtures in all houses built after 1992. However, Las Vegans still use substantially more water than residents of many other Western cities.

Cities measure water use in different ways, so it is difficult to make accurate comparisons. For this reason, the Western Resource Advocates (WRA) compare cities on the basis of water use in single-family residences—an apple-to-apple comparison. According to a 2007 report by the Pacific Institute and Western Resource Advocates, "Hidden Oasis: Water Conservation and Efficiency in Las Vegas," residents of single-family residences in Las Vegas consumed 165 gallons per person per day as compared with 110 gallons per day in Albuquerque, New Mexico, and 114 gallons in Tucson, Arizona.

Added to high consumption levels is the fact that the Las Vegas Valley has been one of the fastest-growing areas in the country for many years. The population in the valley is already about 1.8 million people, and much of the power structure there would like to see the population double by 2030.

In terms of supply, Las Vegas today depends on Lake Mead for 90 percent of its water.

The Southwest is already many years into what is currently considered a drought, and Lake Mead has about half the water it contained 10 years ago.

This mix is clearly a recipe for trouble. So, Las Vegas has some hard choices to make to ei-

Christina Roessler

THE PROBLEMS WITH SEAWATER DESALINATION

Ocean desalination—a process that converts seawater into drinking water—is being hailed as the solution to water supply problems. Proponents of desalination claim that this technology will create a reliable, long-term water supply, while decreasing pressure on other over-drawn water sources. But desalination facilities have the potential to create more problems than they solve.

Here are some reasons why communities need to think twice before embracing ocean water desalination:

1. Alternatives Abound.

Smart water agencies are making great strides in adopting efficient water management practices such as conservation, reuse, and recycling. The Pacific Institute report "Waste Not, Want Not; The Potential for Urban Water Conservation in California" found that California can meet its water needs for the next 30 years by implementing off-the-shelf, cost-effective urban water conservation. Draft guidelines released by the state of Massachusetts found that, "Prior to seeking desalinated water, proponents and communities needing additional water should first achieve savings through efficient use and conservation of existing water." Desalination is an expensive and speculative option that could drain resources away from more practical solutions.

2. It's Expensive.

Ocean desalinated water is among the most expensive ways to supply water. Producing water through ocean desalination costs three or more times what it costs to produce water from traditional supplies. It requires multiple subsidies of both water and electricity to break even, and it entails pricey upfront construction and long-term operation and maintenance costs. California American Water Company has demanded an upfront rate increase to provide for construction of its proposed plant in Monterey, California, before it has even produced a drop of water.

3. It Could Exacerbate Global Warming.

Enormous amounts of energy are needed to force ocean water through tiny membrane filters at a high pressure. Ocean water desalination can be greater than ten times more energy intensive than other supply sources. Ocean desalination proponents, such as private corporations Poseidon Resources and American Water, plan to locate plants alongside existing coastal power plants, thus potentially spurring their emission of global warming pollution.

4. It Creates the Potential for Corporate Control and Abuse.

Ocean desalination provides a new opportunity for private corporations to own and sell water. Currently, there is little regulation of these facilities, creating the possibility that private corporations would rate-gouge thirsty populations—similar to what happened in the Enron energy scheme.

A recent Food and Water Watch analysis compared average water rates charged by publicly and privately owned utilities in four states—California, Illinois, Wisconsin, and New York—and found that privately owned water utilities charge customers significantly higher water rates than their publicly owned counterparts: anywhere from 13 percent to almost 50 percent more.

Worse, corporate controlled desalination facilities have performed miserably. Poseidon Resources, whose largest investor is the private equity firm Warburg Pincus, botched a large facility in Tampa Bay, Florida. The facility, at a final price of $158 million, was completed years behind schedule and did not function until the Tampa Bay Water Authority took it over from Poseidon. Poseidon now plans to build several facilities in California, some of which are much larger, including a facility in Carlsbad. Companies like Poseidon view the ocean not as a public resource but as a vast, untapped source of profit, with unlimited potential to supply water to the highest bidder.

5. Fisheries and Marine Environments Will Be Threatened.

Many proposed ocean desalination plants are now planning to rely on "once–through" intake structures—an outdated technology that sucks in ocean water to cool the power plant. These intakes kill fish and other organisms that cannot free themselves from the intakes or that get sucked into the plants.

According to the U.S. Environmental Protection Agency, these intake structures kill at least 3.4 billion fish and other marine organisms annually. This amounts to a $212.5 million loss to anglers and commercial fishermen. California's power plant intake structures, alone, are responsible for the loss of at least 312.9 million organisms each year, resulting in a $13.6 million loss to fishermen.

As power plants begin to shift away from once–through cooling, a real danger exists that some desalination plants will use these intakes, and marine life destruction will continue. Further, the brine, or super salty wastewater created from the desalination process, also has the potential to upset our delicate coastal ecosystems.

6. It Could Pose a Risk to Human Health.

A number of public health experts have expressed concern about using ocean water as drinking water and the effect that new contaminants have on water quality. Some of these new contaminants include boron, algal toxins (for example, red tide) and endocrine disrupters, all of which are concentrated through the desalination process. Another concern is that ocean desalination draws water from coastal areas with sewage and storm water runoff.

7. It Promotes Environmental and Social Injustice.

Costs may be disproportionately borne by existing low–income communities, both those living near the plant who will not receive the water and those inland whose rates will increase to support the desalination plant, while gaining none of the benefits. In California, most proposed desalination plants would serve affluent communities in Marin County, the Monterey area, Cambria, southern Orange County, and northern San Diego County. Low–income communities located near desalination facilities could be harmed if desalination facilities increase air pollution and limit access to the ocean for subsistence fishing. A proposed desalination plant in Huntington Beach, California would extend the life of a power plant that residents have been struggling to shut down for years.

Source: Food and Water Watch

ther increase supply, reduce demand, or both. And reducing demand can be accomplished either by lowering per capita consumption, limiting growth, or a combination.

It probably won't come as a surprise to learn that Las Vegas wants to have it all. So, rather than taking a serious look at limiting growth, the valley is avidly pursuing new sources of water. Las Vegas is heavily invested in a supply-side solution.

The Southern Nevada Water Authority (SNWA) is proposing to build a massive pipeline system that would extract groundwater from a rural area of the state and pump it hundreds of miles to the Las Vegas Valley. Rural residents believe that exporting water from this high desert environment would turn the region into a giant dustbowl and that the farming and ranching communities in the area would be destroyed. They also suspect that, despite promises to the contrary, if the pipeline gets built, the pressure to keep it full will mean that more water will be pumped each year than will ever get replenished. SNWA has never released figures on the cost of the project, but it will certainly be in the billions of dollars.

SNWA would argue that, in addition to supply-side solutions, it has also put tremendous effort and money into promoting water conservation in order to curb demand. While it is true that the authority has instituted water conservation and efficiency programs, the amount of money it has spent on water conservation pales by comparison to the amount projected for the pipeline project. For every dollar invested in water conservation efforts, fourteen dollars are spent on developing new supplies, and close to 90 percent of water conservation spending has been for turf removal.

So what about curbing demand in Las Vegas? Can more comprehensive and aggressive water conservation and efficiency measures meet the needs of a growing Las Vegas? We have already seen that Las Vegans use substantially higher amounts of water than residents of Tucson and Albuquerque.

Why? The simple answer is that Las Vegas is still behind the curve in its adoption of a culture of water conservation and efficiency. A big problem is that the residents of Las Vegas receive mixed messages regarding water. On one hand they're told that Las Vegas is in a water crisis and people need to conserve—but only outdoors. SNWA does nothing to promote indoor water conservation. On the other hand, people are bombarded with visual images of water abundance.

The good news is that Las Vegas can dramatically reduce its overall water use by aggressively pursuing programs that promote both indoor and outdoor conservation. "Hidden Oasis" concludes that if Las Vegas comprehensively adopted readily available water efficiency measures inside and out, it could reduce its water demand by an additional 86,000 acre feet per

Which Desert City Is Most Water Conscious?

Albuquerque	110 gallons/person
Tucson	114 gallons/person
Las Vegas	165 gallons/person

year—close to a third of its annual allocation from Lake Mead.

Albuquerque: Developing a Culture of Conservation

Driving around Albuquerque, New Mexico, today, it's hard to believe that until the mid-1990s the residential areas, thanks to the profusion of green lawns, looked a lot like parts of the Midwest. Like other places in the West and Southwest, Albuquerque began growing by leaps and bounds in the 1960s. This growth spurt coincided with one of the wettest periods ever recorded in the history of the region. Every year the summer monsoons would come, the winter snows would accumulate as snowpack in the mountains, and it seemed there was water enough for existing residents and more.

The inconvenient truth that Albuquerque did not have boundless supplies of water came as a shock to many of the people living there. Until 1993 the common perception among city residents was that Albuquerque sat over a vast underground water source that was continually being replenished, largely by water from the Rio Grande. Most of Albuquerque's water came from this underground aquifer, and city officials thought it was virtually limitless.

The city got a rude awakening in 1993 when the United States Geological Survey (USGS) released a report concluding that there was a lot less water than people thought. In fact, water levels in the aquifer had dropped about 160 feet since the 1960s. Not only was the water level dropping, but water was not recharging nearly as quickly as

Landscaping (or xeriscaping) with plants native to the desert, such as wildflowers and cacti, eliminate the need for water-guzzling lawns.

people had thought, and water quality was diminishing as water was taken from deeper wells.

When the USGS dropped its bombshell about the depleted aquifer, the city was already in a water crisis—it just didn't know it. The city government had to move very rapidly to change people's perceptions from a sense of bountiful water to an understanding of water scarcity.

In 1994, the city put into motion a process that included extensive citizen participation in order to develop a comprehensive water policy. One of the primary goals of the plan was a 30 percent reduction of per capita water use.

In the next eight years, Albuquerque exceeded its goals and reduced water consumption by 33 percent, moving it from one of the highest per capita users of water in the Southwest to one of the lowest. As of 2006 the average person in a single-family residence in Albuquerque uses 110 gallons of water per day. This stands in stark contrast to the 165 gallons a day used in Las Vegas.

Albuquerque was able to achieve a remarkable shift in water use in a relatively short period of time. The understanding that the city faced a serious water crisis drove the change, but the city also rose to the challenge. One of the keys was a sizable budget—$1 million per year in the early years of the crisis—for promoting water conservation and developing educational materials.

Anyone visiting Albuquerque today can readily see that residents have adopted a culture of water conservation. Desert landscaping is ubiquitous. In 1995, the city adopted codes limiting the use of turf to no more than 20 percent of irrigable acreage on new private development. Albuquerque also offers rebates to help customers convert from water-intensive turf yards to low-water xeriscape landscaping. In addition, residents receive rebates for replacing high-water-use toilets and washing machines with water-efficient models;

together, toilets and washing machines account for over 40 percent of indoor water use in a typical household. These programs and others have been highly effective in helping to reduce Albuquerque's overall water consumption.

However, like Las Vegas, Albuquerque is pursuing a policy of continued growth, which will require difficult choices. The water district has already developed a program to increase supply. In 2008 water from the San Juan and Chama rivers began augmenting the city's drinking water, and the San Juan-Chama Drinking Water Project will ultimately supply up to 70 percent of the metropolitan area's future water. To its credit, however, Albuquerque remains highly ambitious in its efforts to reduce demand and continues to push aggressively for significant reductions in per capita consumption.

Tucson/Civano: A Leader in Water Conservation

If there's any place in the country that leaps to people's minds when they think of a city with a strong desert aesthetic, it's Tucson. Today almost anywhere you go in Tucson, houses are surrounded not by grass but by cacti and other desert landscaping. In fact, you have to really look to find a house with a green lawn. But it wasn't always that way. Until the 1970s, Tucson was full of lawns. Then there was a crisis: not enough water during periods of peak demand.

Rather than call for more water, in 1977 Tucson's water department decided to create a highly visible Beat the Peak campaign, encouraging residents to do their outside watering during off-peak periods. It also raised water rates across the board. And it created a new rate structure that made water more costly as consumers used more of it. Studies consistently demonstrate that

The Beckoning Cistern in Seattle collects roof water for gardens. It is part of a larger, "Growing Vine Street" project to "bring the calming rhythm of nature to the urban setting."

water demand diminishes as the price of water increases, particularly if the jump in rates is steep. Most cities have adopted a rate structure that is relatively incremental and doesn't send a strong price signal to customers. Tucson led the way in instituting substantial increases in water prices as consumption went up. While other cities have also raised rates, few have been willing to adopt Tucson's sharp rate increases, which helps to explain why Tucson is consistently at the low end of the spectrum in terms of water consumption.

The combination of approaches proved to be highly effective. Residents changed their habits, and by the early 1980s desert landscaping and

a conservation ethic were firmly established. Residents now thoroughly embrace the idea that they live in a desert and should act accordingly. Water conservation is seen as a benefit to the community rather than an individual deprivation.

But some residents of Tucson wanted to demonstrate that even more could be done to reduce water and energy consumption. So, in the 1980s a group of people began meeting to plan a new community in Tucson with a goal of significantly reducing water and energy consumption from the standard levels of the time. Planners were quite ambitious about the kind of community they wanted to create. First of all they wanted homes to be affordable rather than aimed at just the high-end market. And they also wanted it to be "an antidote to urban sprawl's five banes: loss of community, loss of open space, traffic conges-

Christina Roessler

tion, air pollution, and poor use of resources."

But what made the concept really stand out was the fact that the planners included concrete goals to reduce potable water consumption by 60 percent and home energy consumption for heating and cooling by 50 percent (over the 1995 Tucson model energy code). The way they planned to achieve these goals was not particularly complicated. In terms of energy, it meant building very tight homes (no leaks) with lots of insulation, high standards in terms of the doors, windows, and skylights, and very efficient furnaces and air conditioners. And all of the homes have solar panels. The community has been able to reduce water consumption by using water-efficient appliances, strict landscaping standards, small lot sizes, and the use of reclaimed water for outdoor watering.

It took many years to make the dream a reality, but in 2000 the first people began moving into their new homes in what is now known as Civano. Driving through Civano today, it looks like a lot of other new subdivisions in Tucson—in an odd way, one of the best things about it is that it is unremarkable. This is not a precious retreat for nostalgic baby boomers. Homes average about 1,600 to 1,800 square feet. Lots of retirees live there, but so do lots of people with young children. Only about 10 percent of the home owners characterize themselves as passionate about the environment. Most residents choose to live here because it's a nice community.

And Civano keeps expanding. Today the homes are built by Pulte, one of the nation's largest homebuilders. Pulte has been able to build homes that are even more efficient in terms of water and energy consumption than the homes built in the first phase of Civano's development (these had multiple builders). And, they're doing it at a price that's only 2 percent higher than comparable homes in the area.

Overall, the houses in Civano consume far less water and energy than "baseline" homes in Tucson. The new Pulte homes use about 47 percent less energy for heating and cooling, 32 percent less energy overall, and 42 percent less potable water than typical Tucson homes. That's really something considering that Tucson's water consumption is already low in comparison to other cities.

Civano's low per-person water and energy consumption is both an inspiration and a ray of hope as we consider our future. This community demonstrates that what constitutes "enough" may be a lot less than we think.

What We Can Learn from Desert Cities

Cities and communities in not just the Southwest, but all over the developed world, will be forced to rethink their water strategies in the years to come, including taking an honest look at the wisdom of current growth patterns in the face of shrinking water supplies. Rather than increasing supply, we need to focus more on decreasing demand.

All of us from east to west, north to south are facing the impacts of climate change and the possibility of water shortages. It's not going to be easy to reduce our water use; we've become accustomed to abundance. But we're going to have to change our concept of what is enough.

Fortunately, there is ample evidence from cities not only in the West, but all over, that smart water use, including conservation, efficiency, and behavioral changes, is the most cost-effective, least destructive, and most enduring approach to handling diminishing water supplies. Lots of cities, and Civano in particular, have proven that we can do much more to reduce our water use. We just have to make that choice.

SLOW THE FLOW

- **Get rid of your lawn.** About 70 percent of water is used outdoors and nice green lawns are a major water guzzler.

- **Choose an automatic irrigation system.** Automatic sprinkler systems can be set to water the lawn for a specified amount of time. A great deal of water can be wasted in short periods of time if sprinklers are left on unnecessarily. Outdoor faucets can flow at rates as high as 300 gallons per hour.

- **Position sprinklers** so that water lands on the lawn or garden, not on areas where it isn't needed, and avoid watering when it's windy—wind causes water to evaporate quickly.

- **Buy water-efficient appliances.** A front-loading washing machine uses one-third less water than a top-loading machine.

- **Check all faucets, pipes, and toilets periodically for leaks.** A faucet drip or invisible leak in the toilet will add up to 15 gallons of water a day, or 105 gallons a week, which adds up to 5,475 gallons of wasted water a year.

- **Install water-saving showerheads.** Low-flow showerheads deliver 2.5 gallons of water per minute or less and are relatively inexpensive. Older showerheads use 5 to 7 gallons.

- **Install a 1.6-gallon low-flow toilet.** Using these could cut indoor water use by as much as 20 percent. Older toilets use 3.5 to 7 gallons per flush.

Chapter 11

NATURAL SOLUTIONS TO OUR WATER CRISIS

By Erin Vintinner and Eleanor Sterling

The Mekong River, "Mother of the Waters," in Lao, winds 3,000 miles from its Tibetan Plateau headwaters to its delta, emptying into the South China Sea. The river, along with its feeder streams in Cambodia, China, Laos, Myanmar, Thailand, and Vietnam, comprise the 300,000-square-mile Mekong River Basin. Approximately 65 million people live in the system, with up to 80 percent supporting themselves with farming and fishing in rural areas. The river system contains almost all of the natural forms freshwater takes on earth—groundwater, lakes, ponds, streams, and wetlands. It is home to over 6,000 known species of vertebrates, and its fish fauna exceeds all but the Amazon and Congo river basins.

During monsoon season, a tributary of the Mekong River reverses direction and flows up into Cambodia's Tonle Sap Lake, advancing shorelines up to 25 miles, nourishing an enormous diversity of fish and birds, and supporting rice farms. Tonle Sap Lake is the largest freshwater lake in Southeast Asia, with impacts on Cambodia's geography, culture, and economy. The rising and falling waters influence nearly everything about life on the lake—houses and entire villages are built on stilts or float on pontoons.

Teeming with biodiversity, the Mekong is one of the most important freshwater ecosystems in the world, and it is one of the world's only major rivers with few mainstream dams. However, upstream hydroelectric dams in Laos, Thailand, and China have begun interfering with the natural water and sediment fluctuations that sustain the river basin's living systems. And more dams are slated for construction.

These threats combine with increasing water extractions, pollution, invasive species, and overfishing to paint a bleak picture for the basin's future. But these are also the same threats that are affecting freshwater ecosystems around the world, as a growing human population and calls for economic growth make ever-greater demands on freshwater.

As we know, water is essential to the existence and evolution of life on Earth, yet less than 1 percent of the world's water is both fresh and available to humans and all other freshwater-dependent species. As we confront the global water crisis, we must consider both our role and responsibility toward ensuring adequate water for other species and how we can work with nature to find solutions.

While they represent a relatively small area of the planet's surface, freshwater ecosystems, such

A restored area of the Mesopotamian Marshes, located between the Tigres and Euphrates Rivers in southern Iraq, which was historically one of the world's most important wetland environments.

Erin Vintinner and Eleanor Sterling

as rivers, streams, lakes, ponds, and wetlands (like marshes and swamps), harbor a disproportionate amount of the world's biodiversity.

Freshwater ecosystems contain an estimated 41 percent of the world's fish species and one quarter of the world's invertebrate species.[1,2] This amazing biodiversity includes everything from the endangered Mekong giant catfish (*Pangasianodon gigas)* that can weigh more than 550 pounds to the tiny 12-spot skimmer dragonfly (*Libellula pulchella*) that lives part of its life in the ponds and lakes of North America. These ecosystems also carry out many important functions that are crucial for the health of the animals and plants that live in them, the terrestrial and marine ecosystems they are connected to, and human populations that depend on them.

These functions, also known as "ecosystem services," include cycling water and nutrients throughout the atmosphere and the biosphere, modifying floods and droughts, delivering nutrients to coastal areas and floodplains, and providing habitat for aquatic plants and animals. In addition to benefiting from freshwater ecosystems through all these processes, humans also use these systems more directly for travel and transport routes, energy production through hydropower, harvesting of plants and animals for food, recreation, drinking water, waste removal, and water purification.

It is difficult to calculate a monetary value for all the services provided by freshwater ecosystems, but some scientists have estimated the value of wetlands alone to be in the trillions of U.S. dollars per year. Whatever the exact amount, it is clear that humans and freshwater ecosystems are tightly interconnected, and the health of human populations depends heavily on the healthy functioning of freshwater ecosystems.

And yet these ecosystems have the highest proportion of species threatened with extinction as they are increasingly besieged by a range of human activities, including water extraction, pollution, and physical alteration.

But there are ways to help save the ecosystems that those species and the rest of us depend on for survival–the key is to work with nature, instead of against it, to harness the power of ecosystem services to solve our water woes.

High-Impact Approaches: Building Massive Infrastructure

The history of human civilization has been tightly linked with freshwater resources. Many of the world's greatest cities are sited along lakes and rivers. In order to reap the benefits provided by these resources for human development, societies have taken a utilitarian view: damming and diverting flows for irrigation, drinking water, flood control, and hydropower; altering the natural courses of waterbodies for navigation; and directing waste streams into local rivers, lakes, and coastal marine environments.

In 1996 the world's human population was using over half of all the world's renewable fresh water contained in rivers, lakes, and accessible underground aquifers. This percentage is conservatively projected to climb to at least 70 percent by 2025, reflecting human population growth alone, and by much more if per capita consumption increases.[3,4]

"The key is to work with nature, instead of against it, to harness the power of ecosystem services to solve our water woes."

Industrialized societies in particular have been remarkably successful at delivering vast quantities of water, whenever and wherever required, by employing large-scale, capital intensive approaches with centralized management, also known as "high impact" approaches,[5] which include large dams and networks of pipes and canals that carry massive amounts of water over long distances.

But the cost for these projects continues to increase with population and the continual upkeep that these projects demand. The most-cited estimate of the cost of meeting the world's future infrastructure needs for water is $180 billion per year until 2025 for water supply, sanitation, wastewater treatment, agriculture, and environmental protection. This figure assumes that future global demand for water and water-related services will match the current level of industrialized nations and that high impact approaches will provide those services.[6]

Many of these infrastructure- and energy-intensive high-impact approaches of hydrologic control have benefited millions of people through reliable access to safe water, improved public health, expanded hydropower generation, agriculture, and reduced risks of seasonal floods and droughts. They focus on the provision of more water to meet growing human demands because planners often equate the idea of using less water with a loss of well-being.[7]

However, there are substantial social, economic, and ecological costs that are often unanticipated in the quest for high-impact approaches. Tens of millions of people have been displaced from their homes by large-scale water projects over the past century. And we regularly neglect the consequences for nonhuman species and ecological systems. Over one-quarter of all North American freshwater fauna populations of fishes, mollusks, crayfishes, amphibians, and insects are now considered threatened with extinction.[8] As humankind withdraws and pollutes a growing share of Earth's freshwater, less remains to maintain the vital ecosystems on which we also depend.[9]

In addition to water quantity, water quality is an issue for organisms downstream from us in the water cycle. Wastewater treatment, for example, cannot remove all the impurities that enter waste streams, such as chemicals from pharmaceutical and personal care products. These products, which include prescription and over-the-counter drugs, antibacterial soaps, antiseptic cleaning agents, and cosmetics, contain chemicals that move unchanged through the waste stream, ending up eventually in freshwater ecosystems and coastal areas. For example, Triclosan, the active ingredient in many antibacterial products, is now found in detectable concentrations in bodies of water across the United States. Recent research has shown that this chemical negatively impacts the hormonal system of developing frogs.[10]

Low-Impact Approaches: Ecologically Sensible Solutions

The limitations of the high-impact approach for water, combined with the sheer social and economic cost of infrastructure, indicate the need for an alternative "low-impact" approach that focuses on flexible, sustainable solutions that match in scale and geographic distribution to human populations and their needs.[11]

Low-impact approaches are local-scale, efficient, and ecologically sensitive solutions to the problem of water management. According to the Pacific Institute's *The World's Water 2002-2003*, these approaches provide genuine alternatives to the more traditional high-impact approach of centralized infrastructure. Low-

Erin Vintinner and Eleanor Sterling

impact advocates strive to improve the productivity of water use rather than seek endless sources of new supply. Society's goal becomes not the use of water, but improved social and individual well-being per unit of water used.[12]

Under a low-impact water regime, the role of management shifts from building and maintaining water-supply infrastructure to providing water services, such as new forms of sanitation, drought-resistant landscapes, urban redesign for conservation, and water reuse and recycling, for example. This approach also incorporates constraints that limit the amount of water humans can withdraw so that shortages do not disrupt how ecosystems function. These alternative approaches offer a comprehensive toolbox of possible solutions.[13]

The Value of Wetlands

A good portion of the total freshwater available in the hydrological cycle is needed to sustain aquatic ecosystems, such as lakes, rivers, wetlands, and the multitude of species that they shelter.[14] For centuries, wetlands were mistreated and misunderstood. Generally called swamps or marshes, they were considered useless, waterlogged, even dangerous land better off filled, farmed, and developed. That's one reason why over half the original wetlands in the lower 48 states have been lost and much of the rest degraded.

Wetlands provide key wildlife habitat and are also culturally significant across the world. They are found from the equatorial tropics to the frozen plains of Siberia and are crucial to the planet's well-being.[15] Healthy natural wetlands are indispensable regulators of water quantity and quality. For example, flood plain wetlands soak up and store water when rivers flood their banks, reducing downstream dam-

age. Wetlands also filter pollutants and sediments, and provide valuable products, such as food, medicinal plants, fuel sources, fiber, and timber. The value of these environmental services to humankind is immense.

Across the world, and in the United States, people are coming to appreciate wetlands for what they offer and take advantage of their ability to purify both wastewater effluent and stormwater overflows.

For example, the Carolina Bay Natural Land Treatment Program relies on a natural wetland as the final treatment stage for wastewater effluent that has already undergone primary and secondary treatment to remove solids and treat biological matter at a nearby facility.[16]

Similar systems exist in many states, from California to Florida. Especially in urbanized areas where construction and paving have increased the amount of impervious surface area, rainfall cannot percolate into the soil and is converted into overflow runoff that washes urban pollutants into nearby bodies of water or sewage systems. Excess runoff can exceed the drainage capacity of existing wastewater treatment systems, and during heavy storms cities regularly have to direct untreated wastewater into nearby streams and rivers. Across the U.S, over 700 cities and communities with about 40 million people rely on these "combined sewer systems."[17] In New York City, for example, overflow from this combined system results in 270 billion gallons of untreated wastewater flowing into New York Harbor annually.[18]

Using Rainwater as a Resource

Relatively clean rainwater that is directed into sewers makes little sense if alternatives exist, such as redirecting rainwater into parks or wetlands (though it is important to ensure that the

A floating village along Tonle Sap in Cambodia, one of the largest freshwater lakes in southeast Asia with impacts on the region's economy, culture, and ecosystems.

waste stream is managed so as not to degrade the wetlands). Another low-impact alternative is the use of permeable pavement, which is a pavement system that allows water to seep through the surface, permitting natural filtration of water through soil, rather than runoff into storm drains.

Green roofs are a further example of a low-impact solution to the problem of stormwater runoff. Various green roof designs exist, but the fundamental principle involves layering of waterproofing materials, soil support system, and appropriately chosen drought-resistant plants. Besides the ability of green roof systems to absorb rain and moderate against pulses of storm runoff, the thermal insulation provided by the soil layer can provide energy savings over conventional roofing. One such system was installed in 2002 on top of the Justice Center in Seattle, Washington, as part of the city's sustainable building program. This green roof requires minimal maintenance and is estimated to reduce annual storm water runoff from the building by 50 to 75 percent.[19] Given the extensive costs of high-impact wastewater and storm water treatment, exploring the use of low-impact water treatment options makes ecological and economic sense.

The Growing Field of Ecological Design

The Environmental Protection Agency notes that constructed wetlands are also being used to treat petroleum refinery wastes, landfill

Erin Vintinner and Eleanor Sterling

High vs. Low Impact Solutions: Working Against or with Nature

High Impact: There are substantial social, economic, and ecological costs that are often unanticipated. Tens of millions of people have been displaced from their homes by large-scale water projects over the past century. And we regularly neglect the consequences for nonhuman species and ecological systems. Examples of high-impact approaches include:

● Damming and diverting rivers for irrigation, drinking water, flood control, and hydropower

● Altering the natural course of water bodies for navigation

● Directing waste streams into local rivers, lakes, and coastal marine areas

Low Impact: Under a low-impact water regime, the role of management shifts from building and maintaining water-supply infrastructure to providing water services. These include:

● Employing drought resistant landscaping

● Redesigning urban spaces for water conservation

● Resusing and recycling water

leachates, and pretreated industrial wastewaters, such as those from pulp and paper mills. A large number of wetlands have been constructed to treat drainage from active and abandoned coal mines, particularly in Appalachia.[20]

The emerging fields of ecological design and ecological engineering are informing the practice of wetland construction. Ecological designers use appropriate technology and ecological principles to engineer low-impact solutions to environmental problems. One remarkable ecologically designed installation transformed a canal in Fuzhou, China, that was polluted with sewage. The artificial wetland constructed on the site, called an "eco machine," used a combination of plants, microorganisms, and an aeration system to restore the canal.

Today, the canal has reduced floating solids and odors, and it no longer negatively impacts downstream aquatic ecosystems.[21] Another such facility in South Burlington, Vermont, is using the principles of ecological design and constructed wetlands to successfully treat 80,000 gallons of wastewater diverted daily from the city's conventional waste treatment plant.[22]

Wastewater Is Not Always a Waste

Wastewater recycling is another potential low-impact solution to the problem of water management, as the next chapter shows. This approach emphasizes the value of wastewater as not just a "waste" product but as a potential source of water that can be put to use. In some cases, treated wastewater effluent can be used for irrigation or in situations where the use of nonpotable water is acceptable, such as for flushing toilets. However, the utility of recycled wastewater may also be extended to drinking water sources in carefully designed systems. In order to address the challenge of meeting the water needs of the growing city of Aurora, Colorado, water managers are developing an innovative solution known as the Prairie Waters Project, slated to be completed in 2010.

For this project, the city will continue to draw water from its current source, the South Platte River. Once the water enters the waste stream, it is returned to the river after passing through a treatment facility. About 20–30 miles downstream, the city will drill wells to pull water up from the riverbed, using the gravel and sand as a natural filter.

This extracted water will then be pumped back to Aurora (along the way, treated with chemicals and UV light to soften the water and remove any microbial contaminants picked up during the journey, and then filtered), approximating a closed loop of recycled water.[23] A drop of water used by an Aurora resident would find its way back to the city's taps as a half-drop in 45 to 60 days, a quarter-drop 45 to 60 days after that, and so on.[24] Innovative approaches, such as the Prairie Waters project, will be increasingly necessary as water stress increases in areas such as the southwestern United States due to increasing population and demand on a finite resource.

FACT

Freshwater ecosystems contain an estimated 41 percent of the world's fish species and one quarter of the world's invertebrate species.

Reviving the Ancient Practice of Rainwater Harvesting

One of the oldest recorded hydrological techniques, rainwater harvesting is another example of a sustainable low-impact approach to water management. Since rainwater is relatively clean in comparison with many surface waters, it makes both economical and ecological sense to use rainwater as a resource. On smaller household scales, rainwater harvesting is practiced across the world.

In Southeast Asian countries, rainwater jars are made of durable materials and may hold as much as several thousand liters. Gutters funnel rain from the roof into the mouth of the jar, which is covered with mesh to screen out leaves and other debris. The water can then be drawn from a tap at the bottom of the jar. Collecting rainwater in this way is a popular technique throughout the region, where rainfall patterns vary greatly throughout the year.

In the United States and the United Kingdom, rainwater harvesting systems have been increasingly used in households, gardens, and even commercial venues. Academic institutions, community groups, government agencies, and cooperatives such as the Texas Cooperative Extension, hosted by Texas A&M University, are actively promoting rainwater harvesting as a sustainable way to augment water supplies and reduce demand on municipal water systems. California offers a tax credit for household rainwater harvesting systems. Residents in Australian cities such as Sydney and Brisbane can receive a rebate for installing rainwater harvesting systems for household use.[25,26]

On larger scales, some municipal systems have even incorporated rainwater harvesting. For thousands of years, arid Yemen has relied on

Erin Vintinner and Eleanor Sterling

large cisterns to collect rainwater for public use. In some United States cities, such as Seattle, Washington; Tucson, Arizona; and Austin, Texas, rainwater systems are increasingly being used in larger buildings, public facilities, and schools to irrigate landscaping and supply restroom facilities.

Xeriscaping with Appropriate Plants

Another example of a water management technique that can work synergistically with nature is the practice of xeriscaping, or landscaping that does not require additional watering or irrigation to maintain. Over 50 percent of the total water used in households in the United States is used outside the home to water lawns and gardens, and to maintain pools.[27] The EPA estimates that over 7 billion gallons per day are used in landscape irrigation alone in the United States. Especially in hot and dry climates of many parts of the country, water-intensive lawns and gardens are unnecessarily consuming vast amounts of precious water.

Xeriscaping typically involves the use of appropriate plant species that tolerate or avoid water stress, the practice of hydrozoning (grouping plants with similar watering requirements), and conserving water by using garden designs and soil types that minimize evaporation. Oftentimes, these drought resistant plants and turf are native to the area and are accustomed to the local climate. There are numerous advantages to xeriscaping, including water conservation, reduced water costs and lawn and garden maintenance, and flexibility during times of water restriction or drought.

Investing in Natural Systems Pay Off

Technological solutions to our water woes will always capture our imagination, but they often solve one problem while creating another and carry high costs, both monetary and environmental. Oftentimes, there are natural, intact ecosystems that continue to offer the numerous benefits humankind depends upon.

The Navikubo Swamp, Uganda

The largest wetland in Uganda's Kampala district, the Navikubo Swamp, is a prime example of the vital ecosystem services that natural wetlands provide. Many of the city's residential settlements and some of its industrial facilities are not connected to Kampala's sewage system, and as a result, the wetland receives contaminated water flows that drain from the city's central business area, industrial district, and residential settlements.[28] The Navikubo swamp purifies the discharge before it enters Lake Victoria, which in turn serves as a drinking water source for Kampala.[29,30,31]

The originally extensive Nakivubo wetland has become severely degraded over recent years and is particularly threatened by the spread of agriculture and industrial and residential developments. The areas surrounding Nakivubo, and the wetland itself, are regarded as prime sites for urban expansion for many reasons: their proximity to the city center, land shortage in higher areas of Kampala, and relatively cheap land prices as compared to other parts of the municipality.[32]

FACT

Over 50 percent of the total water used in households in the United States is used outside the home to water lawns and gardens, and to maintain pools.

Pelicans fly over a restored marsh in Sonora, Mexico near the Baja California border. A local Yaqui Indian has restored the marsh for migrating birds. All the water for the marsh is runoff from nearby agricultural fields.

Yet recent studies conducted by the World Conservation Union and the United Nations' World Water Assessment Program have estimated the cost of replacing just the wetland's wastewater processing services with high impact technologies. The study found that the infrastructure required to achieve a similar level of wastewater treatment to that provided by the wetland would incur costs of up to $2 million (U.S.) a year in terms of extending sewerage and treatment facilities.[33,34] If residents lose this resource, they lose a vital environmental and economic asset. Investment in and protection of the Navikubo wetland is essential for the residents of Kampala.

New York City's Water Source

The case of the New York City water supply system is an excellent example of the tremendous benefits of investing in natural systems. The main sources of drinking water for the 9 million people of NYC are the Catskill and Delaware watersheds in upstate New York. The city water supply system from these watersheds is the largest unfiltered system in the world.

Since 1997, NYC has worked with upstate communities to protect and invest over $1.5 billion in the natural water purification services provided by these watersheds. This investment has allowed the city to maintain the high quality of the water from the watersheds and, as a result, avoid the prospect of a multibillion-dollar water filtration plant.

Erin Vintinner and Eleanor Sterling

NYC compensates residents of upstate watershed communities, who are significantly impacted by restrictions on their development activities, for their vital work in ensuring the quality of the water. Compensation avenues include a residential septic rehabilitation and replacement reimbursement program. This case demonstrates that stewardship of water is not an altruistic act, but a rational one of self-preservation; the goods and services that freshwater ecosystems provide are absolutely central to our quality of life. It also demonstrates the hard work it takes to arrive at effective compromises across different stakeholder groups when it comes to investing in natural systems.

Reasons To Be Hopeful

Beyond the story of the New York City water supply system, there are hopeful signs that keeping freshwater habitats intact and healthy is becoming a top global priority. Initiatives by the United Nations, such as the Millennium Ecosystems Assessment and the Ramsar Convention on Wetlands, seek to recognize and preserve the vital functions provided by freshwater ecosystems.

The remarkable Mekong River Basin is one example of such a natural system that deserves investment and protection, as it is one of the world's least degraded river systems. Several transboundary initiatives that may help balance the needs of people and wildlife are emerging between the six nations that share the Mekong. Political mechanisms, such as the Mekong River Commission, are moving towards more holistic management that takes into account environ-mental health and sustainability, though these political mechanisms are dependent on the support of their member governments.

Becoming Water Stewards

Humans and all other species are connected by the global water cycle, and we are truly each downstream from one another. This interconnectedness brings with it responsibility to properly steward our freshwater resources. In doing so, we can invest in natural systems to help us navigate our coming water crisis. There are numerous examples of how nature can help—from investing in natural and constructed wetlands for wastewater purification and storm water control, to employing the principles of ecological design, to local-scale water conservation measures such as rainwater harvesting.

The study of ecosystem services as they relate to water is still developing. Scientists are working to understand how resilient freshwater ecosystems truly are to modification without compromising essential functions. Accurately valuing water, human impacts on water, and the functions of freshwater ecosystems, is a constant challenge, as is clarifying the tradeoffs inherent in confronting the water crisis.

Although restoration and regeneration are possible, they are costly and require long-term commitment. Our best option is to preserve healthy, functioning ecosystems and the natural services that they provide. Actions we take today to reduce or mitigate human impacts on rivers, lakes, and wetlands can ensure their health for generations to come.

COMMUNITIES WORKING WITH NATURE TO SOLVE WATER PROBLEMS

While the protection and maintenance of natural wetlands is preferable, there are numerous examples of low-impact solutions that have been designed to mimic the services they provide.

Boston, Massachusetts

In the shadow of Boston's famed Fenway Park is a remarkable example of a man-made low-impact solution. Over 100 years ago, visionary landscape architect Frederick Law Olmsted designed the Emerald Necklace park system in Boston and Brookline as an engineered series of public parks serving as urban water treatment wetlands and wildlife corridors. Olmstead designed the tidal Back Bay Fens segment of the necklace, for example, to counter storm water drainage problems in Boston. While they have each been challenged by inadequate maintenance and inappropriate additions, the six parks of the necklace still comprise over 1,000 acres of parkland in one of America's busiest cities. The Emerald Necklace today is the backbone of the city's green infrastructure.

Not every city has had the foresight to preserve its wetlands. There are now thousands of constructed wetlands in use in both public and private facilities around the world.

Columbus, Ohio

Scientists at Olentangy River Wetland Research Park at Ohio State University have been demonstrating how constructed wetlands can hold and treat storm water, for example. The 13 acres of constructed wetlands at the site have been removing nitrogen, phosphorus, and sediment from the polluted Olentangy River for over a decade. In many cases, constructed wetlands can be a cost-efficient alternative to building both drinking water and wastewater treatment plants.

Augusta, Georgia

The Phinizy Swamp Nature Park in the Augusta corridor of the Savannah River is one example of this type of treatment design. The constructed wetlands in the park were designed to solve the city's long-standing violation of federal wastewater release laws and have served as Augusta's tertiary wastewater treatment mechanism since 1997. The wetlands have significantly improved water quality in the urban river corridor, and they are also the centerpiece of a unique nature park that supports K-12 environmental educational programs, research projects on constructed wetlands and clay mine restoration, and community outreach events.

Chapter 12

WATER NEUTRAL: NEW TECHNOLOGY AND GREEN DESIGN

by Eric Lohan and Tara Lohan

Every day we create a water footprint. Each shower, each flush, each time we flip on the A/C or water the lawn. And as we know, there are things we can do to cut down on our water consumption–new fixtures on our faucets, less lawn watering, shorter showers. We've read that conservation can take us–and our cities–a long way in helping to stem this crisis and that natural systems like wetlands and green roofs can act as water filtering systems.

But we can also go a step further with these concepts. If we take conservation, mix it with what we know about ecology, and add appropriate technology, we've got a whole new toolbox to work with. Water consciousness isn't just a state of mind, it is a way of thinking that can be applied to how we want our homes, businesses, and even communities, to function.

This synthesis has led to the burgeoning field of "green design," and within the planning, architecture, and engineering professions the term "water neutral" has emerged as a way to measure how sustainably we use water.

It was a decade ago when that term first came into use, although it hasn't garnered as much popularity as its cousin "carbon neutral," which is fast becoming a household concept. Water neutral, though, comes from a similar premise with the basic idea being to find sustainable sources for water entering a system and sustainable sinks for water leaving the system–whether that system is a home, business, or community.

If you're striving to build a water neutral home, for instance, you want to find ways to match, as closely as possible, the natural water cycle that existed in that spot before your home was developed. Think of it as your house borrowing water on its way from the sky to the ground. And if you're moving into or already living in a home that relies on a municipal water supply, you don't want to suck more water out of the system or put more wastewater back in. This requires finding new ways to capture and use water we'd previously be sending down the drain and into the sewers.

Like carbon neutral, water neutral is an ambitious goal. Can it be achieved? And if so, at what scale? To answer those questions, we'll look at some early examples of the synthesis of technology and ecology and explore recent water neutral homes, businesses, and communities. We'll also see how this idea is being used in the developing world.

Restroom signs in the Center for Health and Healing at the Oregon Health and Science University alert visitors to the building's novel water systems.

Early Examples of Water Neutral Design

While the term "water neutral" has been around for a decade, the concept predates it. From 1991 to 1993, eight "biospherians" were enclosed in a three-acre greenhouse in the Arizona desert. Although it garnered a media spectacle, overlooked in all the coverage was the scientific and engineering feat of Biosphere 2, as it was called, which still sets the bar for water neutral projects.

Biosphere

Inside this airtight mini-Earth was an integrated farm, including crops, fish, goats, and chickens, as well various natural ecosystems, such as a rainforest, an ocean, a wetland, a grassland, and a desert. Because of the self-contained environment, the atmospheric and water systems were closely integrated. Air conditioners condensed water from the air to be used for drinking, raising animals, and a portion of the irrigation. Wastewater from humans and animals was treated with a wetland wastewater treatment system composed of bacteria and plants. After biological treatment, water was then disinfected and used for aquaculture and the remainder of the irrigation. Plants and soil evapotranspired water back into the atmosphere to start the cycle over again.

This system provided the exclusive water and food supply for eight people for over two and a half years. While it is an elegant example of a truly water neutral system, the self-contained environment came with an energy cost equal to 700 U.S. homes (mostly from trying to cool the large glass structure). As such, biospheres are clearly not the answer to our water problems, but they do give us a glimpse of what is possible and remind us that water neutrality should never be achieved at the expense of heightened energy consumption. As we aspire to water neutrality, we should also strive for carbon neutrality, or else we trade one dire environmental problem for another.

Earthships

The design of "Earthships," however, has taken both energy and water into consideration.

In the high desert of northern New Mexico, more than 150 families live in homes known as Earthships. They're built like bunkers, with one side bermed into the pinkish dirt and an exposed wall of glass opened up to take in the sun's heat, with solar panels gleaming on the roof.

Earthships are like a home-scale version of the biosphere concept, but they were developed decades before by Earthship Biotecture beginning in 1969. They are what we would think of today as being totally "off the grid." Their remote setting requires that all services be provided by the home, including heating/cooling, electricity generation, water collection, and wastewater treatment.

These homes rely on an average annual rainfall of 12 inches, approximately one-third the national average. In this location, Earthships need about 500 square feet of roof catchment area, 2,000 gallons of cistern capacity for each resident, and thrifty water use. While this model is great for many rural areas, its value is limited in more urban and suburban areas with multistory buildings. The water frugality required of Earthship dwellers also raises the bar significantly for most North Americans.

Contemporary Water Neutral Design

If we can't live in an Earthship, what's a water-conscious person to do? Fortunately, progressive cities and proactive developers and de-

The Earthship Visitor Center in Taos, New Mexico is an example of a building that makes all its own electric power, heats and cools itself, is made out of natural and recycled materials, collects its own water, and treats its own sewage.

signers are beginning to focus on green design initiatives to combat the water problems that we're seeing today. This is becoming especially valuable as human populations are becoming increasingly urbanized around the world.

City of Chicago chief environmental officer Sadhu Johnston notes, "Water is one of our most important resources; in the next 100 years, access to water will determine whether a city thrives, so we are utilizing green technology to fundamentally redefine how we manage water resources."

Right now there are several buildings and communities that are aiming for water neutrality,

but it is important to note that as the term grows in popularity and use, there is not one set definition of what the guidelines are for water neutral.

One of the most common definitions is water neutral "with respect to developed conditions," which is what we'll talk about. What this means is that we're measuring the water footprint according to what kind of water flows already exist in an area that has previous development–such as other buildings and pavement. (This would be markedly different from an area that has a more natural water system, such as a forest or meadow.)

Two Examples of Water Neutral Design in Buildings

We know that in many places we don't have enough water to meet all of our domestic, industrial, and agricultural needs. So we either have to

149

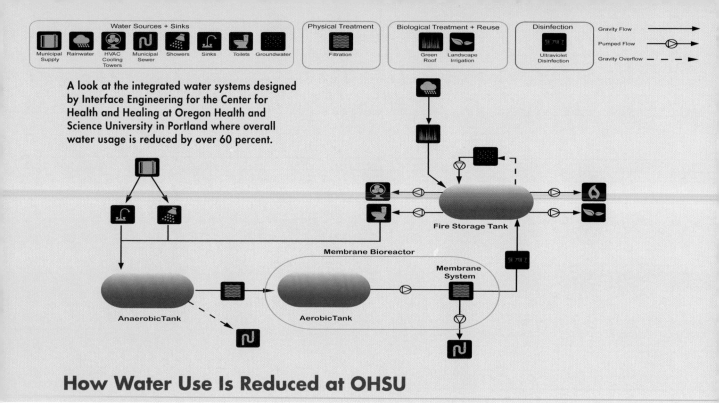

Water Sources + Sinks

Municipal Supply   Rainwater   HVAC Cooling Towers   Municipal Sewer   Showers   Sinks   Toilets   Groundwater

Physical Treatment

Filtration

Biological Treatment + Reuse

Green Roof   Landscape Irrigation

Disinfection

Ultraviolet Disinfection

Gravity Flow
Pumped Flow
Gravity Overflow

A look at the integrated water systems designed by Interface Engineering for the Center for Health and Healing at Oregon Health and Science University in Portland where overall water usage is reduced by over 60 percent.

Fire Storage Tank

Membrane Bioreactor

Membrane System

Anaerobic Tank

Aerobic Tank

How Water Use Is Reduced at OHSU

cut back on how much we use or use water more efficiently. With water neutral design, the aim is to actually do both and also to use water that we might not have known was available.

A number of buildings are taking a stab at becoming water neutral. Although none of these actually achieve total neutrality, as you will read, they do make significant contributions to decreasing water use—way beyond what could be achieved by conservation alone.

The Center for Health and Healing at the Oregon Health and Science University stands 16 stories high and occupies 400,000 square feet along the Willamette River in Portland, Oregon. This structure uses a series of interconnected water systems designed by Interface Engineering to cut down on how much water it needs to take from the municipal system and to eliminate surges of stormwater. While all potable water comes from the municipal supply, highly efficient sinks, showers, and toilets are used throughout the building, and rainwater is captured and stored in a 22,000-gallon cistern for fire suppresion, HVAC (heating/ventilation/air-conditioning) cooling towers, and radiant cooling.

Collected rainwater is also used for a portion of the toilet flushing demand, and building wastewater is treated on-site. Reusing wastewater is one important way to help stretch our water budget. Treated and disinfected water is reused for toilet flushing as well as irrigation. All wastewater is disposed on-site through the irrigation system. A green roof on the building collects a portion of the rainfall and reduces stormwater runoff. With these design changes, the building's potable water demand is reduced by a staggering 61 percent—saving an estimated 5 million gallons of water per year.

The outside of the Center for Health and Healing at the Oregon Health and Science University, which saves 5 million gallons of water per year by using green technologies and design.

In designing water neutral buildings, the most basic premise is to find available sources of water and try to match them with the most appropriate use. As in this example, if you have rainwater that is collected off a building, you can disinfect it and use it for drinking water, irrigating plants, or flushing toilets. Reclaimed water, the captured and treated wastewater, can be used to irrigate and flush but never for drinking.

In order to safely use alternative water sources, three different levels of treatment can be required–removing inorganic materials (like dirt) through filtration; removing organic material (such as that present in sewage) through biological treatment, usually using bacteria to consume it; and removing pathogenic organisms through disinfection, either with a physical treatment like ozone or UV light or a chemical treatment like chlorine, which is what most municipal systems use.

Like sewage that gets pumped out to a centralized treatment plant, reclaimed water will generally require some form of biological treatment to remove organic material. There are two new technologies that have been developed recently to help buildings recycle water right in the structure itself.

The Oregon Health and Science Building contains a "membrane bioreactor" that treats the wastewater for the 16-story building with a system located in the basement. As is typical of large municipal wastewater treatment systems, nutrients in the wastewater are consumed by bacteria. Instead of using passive settling tanks to remove the bacteria, high-pressure membrane filters scrub bacteria from the wastewater. These systems produce very clean water in a relatively small space but the downside is that they require more energy than other technologies and produce a side-stream of sludge, concentrated bacterial cells that requires further treatment. The upside is they allow biological treatment for water reuse in dense urban environments.

New developments in wetland science and engineering have resulted in "advanced wetland systems," such as a Living Machine®, that are both energy and space efficient.

Living Machines mimic natural tidal wetland processes with highly efficient communities of plants, bacteria, and other microorganisms. These systems use approximately 20 percent of the energy of membrane bioreactors and produce no sludge. They do require sunlight and more space, so you can't put them in a basement.

151

Eric Lohan and Tara Lohan

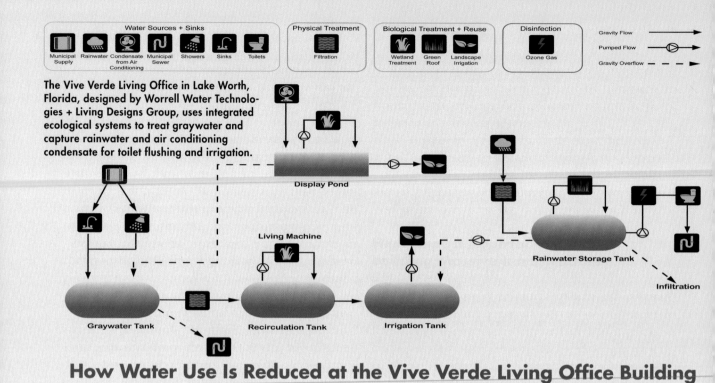

The Vive Verde Living Office in Lake Worth, Florida, designed by Worrell Water Technologies + Living Designs Group, uses integrated ecological systems to treat graywater and capture rainwater and air conditioning condensate for toilet flushing and irrigation.

Display Pond

Living Machine

Rainwater Storage Tank

Infiltration

Graywater Tank

Recirculation Tank

Irrigation Tank

How Water Use Is Reduced at the Vive Verde Living Office Building

One example of a building with a Living Machine is the Vive Verde Living Office Building, a four-story 40,000 square-foot law office in Lake Worth, Florida, that proves efficiency and smart design can also make for a better work environment. Walking into this building, visitors are greeted with an atrium that contains two floors of plants and water features, including a waterfall and a tree that reaches to the roof.

While some of these plants are used to create a natural feel inside the building, many of them are an intrinsic component of building water systems. The building itself has three integrated water systems designed by Living Machines/ Worrell Water Technologies. Rainwater is treated through a green roof system, disinfected, and then used for toilet flushing inside the building. In the second system, graywater is collected from building sinks and showers and then is treated with the Living Machine in the building atrium.

The treated wastewater is then used for irrigation outside the building. Finally, condensate from the air-conditioning system is collected in a small water feature which is recirculated from the second-story atrium to a ground floor pond over a dramatic waterfall. Water coming out of this system is used for indoor irrigation and flows into the graywater reuse system for subsequent exterior irrigation use.

As in the Oregon Health and Science Building, potable water reuse is reduced by about 60 percent, saving an estimated 200,000 gallons per year. The integration of natural systems into the building adds an important aesthetic and educational component. John Szerdi, principal of Living Designs Group, explains, "We sought to go beyond just sustainably using and reusing water to foster an appreciation of 'aquatecture' which

A Living Machine wastewater treatment system that treats wastewater generated by the Las Vegas Regional Animal Campus for reuse again as kennel washdown water. The system saves approximately 1 million gallons of potable water per year.

we define as the sensory delight from the incorporation of water into architecture."

Two Examples of Water Neutral Design in Communities

Using similar technology and design concepts, communities also can aim for water neutrality. Lloyd's Crossing is a 35-square-block mixed-use area of Portland, Oregon, with approximately 3 million square feet of commercial, office, residential, restaurant, and lodging space. By 2050, an additional 8 million square feet of mixed-use buildings and 8,000 new residents are expected. The Portland Development Commission ordered a 2004 Sustainable Urban Design Plan to direct the development of the area over the next 45 years. Its hope is that by 2050 the environmental impacts will be equal to or less than those that existed in 2004. The plan, compiled by the Seattle design firm Mithun and a panel of green design experts, maps out strategies for achieving significantly greater densities while using less water than is currently consumed.

Proposed systems and technologies include high-efficiency fixtures to reduce water use. Rainwater collection and treatment for nonpotable applications, such as building HVAC, is also planned, as is on-site wastewater treatment and reuse for other nonpotable applications, such as toilet flushing. In addition to reducing potable water demands and treating wastewater on site, the plan proposes a network of infiltration swales, which collect stormwater runoff and allow it to naturally percolate into the groundwater.

Costs from infrastructure improvements were estimated at $18 million but are expected to be paid back in 15 years because of the money saved on the decreased need for potable water and sewage disposal, with $40 million in net savings accruing over the next four decades. The proposed water budget predicts a potable water reduction of approximately 60 percent relative to business-as-usual projections.

A similar approach is being proposed for the Thames Gateway Project, a 40-mile stretch along the Thames Estuary from the London Docklands to Essex, which is currently home to 1.26 million residents, with an additional 120,000–165,000 new households expected by 2016. A recent study commissioned by the U.K. Environment Agency compiled a series of scenarios to achieve water neutrality. Relying exclusively on

153

2050 Per Plan Water Use Conditions

Precipitation
64,000,000 gallon/yr

10% of precipitation
Evaporation
6,400,000 gallon/yr

10% of precipitation
Transpiration
6,400,000 gallon/yr

Water metrics summary
©Mithun / KPFF

Potable Water
57,736,439 gallon/yr

45% of precipitation
Stormwater Runoff
28,800,000 gallon/yr

90% of potable water
Waste Water
51,962,795 gallon/yr

10% of potable water
Building System/Occupant Consumptions (System Loss)
5,773,644 gallon/yr

35% of precipitation
Groundwater Recharge
22,400,000 gallon/yr

Note: This concept plan is not intended to represent specific planned or required development proposals

A predicted water budget for Lloyd's Crossing area of Portland, Oregon based on how many people are projected to live there in 2050 and the existing building codes.

upgrading the efficiency of household fixtures such sinks, showers, toilets, and appliances, both in currently developed areas and in future development, the agency predicted it would be possible for this region to become water neutral with an expected cost of $260-360 million. If the project actually plays out as planned, it will be the largest water neutral project in the world.

How Cities Can Become Water Neutral

The question of scale needs to be carefully considered when trying to determine water reuse strategies and achieve water neutral designs. Municipalities throughout the United States and across the world have already invested substantially in collection infrastructure, and a number of large municipal water reuse proj-

ects have been implemented around the country. Of course, wastewater reuse should not be at the expense of preventing water contamination or failing to fund safe public water systems. As infrastructure ages and needs to be replaced, it is important that we continue to advocate for continued public funding to help maintain and rebuild, but also that, where appropriate, we replace outdated technology with more environmentally-friendly approaches.

In many areas of the western United States, municipalities are expanding infrastructure to provide water reuse services as well as treatment. The West Basin Water Recycling Facility in suburban Los Angeles is the largest recycled water plant of its type in the United States. It turns 8 billion gallons of treated wastewater every year into a variety of grades of reclaimed water for

Precipitation
64,000,000 gallon/yr
100%

10% of precipitation
Evaporation
6,400,000 gallon/yr

2% of precipitation
Transpiration
1,280,000 gallon/yr

Potable Water
160,378,998 gallon/yr
100%

88% of precipitation
Stormwater Runoff
56,320,000 gallon/yr

90% of potable water
Waste Water
144,341,098 gallon/yr

10% of potable water
Building System/Occupant Consumptions (System Loss)
16,037,900 gallon/yr

Groundwater Recharge
negligible

A technical advisory committee led by Mithun developed a comprehensive water neutral plan to reduce projected potable water use to less than current water use.

landscape irrigation, high-tech industrial reuse, and aquifer recharge.

Customers for the reclaimed water include Toyota, Chevron, Goodyear, and the Home Depot National Training Center. The large scale of the project assures water quality appropriate for a number of uses and employs a team of experienced operators to maintain the system. The regional scale, however, greatly increases the cost of transporting water across the city from where it is generated to where it is treated and then back to where it is reused.

Expanding the Water Neutral Context

The examples of water neutral and proto-water neutral projects above all focused on reuse for residential or commercial developments in the developed world. But to effectively address our global water problems, this conversation needs to be expanded to incorporate water neutral design in a number of other spheres, including nondomestic urban applications, environmental remediation, and applications for the developing world.

The City of Las Vegas recently built a Regional Animal Campus to facilitate the care and adoption of stray animals. This large facility requires 22,000 gallons of water per day to clean animal kennels. A reuse system was built to collect and treat wash-down water from kennel cleaning with a Living Machine and a three-stage disinfection system. Reclaimed water is then reused for kennel washing. Solar panels were installed to offset energy required by the already energy-efficient system. By reducing the potable requirements for wash-down by up to

Eric Lohan and Tara Lohan

70 percent, this system saves approximately 1 million gallons of water per year, enough to supply 100 homes.

Significant water reuse potential exists in industrial applications and in environmental remediation. Out in Casper, Wyoming, BP is spending the next 100 years or more cleaning up petrochemicals that have leached into the soil and contaminated groundwater. One of the ways they are doing this is through an advanced wetland system designed by North American Wetland Engineers that reclaims almost 1 billion gallons of water per year that is then used for irrigation. This energy-efficient process was also cost-effective, saving BP at least $12 million over other alternatives.

Due to capital costs, operations costs, and availability of reliable electrical power, a much smaller portion of the spectrum of available technologies is appropriate for developing world applications. In most areas of the developing world, water quality problems are of greater concern than water quantity problems. Irrigation water is often obtained directly from open sewers, and 25,000 people, mostly children, die each day from waterborne diseases.

The creativity and financial resources committed to the examples above also need to be directed toward the developing world, where water quality impairment and water shortages are still a matter of life and death.

A number of NGOs and innovative companies are trying to tackle these problems. "Community wastewater treatment can be a catalyst for economic development, in addition to improving public health and fostering protection of our environment," said Edward Karkari of Canada International Development Agency, describing a recent project in Tema, Ghana, where wastewater from a small community is treated by a Living Machine System and used for irrigation of a community vegetable garden. The system itself uses only three pumps and one sensor and is controlled by an inexpensive microcomputer. It is cheap to build and operate, utilizing local equipment and expertise, and is designed to withstand weekly power outages. Five families are currently using treated effluent from the system to irrigate vegetable gardens for consumption and sale.

While this type of system could be applicable elsewhere in the developing world, other new technologies are available to clean water, and there is a growing call to return to basics, like rainwater harvesting, in appropriate areas. Chennai, India, a city of over 7 million people, has no major rivers and is running out of groundwater. However, it does have rain—about 48 inches a year. Efforts are now being made to funnel rainwater that comes off roads and roofs into filtration pits and then tanks for storage, or to allow it to seep back into the ground and recharge the aquifer. Other parts of India are also using age-old systems to harvest water and help water recharge, including in Rajastan, where they have made huge improvements in the quality of life.

Our Water Neutral Future

As these examples have shown, water neutral applications are still in their infancy and the definition of the term is still evolving. But the potential exists to change the way we think about the role of water in future development.

Our water crisis does not have a techno-fix, nor is there a one-size-fits-all solution. But what are emerging are new thinking, new technologies, and new systems that seek to comprehensively address our water problems. As Peter Gleick notes, "Just as education is important, just as regulatory policies are important, just as prop-

WHAT IS WATER NEUTRAL?

- Similar to its cousin, carbon neutral, which is fast becoming a household concept, it relies on innovative design to work towards an ambitious goal

- The basic idea behind water neutral is to find sustainable sources for water entering a system and sustainable sinks for water leaving the system—whether that system is a home, business, or community

- For a water neutral home, you want to find ways to match, as closely as possible, the natural water cycle that existed in that spot before your home was developed
- It requires finding new ways to capture and use water we'd previously be sending down the drain or into the sewers
- Water neutral design is being attempted by homes, businesses, and even communities

er economics is important, there's a critical role for technology."

But in using the term water neutral as a rallying cry for water conservation, we walk a tightrope between inspiring constructive action and devolving into meaningless greenwashing. We have to ensure that as water neutral grows in popularity, its parameters are not compromised. Landscape architect Julie Bargman explains, "Eco–sound bites, like water neutral, are doing their job like any other sound bite–they catch our ear but rarely engage our brain or soul. Our projects, urban or rural, big or small, need to recognize that water is our most important concern. Beyond sound bites we need to continue to refine the goals we aspire to achieve and further develop the tools needed to achieve them until so-called 'sustainability' finally just becomes common sense."

It is likely these tools will be drawn from a spectrum of technologies and applied at a number of different scales. Advances in the understanding of ecological processes and their incorporation into engineered systems is catalyzing an ecological design revolution that has the potential to generate our most important tools for achieving both water and carbon neutrality.

As long as we consider the requirements of each watershed and the proper scale and use of appropriate technologies, and make decisions on local, ecoregional levels, we can help ease the world's strain. Learning to live with less water is an opportunity for us to rethink our policies on growth, development, and consumption. With the right tools and mindset, we can design a world that includes safe, clean water for everyone, with enough water for healthy natural systems and communities of all kinds.

Eric Lohan and Tara Lohan

WATER

WHAT WILL IT TAKE FOR US TO LEARN TO CONSERVE OUR WATER RESOURCES, WORK IN HARMONY WITH THE NATURAL WORLD, AND EQUITABLY SHARE WHAT WE HAVE LEFT?

TO CREATE A SECURE WATER FUTURE, WE NEED NEW POLICY AND NEW THINKING THAT REFLECTS THE SHARED BELIEF THAT WATER IS A FUNDAMENTAL HUMAN RIGHT TO BE SHARED BY ALL—NATURE, TOO.

THIS WILL INCLUDE DUSTING OFF THE LONG-CHERISHED BELIEF IN WATER'S SACREDNESS AND BEGINNING TO VALUE IT FOR MORE THAN ITS ALLEGED MARKET WORTH. WE'LL ALSO NEED A CODE OF ETHICS TO GUIDE EQUITABLE DISTRIBUTION, PRINCIPLES TO DEVELOP OUR WATER CONSCIOUSNESS, AS WELL

FUTURE

AS LAWS THAT PROTECT THE RIGHT TO WATER, REGARDLESS OF INCOME. WE'LL HAVE TO SUPPORT GRASSROOTS MOVEMENTS FIGHTING TO PROTECT WATER AND REINFORCE THEIR WORK WITH NEW POLICY FROM THE LOCAL LEVEL ALL THE WAY UP TO THE INTERNATIONAL LEVEL.

FORTUNATELY, THIS WORK HAS ALREADY BEGUN AND STRUGGLES FOR CLEAN, AFFORDABLE WATER AND LOCAL CONTROL OF WATER RESOURCES ARE LINKING COMMUNITIES FROM URUGUAY TO INDIA AND FROM SOUTH AFRICA TO THE UNITED STATES, THREATENING TO MAKE THE MOVEMENT FOR WATER JUSTICE ONE OF THE STRONGEST AND MOST INSPIRING THE WORLD HAS SEEN.

Chapter 13

ON DEVELOPING "WATER CONSCIOUSNESS": EIGHT MOVEMENT BUILDING PRINCIPLES

By Tony Clarke

I often wonder what it is that makes us so oblivious about the essence of life itself on this planet, namely, water. If one lives in conditions where water is scarce at certain times of the year, then perhaps one is bound to be more aware of the value of water itself, where it comes from, who owns and controls it, how much of it should be used, and how to treat it with care and respect. But, if we live in places where there is adequate access to abundant sources of water, then we tend to take water for granted in our daily lives, not knowing the local watershed from where it comes, let alone who controls it, how to use it, or treat it with respect.

In effect, our consciousness about water largely remains underdeveloped. Yet, as this book shows, the signs of a red alert are everywhere—the poisoning of our freshwater systems through the relentless contamination and pollution of lakes, rivers, and streams; the continuous damming of rivers, the tearing down of forests, and the disappearance of our wetlands; the over-irrigation of our farmlands along with the non-stop mining of our groundwater systems; plus the spread of urban sprawl and the increasingly

A stream at the Braulio Carrillo National Park, 60 miles from the Costa Rican capital San Jose.

heavy use of water by certain high-tech industries—all signifying the assault and damage being waged against the Earth's freshwater sources. Add to this the impacts of global warming, which will dramatically increase the hot spots around the world while reducing annual water runoffs for rivers from melting glaciers.

In short, the time has come to develop a new consciousness about water before it is too late. In varying ways, the chapters in this book provide entry points into this water consciousness. But underlying these chapters is a web of eight themes about water itself. Each of these themes is interrelated and interwoven with the others. Taken together, they can help us deepen our understanding of water, thereby providing a better framework for acting to protect this precious resource.

1. Water Integrity: Recognizing Water's Unique Properties

For the most part, indigenous peoples and cultures have always had a deep understanding of, and relationship with, water. Through their traditions, indigenous peoples have recognized that water has special characteristics and integrity in its own right. As a result, their legends and stories speak about water with a certain sense of mystery and awe. Water is understood to be the blood of Mother Earth, giving life to plants, animals, and humans alike. As such, water is considered by indigenous peoples to be sacred, possessing great value and dignity, and is therefore to be treated with both reverence and respect.

While indigenous cultures have long recognized many special characteristics and properties of water, more recently scientists have made new discoveries about how unique it really is. In a variety of ways, water scientists are using the new technologies available to them to better understand the molecular characteristics and properties of water. For example, the fact that water in trees will expand or contract in response to changing moon cycles during different seasons of the year suggests that there are unique characteristics and properties of water that need to be better understood.

One method used by scientists today is studying the diverse crystal formations of water. When water is frozen, crystal formations take place. Viewed under a microscope, however, these water crystals take on very different shapes and forms. What these scientists have also found is that water crystal formations do change as water passes naturally through different kinds of terrain and foliage like flowers, trees, or shrubs. Moreover, there is even some evidence that water crystals will alter their formation in response to changing colors.

In short, water has special characteristics and properties that give it a unique integrity. By knowing and appreciating the special characteristics of water, we begin to learn more about the integrity of water, which in turn, brings us in touch with the essence of our water consciousness.

2. Water Commons: Sharing with People and Nature

The very fact that water is essential to life on this planet means that water belongs to all people and nature. Neither humans, plants, or animals can survive on this planet without water. Like the air we breathe, water is an essential ingredient of the space and life we share in common with each other as human beings and with nature itself. As an essential part of the commons, therefore, water must be available to all people and nature.

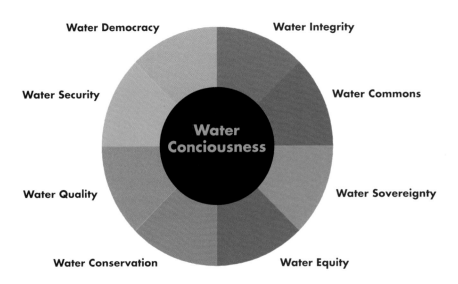

Today, however, we live in a world where everything is for sale. While most human societies and civilizations have traditionally recognized the water commons, our modern world is rapidly moving in the opposite direction by commodifying water as a product to be bought and sold in the marketplace. Instead of viewing water as a life-giving source, it is considered an economic good or commodity to be sold in the market like cars, perfume, or shoes. And once the market becomes the mechanism for the distribution of water, it is made available to those who have the ability to pay, rather than universally available to all people and nature.

The notion of the water commons, therefore, is an important part of developing our water consciousness. It sets the parameters for deepening our understanding of why it is imperative to preserve and protect this precious resource. For humans, it can also be deeply personal. After all, depending on our age, somewhere between 55 and 75 percent of our bodies is composed of water. As a constitutive part of our existence, it is essential for our very survival. We hold this in common with all other humans and with nature itself. Resisting the commodification of water in our lives is an important step in preserving our common humanity on this planet.

3. Water Sovereignty:
Enhancing Local Community Control

Who owns and controls water? If we accept the principle of the water commons, then water essentially belongs to people and to nature. From this perspective, water is not to be owned and controlled by for-profit corporations or the private sector. Nor is it necessarily to be owned and controlled by governments or the public sector. If water really belongs to the people, for example, then local communities should be able to exercise ownership and control over their local watersheds.

Today, we find this notion of water sovereignty constantly being twisted and distorted through the commodification and privatization of water. Under the guise of private-public-partnerships, for-profit corporations are increasingly taking control over the management of water supplies and the delivery of water services in cities and towns. At the same time, governments and corporations are constructing massive dams to redirect the natural flow of rivers to provide hydropower and water sources for cities, thereby often draining much needed water from food producing lands and rural communities. As a result, corporations and governments are seizing control over the water sovereignty of communities and nature itself.

This is why the issue of water sovereignty is key to developing our water consciousness. Above all else, water is local. Local watersheds exist to serve the needs of people and nature in their surroundings. Governments can play an important role in managing and regulating water as a public or an ecological trust, but ultimately water sovereignty should reside in people and nature.

4. Water Equity:
Ensuring Equal Distribution

Water is essential to human survival and should be made available to all people equitably on the planet. Access to clean and adequate supplies of water is a universal human right. Accordingly, governments have an obligation to ensure that their people have adequate access to clean water on an equitable basis. For these reasons, water justice activists put a major priority on advocating that water services be delivered to people through public rather than private systems.

Tony Clarke

Once the private sector is in charge of water services, market mechanisms determine who gets access to water on the basis of the ability to pay.

Horror stories from around the world illustrate how poor people have had their water cut off simply because they are unable to pay the high water rates charged by for-profit corporations that have taken over the running of local water utilities. In virtually every case where a private company takes over the operations of a public water utility (through concessions, contracts or outright ownership), one of the first measures introduced is the spiking of water fees, not just to generate sufficient revenues to improve services but also to accumulate profits to meet the bottom line of its shareholders. As a result, millions of people in developing countries have experienced water cutoffs at the hands of private water companies and their water meters.

Understanding and acting on issues of water equity is an important part of the process of developing and deepening one's water consciousness. Unless we understand that water is a universal human right that must be made available through mechanisms of equitable distribution, there can be no solution to the impending worldwide water crisis.

5. Water Conservation: Using Only What We Need

As noted above, people living in conditions of water scarcity, drought, and deserts know much more about the need to practice water conservation than those living in places of water abundance. In addition, it is generally assumed that water is not finite but instead is a renewable resource. But this is largely a myth. The hydrologic cycle, whereby the earth's freshwater supplies are renewed through precipitation that falls and seeps into the ground then evaporates again later, has been damaged by the expansion of urbanization, industrialization, and now global warming.

As a result, the earth is gradually drying up in many regions and the world as a whole is running out of freshwater. This has already become clear in many regions of the United States, ranging from the southwestern states of Arizona, California, New Mexico, and Nevada to the farm belt states of the Midwest and the southeastern states, including Florida, Alabama, Georgia, and the Carolinas. Moreover, water scientists are predicting the return of drought conditions to the Great Plains region of the Midwest, spurred on by global warming conditions. While water conservation practices have improved in several states, the United States and Canada continue to be the highest per capita consumers of water in the world.

Water conservation is one of the main keys for developing a deeper water consciousness. Very often it is only when people experience water scarcity and understand what it means to be water poor that they cultivate an awareness and appreciation of the essential value and importance of water. By the same token, it is through the activity of practicing water conservation that people learn how to deepen their respect and care for water as the source of life itself.

6. Water Quality: Protecting Healthy Ecosystems

Being conscious about the water around us is not only a matter being aware of water shortages, or unjust distribution, or who controls or governs, but also the quality of water and the issue of clean water. Fundamentally, this is a matter of health affecting people, animals, and plant life. If a watershed or groundwater system is polluted or contaminated by a nearby city dump or waste

A boy drinks the remaining water from a pitcher as he waits in line for the arrival of an army vehicle, which will supply drinking water at Mohammadpur in Dhaka, Bangladesh.

disposal from a neighboring farm, then this poses a direct threat not only to human health in the area but also to animal and plant life.

Throughout the world, the poisoning of our rivers, lakes, and groundwater systems continues apace, almost unabated. Industries such as mining, oil production, and auto and computer manufacturing, use huge volumes of water every day that becomes contaminated with toxic chemicals during their production processes. In the Great Lakes, the largest freshwater system on the planet, high levels of dioxins, polychlorinated biphenyls (PCBs), mercury, lead, and countless other chemicals have been found in all the lakes at every depth, thereby polluting surrounding watersheds with up to a 100 million tons of hazardous wastes each year.

What happens when we continue to pollute our natural water systems? Not only do we contaminate a portion of nature but we reduce the amount of freshwater sources that are available for people, animals, and plant life. Being water conscious requires protecting and preserving healthy ecosystems, which, in turn, means being vigilant in resisting and preventing the polluting and poisoning of our lakes, rivers, and groundwater systems.

7. Water Security: Preventing Water Wars

In relations among countries, regions, and peoples around the world, disputes over

Tony Clarke

water are at the center of conflicts and wars. The struggle for water security has been a central factor in community survival since humans have been competing with each other for resources. By the same token, the pursuit of water security through the sharing of a common water source has also been the basis of peace and unity among peoples.

Throughout the world today we see conflicts and wars brewing over the struggle for water security. Although it is generally acknowledged that the war in Iraq has been largely about securing control over oil sources in the Middle East, it has also been about securing access to and control over water sources. One of the two largest river systems in the Middle East, the Euphrates River, runs through Iraq, and control over this water source is of high strategic importance for relations between peoples and nations in this region. And, in the United States, as problems of water scarcity mount in different regions, conflicts have already begun to intensify.

The struggle for water security, which is so intertwined with the other themes we have been discussing, provides another key to developing and deepening water consciousness. At their core, struggles for water security generally have to do with matters of life and death. This doesn't just apply to the drinking water that people need in order to survive. Like oil, water too has become the lifeblood of our industrialized society. Whether we are talking about the agriculture, energy, mining, or manufacturing sectors of our economy, the production processes involved in these industries require ever increasing amounts of freshwater. The struggle for water security has become imperative for the survival of our society. In turn, this serves to intensify potential conflicts.

8. Water Democracy: Working Together as Water Guardians

The operating principles of developing water consciousness include the recognition that water belongs first and foremost to people and nature, that it is deeply personal, and that it is local. In our capacity as citizens, people can become the primary water guardians. By working together to protect and preserve their local watersheds, citizens and communities actively engage in a process of water democracy. This process, in turn, involves a grassroots, bottom-up approach.

Around the world today, there are myriad examples of water democracy taking place in local communities where people have organized themselves to become water guardians. They include urban community groups who have organized to prevent the privatization of their municipal water utilities; peasants and indigenous peoples who have bonded together to stop the construction of dams and river diversions in rural areas; the local community environmental activists who are working with nature to protect their watersheds and wetlands while promoting rainwater harvesting; plus the growing networks of people who are building community resistance to bottled water consumption and calling for major water conservation initiatives in agriculture and other industries.

In effect, it is through our actions as water

"Governments can play an important role in managing and regulating water as a public or an ecological trust, but ultimately water sovereignty should reside in people and nature."

guardians that we give full expression to the principle of water democracy. And, it is by giving expression to water democracy that we, in turn, ignite our water consciousness, for it is through our actions as water guardians that our passion and our determination to preserve and protect this precious resource comes fully alive. It is also through our concrete actions with others in fighting for and defending water that we come in touch with the other themes of our water consciousness. What's more, if our actions in defense of water are rooted in local, community-based, grassroots activities, then, like free flowing water itself, we embody the essence of living democracy.

Translating Water Consciousness into Action

Taken together, these eight themes—water integrity, water commons, water sovereignty, water equity, water conservation, water quality, water security, and water democracy—are a set of keys for unlocking the doors of our consciousness about water itself. It is through these themes that we can come to develop and deepen our water consciousness, which is essential for the future of humanity and the planet itself. As we have seen, none of these themes exist in isolation from the others. They are all interrelated and interdependent with one another. Entering through one theme such as "water equity" can open up an awareness of the others like the importance of "water quality" and "water conservation" or the implications of "water commons" or "water democracy" itself.

Yet, these are not just themes to trigger or ignite our consciousness about water. They are also principles to motivate and inform our actions about water. Each of these eight themes is, at the same time, a principle for action that we can use as citizens and communities in preserv-

ing and protecting water as a precious resource. Community groups actively organizing and protesting against the privatization of their public water utilities are likely to emphasize "water equity" and "water democracy" as basic principles for their actions, while community groups fighting to protect their local watersheds are more likely to focus on the principles of "water conservation" and "water quality." Yet, just as a community's local watershed and public utility are interlinked, so too are these and related principles for action connected, as well.

In effect, these eight principles, taken together, are essential for cultivating and building a water justice movement. When it comes to social movement building, it's highly important to be conscious of what we are doing. Cultivating any movement involves enabling people to come together and unite around a shared vision of the future. And this, in turn, embodies key ideas and principles as foundation stones for the kind of society we want to build. This is also true with the building of the water justice movement, which is made up of diverse community-based struggles going on all around the world.

Together, these eight principles can help us to broaden and deepen our consciousness about water itself as the basis for our actions. This is imperative for the long haul when it comes to building a movement. Having a shared vision that can be broadened and deepened is an important part of ensuring that the movement endures.

In short, to become effective water guardians, we need to develop the discipline of working with these eight principles as an integral part of our actions to preserve and protect water as a precious resource on this planet. In so doing, we will contribute to the building of an authentic water justice movement—in our own communities and in regions throughout the world.

Chapter 14

THE SACRED WATERS

By Vandana Shiva

"Water is the source of all life"
—The Qur'an

"Apo hi stha mayobhuvas"("Water is the greatest sustainer and hence is like a mother")
—Taittiriya Samhita

Throughout history, water sources have been sacred, worthy of reverence and awe. The advent of water taps and water bottles has made us forget that before water flows through pipes and before it is sold to consumers in plastic, it is a gift from nature.

In India, every river is sacred. Rivers are seen as extensions and partial manifestations of divine gods. According to Rigvedic cosmology, the very possibility of life on earth is associated with the release of heavenly waters by Indra, the god of rain. Indra's enemy Vrtra, the demon of chaos, withheld and hoarded the waters and inhibited creation. When Indra defeated Vrtra, the heavenly waters rushed to earth, and life sprung forth.

According to Hindu mythology, the Ganges River originates in the heavens. The Kumbh Mela, a great festival centered around the Ganges, is a celebration of creation. According to one fable, the gods and demons were fighting over the *kumbh* (pitcher) filled with *amrit* (nectar), created by *sagar manthan* (the churning of the oceans). Indra's son Jayant ran away with the *kumbh* and for 12 consecutive days the demons fought the gods for the pitcher. Finally, the gods won, drank the *amrit*, and achieved immortality.

During the battle over the *kumbh*, five drops of *amrit* fell on earth at Allahabad, Haridwar, Nasik, and Ujjain, the four cities where the Kumbh Mela is still held. To this day, each city holds its own *mela* every 12 years. Allahabad's Maha Kumbh Mela in 2001 was one of the most spectacular festivals to date. Close to 30 million people gathered in the holy city to bathe in the sacred river Ganges.

The oldest and best known myth about the creation of the Ganges is the story of Bhagirath. Bhagirath was the great-great-great-grandson of King Sagar, the ocean king. King Sagar had slain the demons on the earth and was staging an *aswamedh-yagya* (a horse sacrifice) to declare his supremacy. Indra, the rain god and the supreme ruler of the kingdom of gods, feared losing his power of the *yagya* and stole Sagar's horse and tied it to the ashram of the great sage Kapil. At

A Hindu woman worships the god of the sun "Surya" at Sagar Island while taking a holy dip in the confluence of the Ganges River and the Bay of Bengal at Sagar Island, about 93 miles south of the Indian city of Kolkata.

169

the time, Kapil was in deep meditation and unaware of Indra's mischief.

When King Sagar learned of his missing horse, he sent his 60,000 sons in search of it. The sons finally discovered the horse near the meditating sage and began to plot their attack on him. When the sage opened his eyes, he was angered to find the scheming brothers and reduced them to ashes.

King Sagar's grandson Anshuman was eventually successful in recovering the horse from Kapil. Anshuman reported to his grandfather that the sage had burned the 60,000 sons out of anger; the only way for the sons to reach their heavenly abode was if the Ganges could descend from Heaven so its water could cleanse the sons' ashes. Unfortunately, Anshuman and his son Dilip failed in bringing the Ganges to earth.

Finally, Anshuman's grandson Bhagirath went to the Himalayas and started meditating at Gangotri. After a long meditation, the Ganges appeared to him in bodily form and agreed to descend to the earth if someone could break her mighty fall, which would otherwise destroy the earth. King Bhagirath appealed to Shiva, who eventually agreed to use his hair to soften the descent of the Ganges. The river followed Bha-

girath to where the ashes of King Sagar's sons were piled, purified their souls, and paved their way to the heavens.

Because the Ganges descends from heaven, she is a sacred bridge to the divine. The Ganges is a *tirtha*, a place for crossing over from one place to another. The *Gangastothra-sata-namavali* is an ode to the river, and reveals the profound effect of the river in India. The salute has 108 sacred names for the river.

The Ganges' role as mediator between this world and the divine is embodied in death rituals among Hindus. The ashes of our ancestors and kin are cast in the Ganges, so that, like the sons of Sagar, they too will be ensured a transition to the heavens. I was born and brought up in Doon Valley, bounded by the Ganges on the east and the Yamuna on the west. The rivers have nurtured me and shaped my sense of the sacred from childhood. One of the most moving experiences I had in recent years was immersing my father's ashes in the Ganges at Rishikesh.

Like the Ganges, the Yamuna, the Kaveri, the Narmada, and the Brahmaputra are all sacred rivers and are worshiped as goddesses. They are believed to cleanse and wash away spiritual and material impurities. Their reputed purifying characteristics are the reasons why, at their daily bath, devout Hindus chant, "O Holy Mother Ganga, O Yamuna, O Godavari, Oh Sarasvati, O Narmada, O Sindhu, O Kaveri. May you all be pleased to manifest in these waters with which I shall purify myself."

The Ganges does not merely possess the purifying qualities of water; it is saturated with antiseptic minerals that kill bacteria. Modern bacteriological research has confirmed that cholera germs die in Ganges water. Dr. F.C. Harrison writes:

A peculiar fact, which has never been sat-

"When time comes for us to again rejoin the infinite stream of water flowing to and from the great timeless ocean, our little droplet of soulful water will once again flow with the endless stream."

—William E. Marks, *The Holy Order Of Water*

isfactorily explained, is the quick death, in three to five hours, of the *Cholera vibrio* in the waters of Ganga. When one remembers sewage by numerous corpses of natives, often cholera casualties, and by the bathing of thousands of natives, it seems remarkable that the belief of the Hindus, that the water of this river is pure and cannot be defiled and that they can safely drink it and bathe in it, should be confirmed by means of modern bacteriological research.[1]

It is no wonder that the Indian people hold the Ganges and other rivers dearly and believe they possesses mysterious powers. It is not surprising that despite the colonization of India by Coca-Cola and McDonald's, millions of people feel drawn to the Ganges on the occasion of Kumbh Mela.

An Ecological Tale

Ganga, whose waves in swarga flow,
Is daughter of the Lord of Snow.
Win Shiva, that his aid be lent,
To hold her in her mid-descent.
For earth alone will never bear
These torrents traveled from the upper air.[2]

The treks to the source of the Ganges are among my fondest memories of childhood. At an altitude of 10,500 feet stands the Gangotri, where a temple is dedicated to Mother Ganga, who is worshiped as both a sacred river and a goddess. A few steps from the Ganga temple is the Bhagirath Shila, a stone upon which King Bhagirath supposedly meditated to bring the Ganges to the earth. The shrine opens every year on Akshaya Tritiye, which falls during the last week of April or the first week of May. On this day, farmers prepare to plant their new seeds. The Ganga temple closes on the day of Deepavali, the festival of lights, and the shrine of the goddess Ganga is then taken to Haridwar, Prayag, and Varanasi.

The story of the descent of the Ganges is an ecological story. The above hymn is a tale of the hydrological problem associated with the descent of a mighty river like the Ganges. H.C. Reiger, the eminent Himalayan ecologist, described the material rationality of the hymn in the following words:

In the scriptures a realisation is there that if all the waters which descend upon the mountain were to beat down upon the naked earth, then earth would never bear the torrents. ... In Shiva's hair we have a very well known physical device, which breaks the force of the water coming down, ... the vegetation of the mountains.[3]

The Ganges is not just a giver of peace after death—she is a source of prosperity in life. The Gangetic plain is one of the most fertile regions of the world. At the beginning of the ploughing season in Bihar, farmers, prior to planting their seeds, put Ganges water in a pot and set it aside in a special place in the field to ensure a good harvest. It is this treatment of the organic as sacred that inspired geographer Diana Eck to call the Ganges an "organic symbol." Eck writes:

For the Ganga's significance as a symbol is not exhaustively narrative. First, she is a river that flows with waters of life in a vibrant universe. Narrative myths come and go in history. They may shape the cosmos and convey meaning for many generations, and then they may gradually lose their hold upon the imagination and may finally be forgotten. But the river remains, even when the stories are no longer repeated.[4]

Fourteen miles beyond Gangotri is Gaumukh, a glacier formed like the snout of a cow that gives rise to the Ganges. The Gaumukh glacier, which is 24 kilometers in length and 6 to 8 kilometers in width, is receding at a rate of 5 meters per year. The receding glacier of the Ganges, the lifeline for millions of people in the Gangetic plain, has serious consequences for the future of India.

Christianity and the Sacred Waters

The sacredness of water has been inspired both by the power of rivers and by water as a life force. T. S. Eliot once wrote about the Mississippi River, "I do not know much about gods, but I think the river is a strong brown god."[5]

All over the world we see the spiritual importance of water: in France, a temple sacred to the goddess Sequana is located at the source of River Seine, and the Marne River gains its name from Matrona, Divine Mother; the ancient name of the Thames River in England is Tamesa or Tamesis, denoting a river deity. In their book *Sacred Waters*, Janet and Colin Bord list 200 ancient and holy wells in England, Wales, Scotland, and Ireland that have survived into modern times.[6]

Spiritual worship of water was wiped out in Europe with the rise of Christianity. The new religion called water worship pagan and denounced it as an abomination. At the Second Council of Arles, held around A.D. 452, a canon declared, "If in the territory of a bishop, infidels light torches or venerate trees, fountains or stones, and he neglects to abolish this usage, he must know that he is guilty of sacrilege."[7] In A.D. 960, Saxon King Edgar issued a decree requiring that "every priest industriously advance Christianity, and extinguish heathenism, and forbid the worship of fountains."[8] Such edicts continued to be issued well into the 12th century.

In the 15th century, the Hereford Diocese Cathedral Registers passed a decree banning the worship of wells and other water sources in Turnaston, England:

Although it is provided in the divine laws and sacred canons that all who shall adore a stone, spring or other creature of God, incur the charge of idolatry. It has come to our ears, we grieve to say, from the report of many credible witnesses and the common report of the people, that many of our subjects are in large number visiting a certain well and stone at Turnaston in our diocese where with genuflections and offerings they, without authority of the Church, wrongfully worship the said stone and well, whereby committing idolatry; when the water fails they take away with them the mud of the same and treat and keep it as a relic to the grave peril of their souls and a pernicious example to others. Therefore we suspend the use of the said well and stone and under pain of greater excommunication forbid our people to visit the well and stone for purposes of worship. And we depute to each and all of you and firmly enjoin by virtue of holy obedience, to proclaim publicly in your churches and parishes that they are not to visit the place for such purposes.[9]

Despite the ban on water worship, people's deep faith in the sacredness of water persisted. In order to protect holy rituals, people converted sacred places for Christian use; old customs were absorbed into Christian rituals and water worship hid behind a Christian facade.[10] Water maintained its sacredness in rituals of baptism and hand washing. Baptism sites and churches were built close to and, at times, over wells.

Giving "Value" to Water

The word *value* is derived from the Latin term *valere* meaning "to be strong or worthy." In communities where water is sacred, the worth of water rests on its role and function as a life-force for animals, plants, and ecosystems. However, commodification of water reduces its value only to its commercial value. The *Oxford English Dictionary* now defines *value* in primarily economic terms: "that amount of some commodity, medium of exchange, etc, which is considered to be an equivalent for something else; a fair or adequate equivalent or return." Like the term *value, resources* also has an interesting root. It originated from the word *surge*, meaning "that which has the capacity to rise again." Unfortunately, the term now means that which gains value as raw material for industry.

The proposal to give market values to all resources as a solution to the ecological crisis is like offering the disease as the cure. With the arrival of the industrial revolution, all value became synonymous with commercial value, and the spiritual, ecological, cultural, and social significance of resources was eroded. Forests were no longer living communities; they were reduced to timber mines. Minerals were no longer veins of the earth; they were merely raw material. We are now witnessing the commodification of two vital resources—biodiversity and water—which, for a long time, were beyond the reach of forest industrialization. Biodiversity is now a mere genetic mine and water a commodity.

The water crisis results from an erroneous equation of value with monetary price. However, resources can often have very high value while having no price. Sacred sites like sacred forests and rivers are examples of resources that have very high value but no price. Oceans, rivers, and other bodies of water have played important roles as metaphors for our relationship to the planet. Diverse cultures have different value systems through which the ethical, ecological, and economic behavior of society is guided and shaped. Similarly, the idea that life is sacred puts a high value on living systems and prevents their commodification.

Protection of vital resources cannot be ensured through market logic alone. It demands a recovery of the sacred and a recovery of the commons. And these recoveries are happening. A few years ago, a few thousand pilgrims used to walk from villages across north India to Hardwar and Gangotri to collect Ganges water for Shivratri, the birthday of the god Shiva. Carrying *kavads* (yokes from which two jars of holy water dangle and are never allowed to touch the ground) the *kavadias* now number in the millions. The highway from Delhi to my hometown, Dehra Dun, is shut during the weeks of the pilgrimage. Villages and towns put up free resting and eating places along the entire 200-kilometer pilgrimage route. The brightly decorated *kavads* containing Ganga water are a celebration of and dedication to the sacred.

No market economy could make millions walk hundreds of kilometers in the muggy heat of August to bring the blessings of the sacred waters to their villages. The 30 million devotees who went to bathe in the sacred Ganges for the Kumbh Mela did not see the value of the water

> **"The proposal to give market values to all resources as a solution to the ecological crisis is like offering the disease as the cure."**

Vandana Shiva

in terms of its market price but in terms of its spiritual worth. States cannot force devotees to worship the water market.

Sacred waters carry us beyond the marketplace into a world charged with myths and stories, beliefs and devotion, culture and celebration. These are the worlds that enable us to save and share water, and convert scarcity into abundance. We are all Sagar's children, thirsting for waters that liberate and give us life—organically and spiritually. The struggle over the *kumbh*, between gods and demons, between those who protect and those who destroy, between those who nurture and those who exploit, is ongoing. Each of us has a role in shaping the creation story of the future. Each of us is responsible for the *kumbh*—the sacred water pot.

People gather at the Osun sacred river to collect water during an annual festival held to worship a river goddess in Osogbo, southwest Nigeria.

Chapter 15

MAKING WATER A HUMAN RIGHT

By Maude Barlow

Finally, the global water justice movement is demanding a change in international law to settle once and for all the question of who controls water. It must be commonly understood that water is not a commercial good, although of course it has an economic dimension, but rather a human right and a public trust. What is needed now is binding law to codify that states have the obligation to deliver sufficient, safe, accessible, and affordable water to their citizens as a public service. While "water for all, everywhere, and always" may appear to be self-evident, the fact is that the powers moving in to take corporate control of water have resisted this notion fiercely. So have many governments, either because, in the case of rich governments, their corporations benefit from the commodification of water or, in the case of poor governments, because they fear they would not be able to honor this commitment.

So groups around the world are mobilizing in their communities and countries for constitutional recognition of the right to water within their borders and at the United Nations for a full treaty that recognizes the right to water internationally. (The terms "covenant," "treaty" and "convention" are used interchangeably at the U.N.)

Rosmarie Bar of Switzerland's Alliance Sud explains that behind the call for a binding convention or covenant are questions of principle. Is access to water a human right or just a need? Is water a common good like air or a commodity like Coca-Cola? Who is being given the right or the power to turn the tap on or off–people, governments, or the invisible hand of the market? Who sets the price for a poor district in Manila or La Paz– the locally elected water board or the CEO of Suez? The global water crisis cries out for good governance, says Bar, and good governance needs binding, legal bases that rest on universally applicable human rights. A U.N. covenant would set the framework for water as a social and cultural asset, not an economic commodity. As well, it would establish the indispensable legal groundwork for a just system of distribution. It would serve as a common, coherent body of rules for all nations, rich and poor, and clarify that it is the role of the state to provide clean, affordable water to all of its citizens. Such a covenant would also safeguard already accepted human rights and environmental principles in other treaties and conventions.

Michigan lawyer Jim Olson, who has been deeply involved in the fight against Nestlé, says the point must be "repeated and repeated" that

A Kashmiri refugee drinks water at the Thuri Park refugee camp on the outskirts of the earthquake-devastated city of Muzaffarabad in Pakistan-administered Kashmir.

privatization of water is simply incompatible with the nature of water as a commons and, therefore, with fundamental human rights. "Water is always moving unless there is human intervention. Intervention is the right to use, not own and privatize to the exclusion of others who enjoy equal access to use water. It is important to distinguish between sovereign ownership and control of water, enjoyed by states or nations through which water flows or moves, and private ownership. Sovereign state ownership is not the same and has to do with control and use of water for the public welfare, health and safety, not for private profit." If on the other hand, says Olson, the state sides with the World Bank and negotiates private rights to its water with corporations, that state has violated the rights of its citizens, who would have redress under the principle of human rights if the covenant is well crafted.

A human rights convention or covenant imposes three obligations on states: the Obligation to Respect, whereby the state must refrain from any action or policy that interferes with the enjoyment of the human right; the Obligation to Protect, whereby the state is obliged to prevent third parties from interfering with the enjoyment of the human right; and the Obligation to Fulfill, whereby the state is required to adopt any additional measures directed toward the realization of that right. The Obligation to Protect would oblige governments to adopt measures restraining corporations from denying equal access to

"Water is life's matter and matrix, mother and medium. There is no life without water."
—Albert Szent-Gyorgyi, Hungarian biochemist and winner of Nobel Prize for Medicine.

water (in itself an incentive for water companies to leave) as well as polluting water sources or unsustainably extracting water resources.

At a practical level, a right-to-water covenant would give citizens a tool to hold their governments accountable in their domestic courts and the "court" of public opinion, and for seeking international redress. Says the World Conservation Union, "Human rights are formulated in terms of individuals, not in terms of rights and obligations of states *vis-à-vis* other states as international law provisions generally do. Thus by making water a human right, it could not be taken away from the people. Through a rights-based approach, victims of water pollution and people deprived of necessary water for meeting their basic needs are provided with access to remedies. In contrast to other systems of international law, the human rights system affords access to individuals and NGOs."

The union also states that a right-to-water covenant would make both state obligations and violations more visible to citizens. Within a year of ratification, states would be expected to put in place a plan of action, with targets, policies, indicators, and timeframes to achieve the realization of this right. As well, states would have to amend domestic law to comply with the new rights. In some cases, this will include constitutional amendments. Some form of monitoring of the new rights would also be established and the needs of marginalized groups such as women and indigenous peoples would be particularly addressed.

A covenant would also include specific principles to ensure civil society involvement to convert the U.N. convention into national law and national action plans. This would give citizens an additional constitutional tool in their fight for water. As stated in a 2003 manifesto on the right to water by Friends of the Earth Paraguay, "An inseparable part of the right is control and sovereignty of local communities over their natural heritage and therefore over the management of their sources of water and over the use of the territories producing this water, the watersheds, and aquifer recharge areas."

A right-to-water covenant would also set principles and priorities for water use in a world destroying its water heritage. The covenant we envisage would include language to protect water rights for the Earth and other species, and would address the urgent need for reclamation of polluted waters and an end to practices destructive of the world's water sources. As Friends of the Earth Paraguay put it, "The very mention of this supposed conflict, water for human use versus water for nature, reflects a lack of consciousness of the essential fact that the very existence of water depends on the sustainable management and conservation of ecosystems."

Progress at the United Nations

Water was not included in the 1947 United Nations Universal Declaration of Human Rights because at that time water was not perceived to have a human rights dimension. The fact that water is not now an enforceable human right has allowed decision making over water policy to shift from the U.N. and governments toward institutions and organizations that favor the private water companies and the commodification of water such as the World Bank, the World Water Council, and the World Trade Organization.

However, for more than a decade, calls have been made at various levels of the United Nations for a right-to-water convention. Civil society groups argued that, because the operations of the water companies had gone global and were being backed by global financial institutions, nation-state instruments to deal with

water rights were no longer sufficient to protect citizens. International laws were needed, we argued, to control the global reach of the water barons. We also noted that at the 1990 Rio Earth Summit, the key areas of water, climate change, biodiversity, and desertification were all targeted for action. Since then, all but water have resulted in a U.N. convention.

This lobbying started to pay off and the right to water was recognized in a number of important international U.N. resolutions and declarations. These include the 2000 General Assembly Resolution on the Right to Development, the 2004 Committee on Human Rights resolution on toxic wastes, and the May 2005 statement by the 116-member Non-Aligned Movement on the right to water for all. Most important is General Comment Number 15, adopted in 2002 by the U.N. Committee on Economic, Social, and Cultural Rights, which recognized that the right to water is a prerequisite for realizing all other human rights and "indispensable for leading a life in dignity." (A General Comment is an authoritative interpretation of a human rights treaty or convention by an independent committee of experts that has a mandate to provide states with an interpretation of the treaty or convention. In this case, the interpretation applies to the International Covenant on Economic, Social, and Cultural Rights.) General Comment Number 15 is therefore an authoritative interpretation that water is a right and an important milestone on the road to a full binding U.N. convention.

But as John Scanlon, Angela Cassar, and Noemi Nemes of the World Conservation Union point out in their 2004 legal briefing paper *Water as a Human Right?*, General Comment Number 15 is an interpretation, not a binding treaty or convention. To clearly bind the right to water in international law, a binding covenant is needed. So the pressure for a full covenant intensified. In early 2004, Danuta Sacher of Germany's Bread for the World and Ashfaq Khalfan of the Right to Water program at the U.N. Center on Housing Rights and Evictions called a summit, and a new international network called Friends of the Right to Water was born. The network set out to mobilize other water justice groups and national governments to join the campaign to strengthen the rights established in General Comment Number 15 and put in place the mechanisms to ensure implementation of the right to water through a covenant.

In November 2006, responding to a call from several countries, the newly formed U.N. Human Rights Council requested the Office of the High Commissioner for Human Rights to conduct a detailed study on the scope and content of the relevant human rights obligations related to access to water under international human rights instruments, and to include recommendations for future action. While the request does not specifically refer to a covenant, many see this process as having the potential to lead to one. In April 2007, Anil Naidoo of the Council of Canadians' Blue Planet Project, another founding member of Friends of the Right to Water, organized to present a letter of endorsement calling for a right-to-water covenant to U.N. Commissioner Madam Louise Arbour, signed by 176 groups from all over the world.

It has been essential to gain the support of governments in the global South, many of whom fear that their citizens could use a covenant against them if they are unable to immediately fulfill their new obligation. Proponents of a covenant emphasize that the application of a new human rights obligation is understood to be progressive. States without the power to implement the full right are not held accountable for not immediately delivering. What is required is the need to rapidly take minimal steps for implementation that will increase as capacity increases. But some governments are using their incapacity as an excuse to cover real priorities, such as funding the military rather than public services. A rights-based approach to development distinguishes between inability and unwillingness. As agreed at the 1993 U.N. World Conference on Human Rights, "While development facilitates the enjoyment of all human rights, the lack of development may not be invoked to justify the abridgement of internationally recognized human rights." A government that fails to ratify a right-to-water covenant should not try to hide behind capacity arguments.

Nor should relatively water-rich governments such as Canada hide behind a false fear (which Canada is doing) that they will be forced to share the actual water supplies within their territories. A human rights treaty is between a nation-state and its citizens. Recognition of the right to water in no way affects a country's sovereign right to manage its own water resources. What will be expected of First World governments and their development agencies is adequate aid to help developing countries meet their goals and ensure that their aid, and that of the World Bank, is directed toward not-for-profit public water services.

Dueling Visions

While the global water justice movement is excited and encouraged by these developments, there is a growing concern that this process could be hijacked by the water corporations, some northern countries, and the World Bank, and used to create a convention that would enshrine the inclusion of private sector players. There is now a widespread understanding that the right to water is an idea whose time has come and some who opposed it until very recently have decided to drop their opposition and help shape both the process and the end product in their image. The irony here is that this new scenario may just have arisen out of the very success of the global water justice movement's hard work.

Until recently, the global institutions and the big water companies adamantly opposed a right to water convention. So did many European countries such as France, England, and Germany, home to the big water companies. At the World Water Forums in The Hague and Kyoto, World Water Council members and governments refused civil society calls for a right-to-water convention and said that water is a human need, not a human right. These are not semantics: you cannot trade or sell a human right or deny it to someone on the basis of inability to pay.

At the Fourth World Water Forum in Mexico City, the ministerial declaration once again did not include the right to water. But the World Water Council did release a new report called *The Right to Water: From Concept to Implementation*, a bland restatement of many U.N. documents with almost no mention of the private sector (except to say that the right to water can be implemented in a "variety of ways") and with no reference to the public-private debate raging around it. While the report falls far short of recommending a convention on the right to water, the first words of the foreword (written by Loïc Fauchon, president of the World Water Council and senior executive with Suez) capture the essence of the situation in which these corporations and the World Bank now find themselves: "The right to water is an element that is indissociable from human dignity. Who, today, would dare say otherwise?" Who indeed?

The World Water Council is working with Green Cross International, an environmental education organization headed up by Mikhail Gorbachev, which has launched its own high-profile campaign for a U.N. convention on the right to water, and it is just the sort of convention that Loïc Fauchon could live with. Although the Green Cross draft convention admits that there is a problem with "excessive profits and speculative purposes" in the private exploitation of water, it nevertheless places the commercial and human right to water on an equal footing, sets the stage for private financing for water services, allows for the private management of water utilities, and says that water systems should follow market rules. In a legal analysis of the Green Cross draft convention, Steven Shrybman, a Canadian trade expert and legal counsel to Canada's Blue Planet Project, says it is "so seriously flawed as to represent a retreat from current international legal protection for the human right to water." Yet Gorbachev defended his pro-corporate proposal in an interview with the *Financial Times*, when he said that corporations are the "only institutions" with the intellectual and financial potential to solve the world's water problems and that he is "prepared to work with them."

> **"The fact that water is not now an enforceable human right has allowed decision making over water policy to shift from the U.N. and governments toward institutions and organizations that favor the private water companies and the commodification of water such as the World Bank, the World Water Council, and the World Trade Organization."**

Maude Barlow

The global water justice movement would never endorse a convention or covenant of this kind. In submissions to the high commissioner, hundreds of groups have urged the United Nations to take a clear stand in favor of public ownership of water. For them, a covenant must explicitly describe water not only as a human right but also as a public trust. As well, a U.N. covenant on the right to water will have to address the two great shortcomings of existing human rights law if it is to be accepted by civil society. Those shortcomings are their failure to establish meaningful enforcement mechanisms and the failure to bind international bodies.

In his submission to Madam Arbour, lawyer Steve Shrybman said that the most significant development in international law has not been taking place under the auspices of the United Nations, but rather, under the World Trade Organization and the thousands of bilateral investment treaties between governments that have codified corporate rights into international law. "Under these rules, water is regarded as a good, an investment and service, and as such, it is subject to binding disciplines that severely constrain the capacity of governments to establish or maintain policies, laws, and practices needed to protect human rights, the environment, or other non-commercial societal goals that may impede the private rights entrenched by these trade and investment agreements."

Moreover, states Shrybman, these agreements have equipped corporations with powerful new tools in asserting proprietary rights over water with which the state cannot interfere. "The codification of such private rights creates an obvious and serious impediment to the realization of the human right to water." Private tribunals operating under these treaties are now engaged in arbitrating conflicts between human rights norms and those of investment and trade law— a role they are ill-suited to serve. He goes on to challenge the high commissioner to recognize the need to deal with this reality and warns that unless U.N. bodies are able to reassert their role as the fundamental arbiter of human rights, they risk becoming bystanders as private tribunals operating entirely outside the U.N. framework resolve key questions of human rights law. To be effective, the covenant must assert the primacy of the human right to water where there is a conflict with private and commercial interests. As well, this instrument must apply to other institutions beside states, most importantly, transnational corporations, the WTO, and the World Bank.

Grassroots Take the Lead

Clearly, the stage has been set for another form of contest. Having been successful in forcing the United Nations to deal with the right to water, the global water justice movement must now work hard to ensure it is the right kind of instrument. There are many good signs. While several important countries remain opposed to the right to water, most notably the United States, Canada, Australia, and China, many more have come on board in recent years. The European Parliament adopted a resolution acknowledging the right to water in March 2006, and in November 2006, as a response to the 2006 U.N. Human Development Report on the world's water crisis, Great Britain reversed its opposition and recognized the right to water.

As Ashfaq Khalfan of the Centre on Housing Rights and Evictions explains, most countries in one form or another have supported the notion of the right to water in various resolutions at the United Nations and can be counted on to do so again. The challenge is to get support for a

Women take a bath in the natural water which spouts through 22 artistically designed traditional taps at Balaju in Kathmandu.

covenant that will truly be able to deliver on the promise. This is where civil society groups can be so effective. In many countries, water justice groups are hard at work to convince their governments to support the right kind of tool.

But they are not waiting for the United Nations. Many are also working hard within their countries to assert the right of water for all through domestic legislative changes. On October 31, 2004, the citizens of Uruguay became the first in the world to vote for the right to water. Led by Adriana Marquisio and Maria Selva Ortiz of the National Commission for the Defence of Water and Life, and Alberto Villarreal of Friends of the Earth Uruguay, the groups first had to obtain almost three hundred thousand signatures on a plebiscite (which they delivered to Parliament as a "human river"), in order to get a referendum placed on the ballot of the national election, calling for a constitutional amendment on the right to water. They won the vote by an almost two-thirds majority, an extraordinary feat considering the fear-mongering that opponents mounted.

The language of the amendment is very important. Not only is water now a fundamental human right in Uruguay, but also social considerations must now take precedence over economic considerations when the government makes water policy. As well, the constitution now reflects that "the public service of water supply for human consumption will be served exclusively and directly by state legal persons" that is to say, not by corporations.

Maude Barlow

Several other countries have also passed right-to-water legislation. When apartheid was defeated in South Africa, Nelson Mandela created a new constitution that defined water as a human right. However, the amendment was silent on the issue of delivery and soon after, the World Bank convinced the new government to privatize many of its water services. Several other developing countries such as Ecuador, Ethiopia, and Kenya also have references in their constitutions that describe water as a human right, but they, too, do not specify the need for public delivery. The Belgium Parliament passed a resolution in April 2005 seeking a constitutional amendment to recognize water as a human right, and in September 2006, the French Senate adopted an amendment to its water bill that says that each person has the right to access to clean water. But neither country makes reference to delivery.

The only other country besides Uruguay to specify in its constitution that water must be publicly delivered is Netherlands, which passed a law in 2003 restricting the delivery of drinking water to utilities that are entirely public. But Netherlands did not affirm the right to water in this amendment. Only the Uruguayan constitutional amendment guarantees both the right to water and the need to deliver it publicly and is, therefore, a model for other countries. Suez was forced to leave the country as a direct result of this amendment.

Other exciting initiatives are underway. In August 2006, the Indian Supreme Court ruled that protection of natural lakes and ponds is akin to honoring the right to life—the most fundamental right of all, according to the court. Activists in Nepal are going before their Supreme Court arguing that the right to health guaranteed in the country's constitution must include the right to water. The Coalition in Defense of Public Water in Ecuador is celebrating its victory over the privatization of its water by demanding that the government take the next step and amend the constitution to recognize the right to water. The Coalition Against Water Privatization in South Africa is challenging the practice of water metering before the Johannesburg High Court on the basis that it violates the human rights of Soweto's citizens. President Evo Morales of Bolivia has called for a "South American convention for human rights and access for all living beings to water" that would reject the market model imposed in trade agreements. At least a dozen countries have reacted positively to this call. Civil society groups are hard at work in many other countries to introduce constitutional amendments similar to that of Uruguay. Ecofondo, a network of sixty groups in Colombia, has launched a plebiscite toward a constitutional amendment similar to the Uruguayan amendment. They need at least one and a half million signatures and face several court cases and a dangerous and hostile opposition. Dozens of groups in Mexico have joined COMDA, the Coalition of Mexican Organizations for the Right to Water, in a national campaign for a Uruguayan-type constitutional guarantee to the right to water.

A large network of human rights, development, faith-based, labor, and environmental groups in Canada has formed Canadian Friends of the Right to Water, led by the Blue Planet Project, to get the Canadian government to change its opposition to a U.N. covenant on the right to water. A network in the United States led by Food

> **"What is needed now is binding law to codify that states have the obligation to deliver sufficient, safe, accessible, and affordable water to their citizens as a public service."**

and Water Watch is calling for both a national water trust to ensure safekeeping of the nation's water assets and a change of government policy on the right to water. Riccardo Petrella has led a movement in Italy to recognize the right to water, which has great support among politicians at every level. Momentum is growing everywhere for a right whose time has come.

* * *

This, then, is the task: nothing less than reclaiming water as a commons for the Earth and all people that must be wisely and sustainably shared and managed if we are to survive. This will not happen unless we are prepared to reject the basic tenets of market-based globalization. The current imperatives of competition, unlimited growth, and private ownership when it comes to water must be replaced by new imperatives—those of cooperation, sustainability, and public stewardship. As Bolivia's Evo Morales explained in his October 2006 proposal to the heads of states of South America, "Our goal needs to be to forge a real integration to 'live well.' We say 'live well,' because we do not aspire to live better than others. We do not believe in the line of progress and unlimited development at the cost of others and nature. 'Live well' is to think not only in terms of income per capita but cultural identity, community, harmony between ourselves and with mother earth."

There are lessons to be learned from water, nature's gift to humanity, which can teach us how to live in harmony with the earth and in peace with one another. In Africa, they say, "We don't go to water ponds merely to capture water, but because friends and dreams are there to meet us."

CONSTITUTIONS RECOGNIZING THE RIGHT TO WATER

- 1994, Panama: A constitutional amendment recognized the state's responsibility to guarantee water for adequate development
- 1995, Ethiopia: "[P]olicies shall aim to provide all Ethiopians access to [...] clean water"
- 1995, Uganda: The state is obliged to fulfill fundamental rights to social justice and economic development, including clean and safe water
- 1996, Gambia: "The state shall endeavor to facilitate equal access to clean and safe water"
- 1996, South Africa: "Everyone has the right to have access to sufficient food and water"
- 2004, Uruguay: Uruguayans approved a constitutional amendment by popular vote guaranteeing the right to water

Source: Food and Water Watch

Chapter 16

WHY WE NEED A WATER ETHIC

By Sandra L. Postel

Now for the million dollar questions: Why has so much of modern water management gone awry? Why is it that ever greater amounts of money and ever more sophisticated engineering have not solved the world's water problems? Why, in so many places on this planet, are rivers drying up, lakes shrinking, and water tables falling?

The answer, in part, is simple: we have been trying to meet insatiable demands by continuously expanding a finite water supply. In the long run, of course, that is a losing proposition. It is impossible to expand a finite supply indefinitely, and in many parts of the world, the "long run" has arrived.

For sure, measures to conserve, recycle, and more efficiently use water have enabled many places to contain their water demands and to avoid or at least delay an ecological reckoning. Such tried-and-true measures as thrifty irrigation techniques, water-saving plumbing fixtures, native landscaping, and wastewater recycling can cost-effectively reduce the amount of water required to grow food, produce material goods, and meet household needs. The conservation potential of these measures has barely been tapped.

Children watch the river in Pakbeng, a common stop for tourists traveling from Thailand to the old Lao capital of Luang Prabang.

Yet something is missing from this prescription, something less tangible than drip irrigation lines and low-flow showerheads but, in the final analysis, something more important. It has to do with modern society's disconnection from nature's web of life and from water's most fundamental role as the basis of that life. In our technologically sophisticated world, we no longer grasp the need for the wild river, the blackwater swamp, or even the diversity of species collectively performing nature's work. By and large, society views water in a utilitarian fashion—as a "resource" valued only when it is extracted from nature and put to use on a farm, in a factory, or in a home.

Overall, we have been quick to assume rights to use water but slow to recognize obligations to preserve and protect it. Better pricing and more open markets will assign water a higher value in its economic functions and breed healthy competition that weeds out wasteful and unproductive uses. But this will not solve the deeper problem. What is needed is a set of guidelines and principles that stops us from chipping away at natural systems until nothing is left of their life-sustaining functions, which the marketplace fails to value adequately, if at all. In short, we need a water ethic—a guide to right conduct in the face of complex

Sandra L. Postel

WHAT IS THE PRECAUTIONARY PRINCIPLE?

A comprehensive definition of the precautionary principle was spelled out in a January 1998 meeting of scientists, lawyers, policy makers, and environmentalists at Wingspread, headquarters of the Johnson Foundation in Racine, Wisconsin. The Wingspread Statement on the Precautionary Principle, says: "When an activity raises threats of harm to the environment or human health, precautionary measures should be taken even if some cause and effect relationships are not fully established scientifically."

Key elements of the principle include taking precaution in the face of scientific uncertainty; exploring alternatives to possibly harmful actions; placing the burden of proof on proponents of an activity rather than on victims or potential victims of the activity; and using democratic processes to carry out and enforce the principle—including the public right to informed consent.

Source: Science and Environmental Health Network, www.sehn.org

decisions about natural systems that we do not and cannot fully understand.

The essence of such an ethic is to make the protection of freshwater ecosystems a central goal in all that we do. This may sound like an idealistic prescription in light of our ever more crowded world of needs and aspirations. Yet it is no more radical a notion than suggesting that a building be given a solid foundation before adding 30 stories to it. Water is the foundation of every human enterprise, and if that foundation is insecure, everything built upon it will be insecure, too. As such, our stewardship of water will determine not only the quality but the staying power of human societies.

The adoption of such a water ethic would represent a historic shift away from the strictly utilitarian approach to water management and toward an integrated, holistic approach that views people and water as interconnected parts of a greater whole. Instead of asking how we can further control and manipulate rivers, lakes, and streams to meet our ever-growing demands, we would ask instead how we can best satisfy human needs while accommodating the ecological requirements of freshwater ecosystems. It would lead us, as well, to deeper questions of human values, in particular how to narrow the wide gap between the haves and have-nots while remaining within the bounds of what a healthy ecosystem can sustain.

Embedded within this water ethic is a fundamental question: Do rivers and the life within them have a right to water? In his famous essay, "Should Trees Have Standing? Toward Legal Rights for Natural Objects," legal scholar Christopher D. Stone argued more than 35 years ago that yes, rivers and trees and other objects of nature do have rights, and these should be protected by granting legal standing to guardians of the voiceless entities of nature, much as the rights of children are protected by legal guardians.

Stone's arguments struck a chord with U.S. Supreme Court Justice William O. Douglas, who wrote in a famous dissent in the 1972 case *Sierra Club v. Morton* that "contemporary public concern for protecting nature's ecological equilibrium should lead to the conferral of standing upon environmental objects to sue for their own preservation.…The river, for example, is the living symbol of all the life it sustains or nourishes—the fish, aquatic insects, water ouzels, otter, fisher, deer, elk, bear, and all other animals, including man, who are dependent on it or who enjoy it for its sight, its sound, or its life. The river as plaintiff speaks for the ecological unit of life that is part of it."

During the next three decades, U.S. courts heard cases brought by environmental groups and other legal entities on behalf of nature and its constituents. In water allocation, concepts such as "instream flow rights" began to take hold, although these rights often received too low a priority to offer meaningful protection of river health. With freshwater life being extinguished at record rates, a more fundamental change is needed. An ethical society can no longer ignore the fact that water-management decisions have life-or-death consequences for other species. An ethically grounded water policy must begin with the premise that all people and all living things be given access to enough water to secure their survival before some get more than enough.

On paper, at least one government has grounded its water policy in precisely such an ethic. South Africa's 1998 water law establishes a water reserve consisting of two parts. The first is a nonnegotiable water allocation to meet the basic drinking, cooking, and sanitary needs of all South Africans. (When the government changed hands, some 14 million poor South Africans lacked water for these basic needs.) The second part of the reserve is an allocation of water to support ecosystem functions. Specifically, the act says that "the quantity, quality, and reliability of water required to maintain the ecological functions on which humans depend shall be reserved so that the human use of water does not individually or cumulatively compromise the long-term sustainability of aquatic and associated ecosystems." The water determined to constitute this two-part reserve has priority over licensed uses, such as irrigation, and only this water is guaranteed as a right.

At the core of South Africa's policy is an affirmation of the "public trust," a legal principle that traces back to the Roman Empire and says that governments hold certain rights and entitlements in trust for the people and are obliged to protect them for the common good. In addition to the public trust, another rule fast becoming essential for freshwater ecosystem protection is the "precautionary principle," which essentially says that given the rapid pace of ecosystem decline, the irreversible nature of many of the resulting losses, and the high value of freshwater ecosystems to human societies, it is wise to err on the

"Water helped ancient man learn those first lessons about the rights of others and responsibility to a larger society....It became part of the moral and mental legacy parents passed on to their children."

—M. Meyer, *Water in the Hispanic Southwest*

Sandra L. Postel

side of protecting too much rather than too little of the remaining freshwater habitat.

The utilitarian code that continues to guide most water management may fit with prevailing market-based socioeconomic paradigms, but it is neither universal nor unchanging. The American conservationist Aldo Leopold viewed the extension of ethics to the natural environment as "an evolutionary possibility and an ecological necessity." More recently, Harvard biologist Edward O. Wilson noted in his book *Consilience* that ethical codes historically have arisen through the interplay of biology and culture. "Ethics, in the empiricist view," Wilson observes, "is conduct favored consistently enough throughout a society to be expressed as a code of principles."

In other words, ethics are not static; they evolve with social consciousness. But that evolution is not automatic. The extension of freedom to slaves and voting rights to women required leaders, movements, advocates, and activists that collectively pulled society onto higher moral ground. So it will be with the extension of rights to rivers, plants, fish, birds, and the ecosystems of which they are a part.

As societies wrap their collective minds around the consequences of global environmental change—rising temperatures, prolonged droughts, chronic water shortages, disappearing species—it may well be that a new ethic will emerge, one that says it is not only right and good but necessary that all living things get enough water before some get more than enough. Because in the end, we're all in this together.

A woman holds a prayer scroll while bathing at a small waterfall in Mount Banahaw south of Manila, which many Filipinos believe to be a sacred mountain.

AFTERWORD

By Tara Lohan

John F. Kennedy once said, "Anyone who can solve the problems of water will be worthy of two Nobel prizes—one for peace and one for science."

Indeed as we have seen in this book, our water problems are daunting but not insurmountable. However, there won't be any one man or one woman who will be able to claim those two Nobels. The solutions that we need to solve this crisis will require whole communities and nations to band together. We will need individuals to shift their consciousness and world leaders to put access to clean water before profit or politics.

As writers in this book have echoed, "we are all downstream." We will all suffer the consequences of our inactions if we fail to change our course. But we will all reap the rewards of healthy watersheds and healthy communities if we do act. As author John Thorson said, "Water links us to our neighbor in a way more profound and complex than any other." And more simply, as Sandra Postel said, "In the end, we're all in this together."

So what will we decide? After reading this book, we now have the facts. We know which areas are running out of water and we also know how much water we can save by conservation. We know how many lives are lost because of a lack of clean water and we also know that a strong grassroots movement working for equal distribution is growing every day. We know that we've lost half of our wetlands and we also know that communities are implementing green roofs and graywater systems to help filter water naturally and make it available for reuse.

We know that corporations have taken over public water systems and we also know that communities have fought—and won—to get them back.

We know we have the tools we need to make change happen. So how do we get started?

This book contains a list of actions at the end, as well as many scattered throughout each chapter. But one great place to start is with the creation of a public trust for water. If we want clean water for everyone and healthy watersheds and swimmable rivers, we need the money and the infrastructure to make it happen.

In the United States federal money for water infrastructure, all 1.5 million miles of piping, has fallen 70 percent since 1991. According to the U.S. EPA, the funding gap for what is needed to improve our country's aging water infrastructure is now $22 billion a year.

But there is one thing that an overwhelming majority of Americans agree on—83 percent—and that is the creation of a public trust for clean water. We have a public trust fund for highways, for harbor maintenance, for cleaning up oil spills, for botanical gardens, and for restoring wildlife habitat. We need one for water.

A long-term and sustainable fund to ensure clean water has a ripple effect. As Food and Water Watch reported, if we tackled our $22 million a year funding gap with a trust fund, it would "employ more than 1 million people, pay them $28.6 billion, and spur more than $134 billion of economic movement."

Clean water and healthy watersheds can lead to

more "green jobs" and an improved economy. These are the rewards that all of us downstream share. Enacting a public trust for water is one step on a path of change that can ripple across the country and across the world because the politics of water are encompassing. When we work on solutions to our water crisis we also cross paths with issues like indigenous rights, poverty alleviation, environmental justice, education, corporate accountability, and democracy.

When we take action to tackle the water crisis, our efforts multiply across different fronts. The key is, we have get involved. We can take shorter showers and eat local food, but it will take more than that. It will take people working for a public trust for clean water or improved sanitation in another country or ending their city's bottled water contract or stopping polluting industries or fighting for a U.N. resolution on the right to water.

It will take the building of a healthy grassroots movement that can begin to shake the pillars of power all the way up to the top. It is time to put down those roots and water them well.

A sculpture of a faucet is seen at a World Water Day festival in Seoul, South Korea.

Afterword

14 ACTIONS TO PROTECT

1. FIND OUT HOW MUCH WATER YOU USE. Visit the Water Calculator and see what you can do to cut back.

www.h2oconserve.org

2. STOP DRINKING BOTTLED WATER. Choose tap water over bottled water whenever possible. Create a bottled water free zone in your classroom, campus, workplace, union, community center, city hall, environmental organization, or faith-based group.

www.polarisinstitute.org/water
www.thinkoutsidethebottle.org

3. HELP CREATE A CLEAN WATER TRUST FUND. Support public control of water resources and increased funding for public drinking water by signing a petition urging Congress to create a Clean Water Trust Fund.

www.foodandwaterwatch.org/water/trust-fund

4. CONSERVE WATER INSIDE. Retrofit with efficient appliances and fixtures, take shorter showers, check faucets for leaks and drips.

www.awwa.org/waterwiser

5. CONSERVE WATER OUTSIDE. Reduce lawn size and choose drought-tolerant xeriscapes. You can also recycle municipal water and on-site graywater, or harvest rainwater to use in the garden.

www.bewaterwise.com
www.rainwaterharvesting.net

6. DON'T POLLUTE YOUR WATERSHED. Stop using toxic cleaners, pesticides, and herbicides. Properly dispose of pharmaceuticals and personal care products.

www.watoxics.org/homes-and-gardens
www.newdream.org/consumer/personalcare.php

7. LEARN ABOUT YOUR WATERSHED. Form a watershed group. River Keeper organizations, Friends of Creeks groups, and watershed councils are springing up all over the country.

www.4sos.org/wssupport/group_support/form_run.asp

YOU CAN TAKE OUR WATER

8. HELP KEEP YOUR WATERSHED HEALTHY. Support or start water-quality monitoring programs. Citizen-based water-quality monitoring is an accessible and meaningful way to understand the health of your waterways.

www.healthywater.org

9. CLEAN UP AGRICULTURE.
Buy local and organic food. Help with the implementation of on-farm water conservation and protection programs.

www.polarisinstitute.org/water

www.nrcs.usda.gov/programs

10. PROTECT GROUNDWATER FROM DEPLETION AND DEGRADATION.
Help ensure legislation to manage and protect all groundwater. Unlike our system of surface-water rights, the extraction of unlimited quantities of groundwater is largely unregulated.

www.groundwater.org

11. LEARN ABOUT DAMS IN YOUR AREA.
Oppose construction of new dams and always ask if any planned dams are really necessary or if there are better, less destructive ways of conserving water, preventing floods or generating power.

www.internationalrivers.org

12. REDUCE YOUR ENERGY USE.
Producing electricity uses lots of water. You can figure out how much energy you use at Low Carbon Diet.

www.empowermentinstitute.net/lcd/index.html

13. SUPPORT THE RIGHT TO WATER FOR EVERYONE.
Learn more about grassroots movements for water democracy and support for a United Nations covenant on the right to water.

www.blueplanetproject.net

14. HELP SPREAD THE WORD.
Visit WaterConsciousness.org for more information or to buy a copy of this book for a friend.

www.waterconsciousness.org

HOW MUCH DO YOU USE?

TAKE THE WATER CALCULATOR QUIZ

The H2O Conserve Water Calculator is designed to help you measure how much water you use, better understand the ways you use water in your daily life, and get you thinking about what you can do to use less.

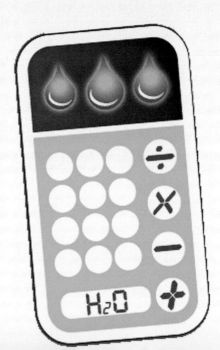

WATER

This lets you know what your "water footprint" is. In other words, it gives you an estimate of the total amount of water you use. Your water footprint takes into account not only the water used in your home, but also the water that is used to produce the food you choose to eat and the products you buy. Your water footprint also includes other factors such as the water used to cool the power plants that provide your electricity, and the water that is saved when you recycle. You may not drink, feel, or see this water, but it makes up the large majority of your water footprint.

It is important to recognize that the H2O Calculator relies on national averages and approximations, and since not everyone's lifestyle is "average," your results should be considered an estimate of your water use and not a scientifically accurate assessment. Regardless, this calculator does provide a general assessment of your water use, as well as the quantity of water used daily by the average American to give you an idea of where you stand in terms of your daily water use.

You can find a more detailed version online at www.H2OConserve.org.

WATER CALCULATOR

1   How many people are in your household?   _____

2   In which state do you live?   _____
Give yourself the corresponding number of points.
Kentucky, Louisiana, North Dakota, Wyoming, West Virginia   18 points
All other U.S. states and Washington, D.C.   6 points

3   Water used for power generation: _____
Multiply the points from your state by the number of people in your household.

4   Domestic Water Use:

a. BATHS
How many baths per week does your household take?
Multiply the number of baths by 5   _____
(Average bath uses 35 gallons H_2O)

b. SHOWERS
On average, how many minutes does a person in your house take a shower?
Multiply the number of minutes by 3. Multiply that by the number of people in your household   _____
(Average shower uses 3 gallons H_2O per minute)

c. TOILETS
Multiply the number of people in your household by 12   _____
(Average person uses 12 gallons per day flushing)

d. SINKS
On average, how many minutes does a person in your household use the sink?
Multiply the number of minutes by 3. Multiply that by the number of people in your household   _____
(Average sink uses 3 gallons H_2O per minute)

e. LAUNDRY
How many loads of laundry per week does your household do?
Multiply the number of loads by 4   _____
(Average load uses 30 gallons)

f. DISHES
How many loads of dishes per day does your household do?
Multiply the number of loads by 10 _____
(Average load of dishes uses 10 gallons)

5   Lawn and Garden
On average, how many times each week do you water your lawn or garden?
Multiply the number of times per week by 171 _____
(Based on 1/4 acre yard, watered once per week, 1200 gallons used)

6   Pool
If you have a pool, give yourself 52 points. _____
If you don't cover your pool, give yourself an additional 16 points. _____

7   Automobile

a. GAS
Give yourself 5 points per car. _____
(Based on 20 gallons per week per car, 1.75 gallons of water per gallon gasoline)

b. CAR WASHING
If you wash your car, give yourself 21 points per car. _____
(Based on 1 car wash per week per car, 150 gallons water per car wash)

8   Diet

a. MEAT EATING
Give yourself 446 points for each vegan in your household. _____
Give yourself 516 points for each vegetarian in your household. _____
Give yourself 1032 points for each meat eater in your household. _____

b. BOTTLED WATER
Multiply the number of people in your household by 1.5 _____
(Based on 1 bottle per day per person, 1.5 gallons used per bottle)

9   Recycling (these values are subtracted from your total)

a. PAPER
Multiply the number of people in your household by 5 (_____)
(Recycling some paper saves you 5 gallons per day per person)

b. PLASTIC
Multiply the number of people in your household by 3   (_____)
(Recycling some plastic saves you 3 gallons per day per person)

c. CLOTHING
Multiply the number of people in your household by 5   (_____)
(Recycling some clothing saves you 5 gallons per day per person)

10 Graywater and Rainwater (these values are subtracted from your total)

a. GRAYWATER
Does your household reuse graywater?
Multiply the number of people in your household by 40   (_____)
(Based on reusing 40 gallons per person per day)

b. RAINWATER
Give yourself 9 points if your household collects rainwater   (_____)
(Based on saving and using 9 gallons of water per day)

TOTAL HOUSEHOLD
(add your values for 3-8; subtract your values for 9 and 10)   _____

TOTAL INDIVIDUAL
(divide the total household value by the no. of people in your household)   _____

WHAT DOES YOUR SCORE MEAN?

The score for the average American is 1,190.

900 and below: Water Warrior

Congratulations, you are doing better than most Americans! Give yourself a pat on the back for being water conscious. You have a thing or two to teach your neighbors, but there may still be ways to cut back on your water use.

901-1,300: Water Activist

Not too shabby! Your water consumption is typical of most Americans. But as we know, Americans are among the highest water users worldwide. The good news is, there are many ways to use less water and decrease your footprint.

1,301 and above: Water Enthusiast

Time for a water-use makeover! Your household is a thirsty one, even by American standards. Now is a great time to think of ways to cut back on your water use — whether it is in the home, outside your home or in your consumption habits.

For more ideas on conservation, read the Learn to Conserve tips or visit www.H2OConserve.org

LEARN TO CONSERVE

Here are some tips for cutting down on water use. For a more detailed list visit www.H20Conserve.org.

● Put a bucket in the shower while you're waiting for the water to warm up, and use the water you catch for watering plants or cleaning.

● To check for a toilet leak, put dye or food coloring into the tank. If color appears in the bowl without flushing, there's a leak that should be repaired.

● Fix those leaky faucets. You may think that a constant drip is just annoying, but it's also a huge waste of water (you can lose about 20 gallons of water per day from a single drippy faucet!).

● Use the garbage disposal less and the garbage more (or even better, start composting!).

● Install a low-flow showerhead. It may cost you some money up front, but your water conservation efforts will save you money down the road.

● Use the water left over from boiling to water your plants (just let it cool down first!).

● Eat meat and dairy foods fewer times a day, or just in smaller portions. The amount of water used to produce animal products far exceeds the amount used for growing vegetables and grains.

● Use your laundry machine only when it's full.

● Use a pool cover! You'll keep leaves and bugs out of the pool, and save thousands of gallons of water from evaporation.

● If your family wants to play with the hose or the sprinkler, make sure they do it in a dry part of the lawn that can use the water.

● Use a drip irrigation system instead of a hose or sprinkler to water your garden.

● Xeriscape! Plant native species that don't require additional watering around your house. Grassy lawns make sense in wet climates, but in dry areas like the southwest they're huge water-wasters. In dry climates, try landscaping with rock gardens, cacti, and native trees and plants that won't require watering.

● Buy re-usable products for your home instead of disposables.

● Your trash is someone else's treasure! Make sure to donate or re-sell your old stuff instead of just throwing things out.

● Set up a rain barrel under a rain gutter outside your house. You can catch hundreds of gallons to use for watering the lawn, washing the car, etc. Just don't drink it, and make sure to keep it covered with a screen so it doesn't breed mosquitoes. Check your local municipal regulations to see if a rain barrel is allowed.

● If you're building a new house, or re-doing the plumbing in your old house, consider setting up a graywater system. These systems allow you to re-use the water from your sinks, laundry machine, and dishwasher for watering plants and flushing toilets. Check your local municipal regulations to see if a graywater system is allowed.

WATER: H2O = LIFE

An Exhibit Putting Water Education in Action

You can also learn about water issues interactively. Water: H2O = Life is an exhibit that illuminates some of the many challenges related to humanity's sustainable management and use of the life-giving, but finite, resource—water. It explores the ways that water shapes life on Earth and makes our planet livable and also suggests actions people can take to help preserve our planet's water.

Exhibition Organization and International Tour

Water: H2O = Life is designed and produced by the American Museum of Natural History's Department of Exhibition under the direction of David Harvey, Vice President for Exhibition and curated by Eleanor Sterling, Director of the American Museum of Natural History's Center for Biodiversity and Conservation (coauthor of Chapter 1 and Chapter 11).

The exhibit is organized by the American Museum of Natural History, New York (www.amnh.org), and the Science Museum of Minnesota, St. Paul (www.smm.org), in collaboration with Great Lakes Science Center, Cleveland; The Field Museum, Chicago; Instituto Sangari, São Paulo, Brazil; National Museum of Australia, Canberra; Royal Ontario Museum, Toronto, Canada; San Diego Natural History Museum; and Singapore Science Centre with PUB Singapore.

The exhibit showed at the American Museum of Natural History from November 3, 2007 until May 26, 2008, when it began an international tour. Currently scheduled stops include:

- The Singapore Science Centre (May 2008 to October 2008)
- The San Diego Museum of Natural History (July to November 2008)
- The Science Museum of Minnesota, St. Paul (January to April 2009)
- The Field Museum of Natural History, Chicago (June to September 2009)
- Great Lakes Science Center, Cleveland (November 2009 to April 2010)
- The National Museum of Australia, Canberra (January to June 2010)
- The Royal Ontario Museum, Toronto (March to September 2011)

The Exhibition

Water: H2O = Life examines the beauty and essential nature of our planet's lifeblood using imaginative presentation techniques, including a 68-inch globe displaying composite satellite images of Earth and three-dimensional video, as well as live animals and walk-through dioramas that give visitors a firsthand experience of the power and importance of water. The exhibition also addresses the most compelling issues facing societies and ecosystems around the globe related to water quality and availability.

If the exhibit doesn't reach a city near you, online visitors can explore Water: H2O = Life by going to the www.amnh.org, and clicking the link in the "On Exhibit" area. The Web site www.amnh.org/water features information and interviews with the curator and other museum scientists; photos, videos, and interactives from the exhibition; fascinating scientific and cultural facts about water; educational resources and an exhibition map.

Visitors enter Water: H2O=Life exhibit through a "fog curtain."

End Notes

Chapter 1

1. Falkenmark, M. Water scarcity: Time for realism. *Populi* 20(6): 11–12. June 1993.

2. Sterling, Eleanor J. and Camhi, Merry D, "Sold Down the River," *Natural History Magazine.* November 1997.

3. AAAS Atlas of Population and Environment pp. 51–54 from: http://atlas.aaas.org/index .php?part=2&sec=natres&sub=water

4. WorldWatch (2007) from http://www.worldwatch.org/ node/811 and Barlow, M. (2008). *Blue Covenant* p. 5.

5. Hinrichsen et al. 1998 Solutions for a Water Short World, *Population Reports Series M*, Number 14.

6. Hinrichsen et al. 1998 Solutions for a Water Short World, *Population Reports Series M*, Number 14, http:// www.infoforhealth.org/pr/m14/m14table.shtml#table1.

7. UNEP. 2002b. Vital Water Graphics: An Overview of the State of the World's Fresh and Marine Resources. From: http://www.unep.org/dewa/assessments/ ecosystems/water/vitalwater/.

8. Postel, S. 1998. Water for food production: will there be enough in 2025?, *BioScience* 48: 629–637.

9. Hinrichsen, et al. 1998 Solutions for a Water Short World, *Population Reports Series M*, Number 14.

10. Fitzhugh and Richter 2004 *Bioscience.*

11. General Accounting Office 2003. Freshwater Supply— from http://www.gao.gov/new.items/d03514.pdf.

12. *Ibid.*

13. *Ibid.*

14. Postel, Daily, and Ehrlich. 1999. Human Appropriation of Renewable Freshwater. *Science* 271:5250.

15. 2006-2007 *World's Water* Peter Gleick Table 2.

16. Gleick 1993, and Seckler, D. 1996. The new era of water resources management. Research Report 1. Colombo, Sri Lanka: International Irrigation Management Institute (IIMI). From: http://www.iwmi .cgiar.org/pubs/pub001/body.htm.

17. Somervile and Briscor Science 2001 – http://www .sciencemag.org/cgi/content/summary/292/5525/2217.

18. http://www.unep.org/geo2000/english/0046.htm.

19. http://www.worldwatch.org/node/5050.

20. http://www.devalt.org/water/WaterinIndia/issues.htm, *Ministry of Water Resources* (MOWR, 2000).

21. http://www.epa.gov/owow/nps/Section319II/intro .html.

22. http://www.paho.org/english/dd/pin/ptoday12_ mar04.htm.

23. http://na.unep.net/AfricaLakes/AtlasDownload/PDFs/ Africas-Preface-Screen.pdf.

24. WHO and UNICEF. 2006. Meeting the MDG Drinking Water and Sanitation Target: The Urban and Rural Challenge of the Decade. Retrieved from: http://www .wssinfo.org/en/40_MDG2006.html.

25. Gleick World's Water 2006-2007 Table 2.

26. UNDP 2006 Human Development Report.

Chapter 5

1. Eskenazi, Stuart. The Biggest Pump Wins, *Dallas Observer,* November 19 25, 1998, http://www.dallas observer.com/1998-11-19/news/the-biggest-pump- wins/; Accessed 16 August 2006.

2. Gleick, Peter H. *The World's Water 2004–2005: The Biennial Report on Freshwater Resources.* Island Press, 2004, p. 17.

3. Flynn, Sean and Kathryn Boudouris. "Democratizing the Regulation and Governance of Water in the U.S.," Excerpt from *Reclaiming Public Water: Achievements, Struggles, and Visions From Around the World*, Transnational Institute and Corporate Europe Observatory, January 2005.

4. Fishman, Charles. "Message in a Bottle," *Fast Company*, July 2007; "Bottled Water: More than just a story about sales growth," Press Release International Bottled Water Association, April 9, 2007, http://www.bottledwater .org/public/2007_releases/2007-04-09_bevmkt.htm; Accessed June 2007.

5. U.S. Environmental Protection Agency. "Analysis and Findings of the Gallup Organization's Drinking Water Customer Satisfaction Survey," August 6, 2003.

6. Eskenazi, *Ibid.*; Farhrenthold, David A. "Bottlers, States, and the Public Slug It Out in Water War," *Washington Post*, June 12, 2006. http://www.washingtonpost .com/wp-dyn/content/article/2006/06/11/ AR2006061100797_pf.html; Accessed 12 February 2008.

7. "The Clean Water and Drinking Water Gap Analysis." Office of Water, *U.S. Environmental Protection Agency*, September 30, 2002. http://www.epa.gov/safewater/gapreport.pdf; Accessed on 11 February 2008.

8. Vega, Cecilia, M. "City pays big for bottled water," *San Franciso Chronicle*, January 27, 2006. http://www.sfgate.com/cgi-bin/article.cgi?f=/c/a/2006/01/27/MNGBEGUHCJ1.DTL; Accessed on 11 February 2008.

9. Chura, Hilary. "$7.7 billion industry: Water war bubbling among top brands," *Advertising Age*, July 7, 2003.

10. Bloom, Jonah ed. "Ad Age Annual," *Ad Age*, January 1, 2007.

11. Bauers, Sandy. "Bottled water's environmental backlash," *Philadelphia Inquirer*, November 3, 2007.

http://www.philly.com/philly/news/20071103_Bottled_waters_environmental_backlash.html Accessed 12 February 2008.

12. Press Release. "The U.S. Conference of Mayors Announces 2007 City Water Taste Test Winners, "USCOM Annual Meeting, June 25, 2007, www.usmayors.org/75thAnnualMeeting/pressrelease_062507b.pdf; Accessed 11 February 2008.

13. Larsen, Janet. "Bottled Water Boycotts: Back-to-the-Tap Movement Gains Momentum," *Earth Policy Institute: Plan B Updates*, December 7, 2007. http://www.earth-policy.org/Updates/2007/Update68.htm; Accessed 12 February 2008.

14. Scanlon, Jessie. "Buy Water, Help Children: Interview with Peter Thum," *BusinessWeek Online*, March 22, 2006. http://www.businessweek.com/investor/content/mar2006/pi20060322_252796.htm; Accessed 12 February 2008.

15. "Nestle Waters Global Business Review," presented by Kim Jeffery, president and CEO, Nestle Waters North America at the Morgan Stanley Global Consumer and Retail Conference, November 15, 2007, New York City, N.Y. http://www.nestle.com/Resource.axd?Id=89D1A0C8-4355-41F0-8A99-AB505CE3D6F3 Accessed 12 February 2008.

16. Carlton, Jim. "Can a Water Bottler Invigorate One Town?" *Wall Street Journal*, June 9, 2005.

17. Indar, Josh. "Drinking Problem," *Sacramento News and Review*, August 18, 2005;

18. Indar, *Ibid.*

19. "Nestlé In McCloud: The Costs," memo from original McCloud Watershed Council Web site, McCloudWater .com; Accessed 22 June 2005. Website has subsequently been updated to www .mccloudwatershedcouncil.org.

20. McCloud Watershed Council, *Ibid.*

21. McCloud Watershed Council, *Ibid.*

22. McCloud Watershed Council, *Ibid*

23. Indar, *Ibid.*

24. Indar, *Ibid.*

25. Gladwell, Malcolm. Blink: *The Power of Thinking Without Thinking.* Little, Brown & Company, 2005.

26. CBS Poll, http://cbs2chicago.com/video/?id=37419@wbbm.dayport.com; Accessed 12 February 2008.

27. Olson, Erik. "Bottled Water: Pure Drink or Pure Hype?" *Natural Resources Defense Council* (NRDC), March 1999, http://www.nrdc.org/water/drinking/bw/exesum.asp; Accessed 8 August 2007.

28. Britton, Charles R.; Ford, Richard K.; and Gay, David, E.R. "The Market for Bottled Water in a "Water Rich" State," *The Forum of the Association for Arid Lands Studies*, Volume XXII, 2006.

29. NRDC, *Ibid.*

30. Review of Dasani product labels produced circa Feburary 2007; more information at www .makeyourmouthwater.com (Dasani Web site).

31. http://www.aquafina.com; Accessed 16 August 2006.

32. Review of Aquafina product labeling, February 2007.

33. Personal communication received by Nick Guroff/Corporate Accountability International from the Industry and Consumer Affairs Division of the Coca Cola Company on September 27, 2007, in response to inquiry.

34 Gleick, Peter H. "The World's Water: The Biennial Report on Freshwater Resources," Vols. 4 and 5. Island Press, 2004/2006.

35. Mercer, Chris. "US: Bottled water pulled in bromate scare," *BeverageDaily.com*, August 14, 2006.

http://www.beveragedaily.com/news/ng.asp?n=69827-wegmans-bromate-bottled-water; Accessed 11 February 2008.

36. Olson, Erik. "Bottled Water: Pure Drink or Pure Hype?" Natural Resources Defense Council (NRDC), March 1999, http://www.nrdc.org/water/drinking/bw/exesum.asp; Accessed 8 August 2007.

37. Basu, Moni and Scott Leith. "Villagers to Coke: 'Go away,'" *Atlanta Journal-Constitution*, May 29, 2005.

38. Simons, Craig. "Report looks at Coke water use in India," *Atlanta Journal Constitution*, January 14, 2008. http://www.ajc.com/business/content/business/coke/stories/2008/01/14/cokeindia_0115.html; Accessed 12 February 2008.

39. Basu, *Ibid.*

40. "Water privatisation to be a key issue in elections," the *Hindu*, January 23, 2004, http://www.thehindu.com/2004/01/23/stories/2004012305921200.htm; Accessed 16 August 2006.

41. Basu, *Ibid.*

42. Date Vidyadhar. "Villagers blame Coca-Cola for water woes in Thane district," *Times of India*, June 5, 2003. http://timesofindia.indiatimes.com/articleshow/6753.cms; Accessed 12 February 2008.

43. Basu, *Ibid.*

44. Jeff Seabright, vice president, Environment & Water Resources. Remarks at the Center for Strategic & International Studies & Sandia National Laboratory–Global Water Futures Workshop: Water Sustainability and Corporate Responsibility, Washington D.C., February 9, 2005. http://www.thecoca-colacompany.com/presscenter/viewpoints_environmental_csis.html; Accessed 12 February 2008.

45. "World Water Forum–Diluting Dissent?" InfoBrief #2, Corporate Europe Observatory, http://www.corporateeurope.org/water/infobrief2.htm; Accessed 12 February 2008.

46. DePorte, Tara. "Talk or Action at World Water Forum?" AlterNet.org, April 22, 2006. http://www.alternet.org/environment/35293/; Accessed 12 February 2008.

47. Coca-Cola Company Press Release, June 5, 2007; http://www.thecoca-colacompany.com/presscenter/nr_20070605_tccc_and_wwf_partnership.html; Accessed 12 February 2008.

48. UN-Water. "Fact Sheet on Water and Sanitation," International Decade for Action: Water for Life, 2005-2015, http://www.un.org/waterforlifedecade/factsheet.html; Accessed 16 August 2006.

49. "California considers new bottled-water rules," U.S. Water News Online, May 2003. http://www.uswaternews.com/archives/arcquality/3calcon5.html; Accessed 12 February 2008.

50. International Bottled Water Association Press Release, June 5, 2003. http://www.bottledwater.org/public/2003_Releases/CorbettAB83.htm; Accessed 12 February 2008.

51. Geissinger, Steve. "Schwarzenegger OKs bills on gay rights, toxic toys," *Oakland Tribune*, October 15, 2007; Editorial. "Bottled Water Mystery: Consumers need more information," *Sacramento Bee*, April 26, 2007. http://www.sacbee.com/110/story/161153.html; Accessed 12 February 2008; Lazarus, David. "What the heck is in those water bottles?" *San Francisco Chronicle*, May 4, 2007. http://www.sfgate.com/cgi-bin/article.cgi?f=/c/a/2007/05/04/BUGUSPKP6D1.DTL; Accessed 12 February 2008.

52. Blanding, Michael. "The Bottled Water Backlash," AlterNet.org, October 19, 2007. http://www.alternet.org/environment/65520/?page=3; Accessed 12 February 2008.

53. "Executive Directive 07-05: Permanent Phase-Out of Bottled Water Purchases by San Francisco City and County Government." Office of the Mayor, City and County of San Francisco, June 21, 2007. http://sfwater.org/Files/Pressreleases/Bottled%20Water%20Executive%20Order.pdf; Accessed 11 February 2008.

54. Vega, Cecilia M. "Mayor to cut off flow of city money for bottled water," *San Francisco Chronicle*, June 22, 2007.

55. Poor, Jeff. "'Nightly News' Continues 'War' on Bottled Water," *Business and Media Institute*, October 18, 2007. http://www.businessandmedia.org/printer/2007/20071018143349.aspx; Accessed 12 February 2008.

56. USCOM Business Council Website [TBD]

57. Swanson, Stevenson. "Some would like to play taps for bottled water," *Chicago Tribune*; reprinted by the *Seattle Times*, July 26, 2007. http://seattletimes.nwsource.com/html/nationworld/2003806269_water26.html; Accessed 12 February 2008.

58. U.S. Conference of Mayors 2007 Adopted Resolutions. Resolution #90: "The Importance of Municipal Water." http://usmayors.org/uscm/resolutions/75th _conference/environment_02.asp; Accessed 11 February 2008.

59. Gitlitz, Jennifer and Pat Franklin. "Water, Water Everywhere: The growth of non-carbonated beverage containers in the United States. *Container Recycling Institute*, February 2007.

60. Goodison, Donna. "Hub protesters: Don't go near the (bottled) water," *Boston Herald*, October 11, 2007. www.bostonherald.com/business/general/view .bg?articleid=1037360; Accessed 11 February 2008.

61. O'Donnell, Maureen. State of Illinois Department of Central Management Services Memorandum, October 29, 2007. http://thecapitolfaxblog.com/Watermemo .pdf; Accessed 11 February 2008.

62. Credeur, Mary Jane. "PepsiCo Adds 'Public Water Source' to Aquafina Label," Bloomberg.com, July 26, 2007. http://www.bloomberg.com/apps/news?pid=20 601205&refer=consumer&sid=aiqSSi38Zp6E; Accessed 12 February 2008.

Chapter 6

1. Clarke, Tony and Barlow, Maude. "The battle for water." Yes! A Journal of Positive Futures, Winter 2004.

2. Pfeiffer, Dale Allen. "Eating fossil fuels: Without oil, families will go hungry, not just their SUVs." *CCPA Monitor, Canadian Center for Policy Alternatives*, Vol. 12, No. 10, pg. 21. April 2006.

3. Clarke, Tony and Barlow, Maude. "The battle for water." *Yes! A Journal of Positive Futures*, Winter 2004.

4. USDA Economic Research Service, *Environmental Resources and Environmental Indicators 2003* at Chapter 2.1.

5. C. Picone and D. Van Tassel. Agriculture and Biodiversity Loss: Industrial Agriculture. Published in Niles Eldredge (Ed.), *Life on Earth: An Encyclopedia of Biodiversity, Ecology, and Evolution*, pp. 99-105. Reprinted with permission by ABC-CLIO, Santa Barbara, California. Published 2002.

6. Pfeiffer, Dale Allen. "Eating fossil fuels: Without oil, families will go hungry, not just their SUVs." *CCPA Monitor, Canadian Center for Policy Alternatives*, Pg. 21 Vol. 12 No. 10. April 2006.

7. *Ibid.*

8. *Ibid.*

9. McConnell, Mike. "Ask for a change: Meat as wedge issue." *Waterkeeper Alliance*, May 2, 2006.

10. Fulhage, Charles D. "How to Size a Farm and Home Water System." University of Missouri. Department of Agricultural Engineering. October 1993

11. A Citizen's "Guide to the Regional Economic and Environmental Effects of Large Concentrated Dairy Operations." Weida, William J. Department of Economics at the Colorado College, Colorado Springs, CO, and The Global Resource Center for the Environment, New York, N.Y., November 19, 2000.

12. Pfeiffer, Dale Allen. "Eating fossil fuels: Without oil, families will go hungry, not just their SUVs." *CCPA Monitor, Canadian Center for Policy Alternatives*, April 2006. P. 21, Vol. 12, No. 10.

13. "Numerical Simulation of Groundwater Flow for Water Rights Administration in the Curry and Portales Valley Underground Water Basins, New Mexico." Musharrafieh, Ghassan and Logan, Linda. March 1999.

14. New Mexico State University, NMSU Dairy Extension. Available at: http://cahe.nmsu.edu/ces/dairy/index .html.

15. Factory farms grow new roots in developing world. Environmental News Service, April 22, 2003. Available at: www.ens-newswire.com/ens/ apr2003/2003-04-22-10.asp

16. USDA ERS, *Environmental Resources and Environmental Indicators 2006*, at Chapter 2.2.

17. C. Picone and D. Van Tassel. Agriculture and Biodiversity Loss: Industrial Agriculture. Published in Niles Eldredge (Ed.), *Life on Earth: An Encyclopedia of Biodiversity, Ecology, and Evolution*, pp. 99-105. Reprinted with permission by ABC-CLIO, Santa Barbara, California. Published 2002.

18. *Ibid.*

19. *Ibid.*

20. Cummings, Claire Hope. "Ripe for change: agriculture's tipping point." *World Watch* magazine, July 1, 2006.

21. Cook, Christopher D. "The Spraying of America: American agriculture dumps a billion pounds of pesticides on food, producing a truly toxic harvest." Earth Island Journal, Spring 2005. Available at: http:// www.thirdworldtraveler.com/Environment/Spraying _America.html

22. Kwa, Aileen. "Agriculture in Developing Countries: Which way forward?" Occasional Papers, South Centre, June 2001. Available at: http://www.focusweb.org/publications/2001/agriculture_which_way_forward.html

23. Keeney, Dennis and Mark Muller, Institute for Agriculture and Trade Policy, "Water Use by Ethanol Plants: Potential Challenges," 2006.

24. Wakker, Eric, "The Kalimantan Border Oil Palm Mega-Project," Friends of the Earth Netherlands/Swedish Society for nature Preservation, Apr. 2006.

25. World Bank, *World Development Report 2008* at 182.

26. World Bank, Independent Evaluation Group, "Water Management in Agriculture: Ten Years of World Bank Assistance, 1994-2004," 2006 at xiii.

27. World Bank, *World Development Report 2008* at 180.

28. Mellor, John W., "Foreign Aid and Agriculture-Led Development," *International Agricultural Development*, Edited by Carl K. Eicher and John M. Staatz, Third Edition, (Baltimore: The Johns Hopkins University Press, 1998), at 63.

29. Hirsch, Jerry and Chu, Henry. "Brazil's rise as farming giant has a price tag." *Los Angeles Times*, Aug. 21, 2005. Available at: http://forests.org/articles/reader.asp?linkid=45413

30. Stewart, Ain. "Desert Bloom." *The New York Jewish Week*, Aug. 11, 2006.

31. "Organic farming can feed the world, U-M study shows." University of Michigan News Service, July 10, 2007.

Chapter 11

1. Dudgeon, D. et al. 2006. Freshwater biodiversity: importance, threats, status and conservation challenges. Biological Reviews 81(1):163-182.

2. IUCN – The Freshwater Biodiversity Crisis, 1999.

3. Postel et al. 1996. Human appropriation of renewable fresh water. *Science* 271: 785-788.

4. Holmes, B. Water, water everywhere... *New Scientist*, Feb. 17, 1996. p. 8.

5. Brooks, D.B. 2005. Beyond greater efficiency: The concept of water soft paths. *Canadian Journal of Water Resources* 30(1): 1-10.

6. Gleick, P. 2003. Global Freshwater Resources: Soft-Path Solutions for the 21st Century. *Science* 302:1524-1528.

7. Brooks, D.B. 2005. Beyond greater efficiency: The concept of water soft paths. *Canadian Journal of Water Resources* 30(1): 1-10.

8. Dudgeon, D. et al. 2006. Freshwater biodiversity: importance, threats, status, and conservation challenges. *Biological Reviews* 81(1):163-182.

9. Gleick, P. 2003. Global Freshwater Resources: Soft-Path Solutions for the 21st Century. *Science* 302:1524-1528.

10. Veldoen et al. 2006. The bactericidal agent triclosan modulates thyroid hormone-associated gene expression and disrupts postembryonic anuran development. *Aquatic Toxicology* 80(3):217-227.

11. Lovins, A. 1976. Energy strategy: The road not taken? *Foreign Affairs* 6(20): 5-15.

12. Gleick, P. 2003. Global Freshwater Resources: Soft-Path Solutions for the 21st Century. *Science* 302:1524-1528.

13. Brandes, O. and D. Brooks. 2007. Ingenuity trumps hard tech: the water soft path is the best bet for Canada's public and ecological needs. Alternatives Journal at http://goliath.ecnext.com/coms2/gi_0199-6935073/Ingenuity-trumps-hard-tech-the.html.

14. Hinrichsen, et al. 1998. Solutions for a Water Short World, *Population Reports Series M*, Number 14.

15. WWF Freshwater Info: http://www.panda.org/about_wwf/what_we_do/freshwater/about_freshwater/index.cfm

16. EPA – 17 case studies of constructed wetlands (1993): http://www.epa.gov/owow/wetlands/pdf/ConstructedWetlands-Complete.pdf.

17. http://cfpub.epa.gov/npdes/faqs.cfm?program_id=5.

18. http://www.riverkeeper.org/campaign.php/pollution/the_facts/986.

19. http://www.greenroofs.com/projects/pview.php?id=311 and http://www.psat.wa.gov/Publications/LID_studies/lid_natural_approaches.pdf.

20. EPA – Handbook of Constructed Wetlands – http://www.epa.gov/owow/wetlands/pdf/hand.pdf.

21. John Todd Ecological Design Case Study – http://www.toddecological.com/case-studies/index.html.

22. John Todd Ecological Design Case Study – http://www.toddecological.com/case-studies/index.html.

23. Prairie Water Project website – http://www.prairiewaters.org/overview.htm.

24. Gertner, J. Oct. 2007. The Future if Drying Up. *New York Times*.

25. http://www.sydneywater.com.au/SavingWater/InYourGarden/RainwaterTanks.

26. http://www.rainharvesting.com.au/rainwater_tank_rebates.asp.

27. Ofwat. 2000. Worldwide Water Comparisons. From: http://www.ofwat.gov.uk/aptrix/ofwat/publish.nsf/AttachmentsByTitle/worldwide_water_comp9900.pdf/$FILE/worldwide_water_comp9900.pdf.

28. Emerton, L., L.Iyango, P. Luwum, and A. Malinga. 1999. *The Present Economic Value of Nakivubo Urban Wetland*, Uganda IUCN – The World Conservation Union, Eastern Africa Regional Office, Nairobi. From: http://www.iucn.org/places/earo/pubs/economic/nakivubo.pdf.

— Emerton, L. and E. Bos. 2004. Value – Counting Ecosystems as Water Infrastructure. Retrieved on July 15, 2007, from: http://europeandcis.undp.org/WaterWiki/images/c/ca/VALUE.pdf.

29. National Water and Sewerage Corporation. 2006. National Water and Sewerage Corporation. From: http://www.nwsc.co.ug/modules/mypage/.

30. World Health Organization/Water, Sanitation and Health Protection and the Human Environment. 2005. *Water Safety Plans: Managing drinking-water quality from catchment to consumer*. From: http://www.who.int/water_sanitation_health/dwq/wsp170805.pdf.

31. AWE (Air, Water, Earth) Limited. 2005. Why Lake Victoria pollution levels are rising. From: http://www.awe-engineers.com/news1.html.

32. Emerton, L., L.Iyango, P. Luwum, and A. Malinga. 1999. *The Present Economic Value of Nakivubo Urban Wetland*, Uganda IUCN – The World Conservation Union, Eastern Africa Regional Office, Nairobi. From: http://www.iucn.org/places/earo/pubs/economic/nakivubo.pdf.

33. Emerton, L., L.Iyango, P. Luwum, and A. Malinga. 1999. *The Present Economic Value of Nakivubo Urban Wetland*, Uganda IUCN – The World Conservation Union, Eastern Africa Regional Office, Nairobi. Retrieved on July 13, 2007, from: http://www.iucn.org/places/earo/pubs/economic/nakivubo.pdf.

— Emerton, L. and E. Bos. 2004. . Retrieved on July 15, 2007, from: http://europeandcis.undp.org/WaterWiki/images/c/ca/VALUE.pdf.

34. UNESCO World Water Assessment Programme. 2006. National Water Development Report: Uganda. Retrieved on July 14, 2007, from: http://unesdoc.unesco.org/images/0014/001467/146760e.pdf.

Chapter 14

1. Swami Sivananda, *Mother Ganges,* (Uttar Pradesh, India: The Divine Life Society, 1994), p. 16.

2. H.C. Reiger, "Whose Himalaya? A Study in Geopiety," in T. Singh, ed., *Studies in Himalayan Ecology and Development Strategies* (New Delhi: English Book Store, 1980), p. 2.

3. *Ibid.*

4. Diana Eck, "Ganga The Goddess in Hindu Sacred Geography" in *The Divine Consort: Radha and the Goddesses of India*, John Stratton Hawley, Donna Marie Wulff, eds. (Berkeley: Graduate Theological Union, 1982), p. 182.

5. Uma Shankari and Esha Shah, *Water Management Traditions in India* (Madras, India: Patriotic People's Science and Technology Foundation, 1993), p. 25.

6. Janet Bord and Colin Bord, *Sacred Waters: Holy Wells and Water Lore in Britain and Ireland* (London; New York: Granada, 1985).

7. *Ibid.*, p. 31.

8. *Ibid.*

9. Robert Mascall, *Bishop of Hereford*, pp. 1404-1417. Also see Bord and Bord, *Sacred Waters*, p. 45.

10. *Ibid.*

Contributor Biographies

Maude Barlow

is the national chairperson of The Council of Canadians, Canada's largest public advocacy organization, and the co-founder of the Blue Planet Project, working internationally for the right to water. She serves on the boards of the International Forum on Globalization, and Food and Water Watch, as well as being a Councilor with the Hamburg-based World Future Council. Barlow is the recipient of six honorary doctorates, the 2005/2006 Lannan Cultural Freedom Fellowship Award, and the 2005 Right Livelihood Award for her global water justice work. She is also the best-selling author or co-author of sixteen books, including *Blue Gold: The Fight to Stop the Corporate Theft of the World's Water* (with Tony Clarke) and the recently released *Blue Covenant: The Global Water Crisis and the Coming Battle for the Right to Water*.

Tony Clarke

is the founder and executive director of the Polaris Institute. He is the author and co-author of nine books, including *Blue Gold: The Fight to Stop the Corporate Theft of the World's Water* (with Maude Barlow). In 2005 he won the Right Livelihood Award for his work on international water and trade issues. Clarke has written numerous articles on water issues for magazines and journals. He has worked with mass social movements of indigenous peoples, peasants, and urban workers in building resistance to the privatization of water. At Polaris, he has spearheaded several new projects on water justice issues, including a sustainable water project for agriculture in California and a city and countryside project on water struggles with counterpart groups in Mexico. Clarke also has a bachelor's degree in political science from the University of British Columbia plus a master's and a doctoral degree from the University of Chicago in social ethics.

Brock Dolman

is the director of Occidental Arts and Ecology Center's WATER Institute and Permaculture Design Program, and he co-directs the Wildlands Biodiversity Program. He co-instructs Basins of Relations and permaculture-related courses. He also co-manages the center's biodiversity collection, orchards, and 70 acres of wildlands. His experience ranges from the study of wildlife biology, native California botany, and watershed ecology, to the practice of habitat restoration, education about regenerative human settlement design, ethno-ecology, and ecological literacy activism towards societal transformation.

Tom Engelhardt

runs the Nation Institute's Tomdispatch.com. A Fellow of the Institute, he is also the co-founder of The American Empire Project (Metropolitan Books). His book, *The End of Victory Culture* (University of Massachusetts Press), has been thoroughly updated in a newly issued edition that deals with victory culture's crash-and-burn sequel in Iraq.

Paula Garcia

is the executive director of the New Mexico Acequia Association. She is a community leader, political activist, and aspiring farmer who dedicates her time to family and community. During her years of service to the NMAA, acequia communities have built a movement around the principle that "el agua es la vida" (water is life), and have achieved major policy changes locally and statewide. The association also launched campaigns and programs to involve youth in agricultural traditions and to increase cultivation of foods of spiritual and cultural significance to native and traditional communities in New Mexico.

Wenonah Hauter

is the executive director of Food & Water Watch. She has worked extensively on water, food, energy, and environmental issues at the national, state, and local level. From 1997 to 2005 she served as Director of Public Citizen's Energy and Environment Program, which focused on water, food, and energy policy. From 1996 to 1997, she was environmental policy director for

Citizen Action, where she worked with the organization's 30 state-based groups. From 1989 to 1995 she was at the Union of Concerned Scientists where, as a senior organizer, she coordinated broad-based, grassroots sustainable energy campaigns in several states. She has an M.S. in applied anthropology from the University of Maryland.

Jacques Leslie

writes narrative nonfiction about the world's most pressing environmental issues. His 2005 book, *Deep Water: The Epic Struggle Over Dams, Displaced People, and the Environment,* won the J. Anthony Lukas Work-in-Progress Award and was named one of the top science books of the year by *Discover Magazine.* A former *Los Angeles Times* foreign correspondent, he has won numerous literary and journalism awards including the Drunken Boat Panliterary Award in nonfiction, the Sigma Delta Chi Distinguished Service Award for Foreign Correspondence, and an Overseas Press Club citation. For more information go to www.jacques leslie.com.

Eric Lohan

is a project manager for Living Machine Research and Development at Worrell Water Technology. He has a B.A. in biology and environmental studies from Oberlin College and a M.S. from The Ohio State University in environmental science with a focus on ecological engineering. Lohan has been involved with research, design and project management of Living Machine systems for eight years. He is co-author of five patents.

Tara Lohan

is an environmental journalist and senior editor at AlterNet. She manages the environment and water coverage. Lohan has worked as a writer, editor, and organizer on environmental and social justice issues for ten years. She has a master's degree in literary nonfiction from the University of Oregon and a bachelor's degree in English and environmental studies from Middlebury College.

Kelle Louaillier

has been with Corporate Accountability International for nearly two decades, serving as director of international outreach, campaign director, development director, and associate director before becoming the organization's executive director in 2007. Under her leadership, Corporate Accountability International (formerly Infact) helped move General Electric out of the nuclear weapons business, spearheaded grassroots efforts behind the passage of the global tobacco treaty, and launched the nationwide "Think Outside the Bottle" campaign. Prior to joining CAI, Louaillier taught math in the Central African Republic and worked to empower homeless youth in Seattle. She holds degrees in French, philosophy, and mathematics from Seattle University.

Bill McKibben

is an environmentalist and writer who frequently writes about global warming, alternative energy, and the risks associated with human genetic engineering. His first book, *The End of Nature,* was published in 1989 and is regarded as the first book for a general audience about climate change. It has been printed in more than 20 languages. He has written over ten books and has been awarded Guggenheim and Lyndhurst Fellowships, and won the Lannan Prize for nonfiction writing in 2000. He has honorary degrees from Green Mountain College, Unity College, Lebanon Valley College, and Sterling College. He is a scholar in residence at Middlebury College.

Sandra Postel

directs the independent Global Water Policy Project, as well as the Center for the Environment at Mount Holyoke College. She is author of *Pillar of Sand: Can the Irrigation Miracle Last?* and of *Last Oasis: Facing Water Scarcity.* She is also co-author (with Brian Richter) of *Rivers for Life: Managing Water for People and Nature.* In 2005, the Worldwatch Institute released her publication *Liquid Assets: The Critical Need to Safeguard Freshwater Ecosystems.* Postel has served as advisor to the Division on Earth and Life Studies of the U.S. National Research Council as well as to American Rivers. She has served on the Board of Directors of the International Water Resources Association, and on the editorial boards of Ecosystems, Water Policy, and Green Futures. She received a B.A. (summa cum laude) in geology and political science at Wittenberg University and an M.E.M. with emphasis on resource economics and policy at Duke University. She has also received two honorary Doctor of Science degrees. Postel has been awarded the Duke University School of Environment's Distinguished Alumni

Award, and a Pew Scholar's Award in Conservation and the Environment.

Christina Roessler

is a consultant and writer working on water issues in the western United States. Before becoming a consultant she was the founding director of the French American Charitable Trust.

Miguel Santistevan

is a Ph.D. student at the University of New Mexico (UNM) in biology. His research interest is in crop diversity and agriculture ecology of the acequia and dryland agricultural systems in northern New Mexico. He is a youth mentor/radio producer for The New Mexico Acequia Association project, "Sembrando Semillas" and a radio show called "¡Que Vivan las Acequias!" He has a B.S. in biology from UNM and a M.S. in ecology from the University of California, Davis. He maintains a small experimental seed-saving farm in Taos called Sol Feliz. Santistevan is a permaculture design course instructor with the Traditional Native American Farmers' Association.

Vandana Shiva

is a world-renowned environmental leader and thinker. Director of the Research Foundation on Science, Technology, and Ecology, she is the author of many books, including *Water Wars: Pollution, Profits, and Privatization* and *Biopiracy: The Plunder of Nature and Knowledge*. Shiva is a leader in the International Forum on Globalization, the founder of Navdanya ("nine seeds"), a movement promoting diversity and use of native seeds. Before becoming an activist, she was one of India's leading physicists. She holds a master's degree in the philosophy of science and a Ph.D. in particle physics. In 1993, Shiva won the Right Livelihood Award.

Alan Snitow and Deborah Kaufman

are award-winning filmmakers whose PBS documentary *Thirst* and its follow-up book (Wiley, 2007) exposed how the corporate drive to control water has become the catalyst for community resistance to globalization. Snitow and Kaufman's earlier PBS films dealt with organizing high-tech workers (*Secrets of Silicon Valley*) and with Black-Jewish relations (*Blacks and Jews*). Snitow is on the board of Food and Water Watch. Kaufman is on the board of the Progressive Jewish Alliance. They are currently working on a film about Jewish power and identity in America.

Eleanor Sterling

is the director of the American Museum of Natural History's Center for Biodiversity and Conservation. She received her B.A. from Yale College and a joint Ph.D. in physical anthropology, and forestry and environmental studies from Yale University. Sterling has more than 25 years of field research experience in Africa, Asia, and Latin America. She has served as an adjunct professor at Columbia University since 1997, and has served as the director of Graduate Studies for Columbia University's Department of Ecology, Evolution, and Environmental Biology since 2003. Sterling sits on the Board of Governors of the Society for Conservation Biology and is the chair of the society's education committee.

Roger Stone

is the director and president of the Sustainable Development Institute. He was formerly a correspondent and news bureau chief for *Time* magazine with three years of service in Brazil. He has also been a vice president of the Chase Manhattan Bank and of the World Wildlife Fund, and president of the Center for Inter-American Relations. He is the author of five published books.

Erin Vintinner

is biodiversity research specialist at the Center for Biodiversity and Conservation (CBC) at the American Museum of Natural History. She provides research and writing support for various CBC projects and contributes content to the Network of Conservation Educators and Practitioners. Prior to coming to the CBC, Vintinner served as research and expedition coordinator for the "No Water No Life" nonprofit photodocumentary project in the Columbia River Basin. She also previously served as a fisheries technician with the USDA Forest Service in Sitka, Alaska and the Bureau of Land Management in Eugene, Oregon. Vintinner holds a M.A. in conservation biology from Columbia University's Department of Ecology, Evolution and Environmental Biology and a B.A. in biology from Boston University.

Photography Credits

Acknowledgments

Water Consciousness is one of the first books from the AlterNet publishing program. The idea to create *Water Consciousness* initially evolved from our ongoing drumbeat of environmental news on water and from conversations with many people about the growing global water crisis. We realized that in addition to our coverage of news on this issue, many diverse creative and educational projects would need to be developed if we were going to address the water challenge and its fundamental connection to our survival. We hoped to create a book that would be one bold statement in that direction, hopefully joined by many others.

Almost simultaneously during these discussions on the water crisis came word of a powerful water exhibit that would be opening in the Fall of 2007 at the American Museum of Natural History, called Water: H20=Life. This powerful exhibition moved to the San Diego Natural History Museum as this book was being published and will keep traveling to many cities in the U.S. and abroad over the next ten years. In a short amount of time it has already come to symbolize the increasing seriousness of the effort to develop both awareness and solutions to a growing crisis. So we developed *Water Consciousness* to complement the fantastic elements of the Water: H20=Life exhibit. Thanks to Eleanor J. Sterling who was one of the masterminds of that exhibit, and a warm supporter and contributor of this book along with Erin Vintinner, and to the people at the San Diego Natural History Museum, who are helping to see that the book and its voices find broad audiences.

From these initial conversations came generous support from the Panta Rhea Foundation. Enormous thanks goes to Hans Schoepflin, the foundation's visionary founder and to Diana Cohn, the foundation's executive director. We thank Hans and Diana for their wisdom, their unflinching commitment to address the global water crisis, and their organizing energy and strategic smarts. We also acknowledge the Compton Foundation with thanks to Edith Eddy and the Compton Board who worked with us to include the critical role of the arts as a central element to the book's design. In addition, an anonymous donor also came through with a generous grant that helped the book become a reality.

The project was also a group effort at AlterNet. Our environmental editor Tara Lohan tackled the project with enthusiasm, becoming the book's editor, recruiting the fabulous line up of writers, and wrangled the photos, charts, graphs, and everything necessary to make this powerful book. She has done an extraordinary job. Other members of the AlterNet book team gave stellar performances, especially Elijah Nella and Valrie Sanders who handled production and book printing. The book team also enjoyed key contributions from Liz Mullaney, Shelana deSilva, Heather Gehlert, and Patrick Hughes for fundraising, editing, and marketing. We also couldn't have done it without many extra sets of eyes from our copy editors Robert Gomez and Suzi Steffen, proofer Debra Gates, and indexer Ken DellaPenta.

A very special thanks goes to Watershed Media–Dan Imhoff, Roberto Carra, and Timothy Rice–for the beautiful design that made the book come alive. We were also helped by a whole bunch of other folks–those at H20Conserve.org and especially Robin Madel who brought the innovative water calculator to print; John Dickerson for the generous use of his photos; and Tim Kingston of International Rivers who provided endless support with photos and information.

Of course there would be no book without the high quality writers and photographers whose work appears, many of whom went beyond the call of duty to help ensure that we produce a book that would make an impact, and one that we would all be proud of. Additional thanks to the *American Prospect* who loaned us some excellent content from their special issue on water.

Indeed this project has taken a whole community of committed people of various backgrounds and it is no surprise. Our water crisis will challenge all of us to come together–scientists, artists, and activists–to solve one of the world's most pressing problems. We've already begun the collaboration, now let's keep going.

–Don Hazen, Executive Editor, AlterNet

Resources

Advocacy, Public Education, Research

AMIGOS BRAVOS
Taos, New Mexico
(575) 758-3874
www.amigosbravos.org
A river conservation organization guided by social justice principles and dedicated to preserving and restoring the ecological and cultural integrity of New Mexico's rivers and watersheds.

BLUE PLANET PROJECT
Ottawa, Ontario, Canada
(613) 233-2773
www.blueplanetproject.net
An international civil society movement begun by The Council of Canadians to protect the world's fresh water from the growing threats of trade and privatization.

CONCERNED CITIZENS
COALITION OF STOCKTON
Stockton, California
(209) 465-3948
www.cccos.org
Made up of organizations and individuals working together to study government actions and inform the public.

CORPORATE ACCOUNTABILITY
INTERNATIONAL
Boston, Massachusetts
(617) 695-2525
www.stopcorporateabuse.org
A nonprofit challenging corporate abuse, including water privatization, for more than 30 years.

FELTON FLOW
(Friends of Locally Owned Water)
Felton, California
(831) 335-3053
www.feltonflow.org
A citizen group fighting for local control of their public water system.

FOOD & WATER WATCH
Washington, DC
(202) 683-2500
www.foodandwaterwatch.org
A nonprofit consumer organization that challenges the corporate control and abuse of our food and water resources.

GLOBAL WATER POLICY PROJECT
Western Massachusetts
www.globalwaterpolicy.org
Promotes the preservation and sustainable use of Earth's fresh water through research, writing, outreach, and public speaking.

GRACE
New York, New York
(212) 726-9161
www.gracelinks.org
A nonprofit environmental organization that promotes sustainable solutions for American's food, energy, and water systems.

INTERFAITH CENTER FOR
CORPORATE RESPONSIBILITY
New York, New York
(212) 870-2295
www.iccr.org
A membership organization that works to engage corporate management on social and environmental issues such as global warming, genetically modified

foods, water, and environmental justice.

INTERNATIONAL RIVERS
Berkeley, California
(510) 848-1155
www.internationalrivers.org
An international nonprofit opposing destructive dams, protecting rivers, and defending communities that rely on rivers.

THE JOHNS HOPKINS CENTER FOR LIVABLE FUTURE
Baltimore, Maryland
(410) 502-7578
www.jhsph.edu/clf
An academic center that promotes research to develop and communicate information about the interrelationships among diet, food production, environment, and human health; to advance an ecological perspective in reducing threats to the health of the public; and to promote policies that protect health, the global environment and the ability to sustain life for future generations.

MICHIGAN CITIZENS FOR WATER CONSERVATION
Mecosta, Michigan
www.savemiwater.org
A group helping Michigan's citizens protect community water supplies.

NAVDANYA
New Delhi, India
(+91) 11 2653-5422
www.navdanya.org
A biodiversity conservation program that helps rejuvenate indigenous knowledge and culture, create

awareness of the hazards of genetic engineering, and defend against biopiracy.

NEW MEXICO ACEQUIA ASSOCIATION
Santa Fe, New Mexico
(505) 995-9644
www.lasacequias.org
Works to protect the acequia system and water as a community resource.

OCCIDENTAL ARTS AND ECOLOGY WATER INSTITUTE
Occidental, California
(707) 874-1557
www.oaecwater.org
Promotes the understanding of healthy watersheds through advocacy and policy development; training and support; education and demonstration; and research.

PACIFIC INSTITUTE
Oakland, California
(510) 251-1600
www.pacinst.org
An independent, nonpartisan think-tank that conducts research on water, community strategies for sustainability and justice, and globalization.

POLARIS INSTITUTE
Ottawa, Ontario, Canada
(613) 237-1717
www.polarisinstitute.org
Helps citizen movements fight for democratic social change, including in the area of water democracy.

Exhibits, Media, Resources

ALTERNET.ORG AND ALTERNET BOOKS
San Francisco, California
(415) 284-1420
www.alternet.org
An award-winning news magazine, online community, and book publisher that focuses on progressive issues, including the environment and water.

ROBERT DAWSON PHOTOGRAPHY
San Francisco, California
www.robertdawson.com
Thirty years of photography focusing on the American West.

H2O CONSERVE WATER CALCULATOR
www.H2OConserve.org
An online tool that enables people to calculate their water footprint and find ways to reduce their consumption.

MARCUS RHINELANDER PHOTOGRAPHY
mqrphoto.com
Documentary photography of Asia.

RIVER OF WORDS
Berkeley, California
(510) 548-7636
www.riverofwords.org
A nonprofit organization, co-founded by U.S. Poet Laureate (1995-1997) Robert Hass and writer Pamela Michael, dedicated to promoting literacy, creative

expression and community awareness of our most critical environmental concern: water. It has a unique watershed education model that integrates art and poetry in a place-based curriculum.

SNITOW-KAUFMAN PRODUCTIONS
Berkeley, California
(510) 841-1068
www.snitow-kaufman.org
A nonprofit that produces film, video and educational media for the general public on social issues from race relations to globalization, including *Thirst*, about water privatization.

WATER: H20=LIFE
http://www.amnh.org/exhibitions/water
An exhibit organized by the American Museum of Natural History, New York, and the Science Museum of Minnesota, St. Paul, in collaboration with Great Lakes Science Center, Cleveland; The Field Museum, Chicago; Instituto Sangari, São Paulo, Brazil; National Museum of Australia, Canberra; Royal Ontario Museum, Toronto, Canada; San Diego Natural History Museum; and Singapore Science Centre with PUB Singapore.

WATERSHED MEDIA
Healdsburg, California
(707) 431.2936
www.watershedmedia.org
An award-winning non-profit publisher that produces visually-

dynamic, action-oriented books about under-reported environmental issues.

Green Design, Architecture, Engineering

2020 ENGINEERING
Belingham, Washington
(360) 671-2020
www.2020engineering.com
Engineering firm dedicated to providing simple and innovative solutions to long-term economic and environment sustainability of local, national, and international communities.

D.I.R.T. STUDIO
Charlottesville, Virginia
www.dirtstudio.com
A landscape architecture firm specializing in urban redevelopment and water-efficient landscaping.

EARTHSHIP BIOTECTURE
Taos, New Mexico
(575) 751-0462
www.earthship.net
A global company offering sustainable designs, construction drawings and details, products, educational materials, lectures/presentations, consultation and guidance toward getting people in sustainable housing.

GLOBAL ECOTECHNICS CORPORATION
Santa Fe, New Mexico
www.globalecotechnics.com

A company engaged in the development and application of innovative ecotechnic projects and biospheric design and engineering, including Biosphere 2.

GREEN ROOFS FOR HEALTHY CITIES
Toronto, Ontario, Canada
(416) 971-4494
www.greenroofs.org
A network that helps increase the awareness of the economic, social, and environmental benefits of green roof infrastructure across North America and rapidly advance the development of the market for green roof products and services.

INTERFACE ENGINEERING
Seattle, Washington
(425) 820-1542
www.ieice.com
Progressive mechanical and electrical engineering.

LIVING DESIGNS GROUP
Taos, New Mexico
(575) 751-9481
www.livingdesignsgroup.com
An architecture firm specializing in the integration of sustainable design elements for residential and commercial projects.

MITHUN
Seattle, Washington
(206) 623-3344
www.mithun.com
A green architecture, planning, and design firm.

NORTH AMERICAN WETLAND
ENGINEERING
White Bear Lake, Minnesota
(651) 255-5050
www.nawe-pa.com
An award-winning ecological
engineering company and leader
in the decentralized water and
wastewater industry.

RAINWATER HARVESTING FOR
DRYLANDS AND BEYOND
Tucson, Arizona
www.harvestingrainwater.com
Books, Web site, presentations,
videos and more on how to
conceptualize, design, and
implement sustainable water-
harvesting systems for home,
landscape, and community.

WORRELL WATER
TECHNOLOGIES/LIVING
MACHINES
Charlottesville, Virginia
(434) 973-6365
www.livingmachines.com
A company dedicated to
developing environmentally
sustainable technologies in the
water purification and wastewater
treatment industries.

Index

A

ABB Ltd., 92
Acequias
    definition of, 112
    global water movement and,
        118–19
    governance of, 115–16, 117
    history of, 113, 114
    social dimension of, 113–14
    spiritual dimension of, 114
    threats to, 116–18
    traditions of, 114–15
Africa, water pollution in, 22
Agriculture
    biofuels, 77–78
    dams and, 88
    "Green Revolution," 74, 79
    livestock operations, 75
    pollution and, 73, 75–76
    sustainability and, 78–81
    transnational corporations and, 74
    water consumption by, 18, 20,
        73, 74–75, 79, 124
Agroecology, 80–81
Albania, 28
Albuquerque, New Mexico, 109,
    125, 127, 129–30
Allahabad, 169
Alliance for Democracy, 70, 71
American Beverage Association, 70
Anasazi, 31–32
Ancestral Pueblo culture, 121
Anderson, Rocky, 69
Ankara, Turkey, 27
Anshuman, 170
Apollo 8, 15
Aquafina, 63, 64, 70
Aquifers. See also Groundwater
    definition of, 16

    mining, 16, 20
    Ogallala, 12, 20, 75
    saltwater intrusion in, 17
Arctic
    ice pack in, 29
    pollution in, 22, 24
Arizona, 12, 75
Arkansas, 17
Army Corps of Engineers, 28, 84, 89
"At Blackwater Pond" (Oliver), 3
Atlanta, Georgia, 27–30, 46, 48,
    49
Augusta, Georgia, 145
Aurora, Colorado, 141
Austin, Texas, 142
Australia
    rainwater harvesting systems in,
        141
    water shortages in, 10, 27, 32

B

Banahaw, Mount, 190
Bangladesh, 18, 165
Bank of New York, 48
Baptism, 172
Bar, Rosmarie, 177
Bargman, Julie, 157
Barlow, Maude, 22
Bechtel, 45
Beef, 23
Beijing, China, 16, 73
Belgium, 184
Bhagirath, 169–70, 170
Biofuels, 77–78
Biosphere, 148
Blue Planet Project, 184
Blumenfeld, Jared, 69
Bonneville Power Administration, 85
Boston, Massachusetts, 145

Bottled water
    exporters and importers of, 61
    growth of, 59–60
    marketing of, 60, 63–64
    myths about, 65
    opposition to, 68, 69–71
    public relations and, 66–67, 69
    regulation of, 64, 66, 69
    water sources for, 59, 61–64, 66
BP, 156
Bracken, David, 29
Braulio Carrillo National Park, 161
Brazil
    deforestation in, 78, 79
    freshwater in, 16, 19
Briscoe, John, 92
Bulgaria, 28
Burr, Aaron, 48

C

CAFOs (concentrated animal feeding
    operations), 75
Cairo, Egypt, 16
Calcutta, India, 16
California
    agriculture in, 18, 124
    bottled water standards in, 69
    dams in, 94
    desalination plants in, 126
    rainwater harvesting systems in,
        141
    water shortages in, 12
Cambodia, 135
Canada
    freshwater in, 16, 19
    right to water in, 184
    water consumption in, 23, 24,
        125
    water treaty between U.S. and, 39

About AlterNet.org

AlterNet.org is an award-winning news magazine and online community that creates original journalism and amplifies the best of dozens of other independent media sources. Its mission is to inspire citizen action and advocacy on the environment, human rights and civil liberties, social justice, media, and health care issues. AlterNet's editorial mix underscores a commitment to fairness, equity, and global stewardship, and to making connections across generational, ethnic, and issue lines. AlterNet has won two Webby Awards for best web magazine and several Independent Press Awards for online political coverage. AlterNet was also named one of National Public Radio's five "Winners on the Internet."

AlterNet Books was created to bring our readers a deeper and more insightful analysis of the progressive issues that matter.

Visit AlterNet.org/books today to order our other books!

Launched with *Young Dick Cheney: Great American,* AlterNet Books is a source of provocative thinking and high-quality writing.

Shock Jocks: Hate Speech and Talk Radio, our second book, highlights the politicized and often factually challenged world of talk radio and profiles the progressive alternatives fighting for airtime.

Want to make sure partisan maneuvering, mismanagement, and bad machines don't compromise the upcoming election? *Count My Vote: A Citizen's Guide to Voting* gives voters the information they need to cast their ballots with confidence. Author Steven Rosenfeld uncovers the obstacles facing voters in this watershed year. Rosenfeld argues that the extended primary and caucus season in early 2008 has shown—in state after state—that numerous problems face voters. Drawing on articles and analysis, reports by activists and voters across America, this must-have handbook provides tips on avoiding snags in all 50 states, as well as suggestions for voters who find their vote endangered. *Count My Vote* includes 50 state pages with information on election officials and state-specific problems to look out for. *Count My Vote* has all the voting rules for every individual state, plus special sections for students, seniors, and people who moved, information about new voting machines, and much more. *Count My Vote* empowers voters with the information needed to guarantee a clean and fair election this November!

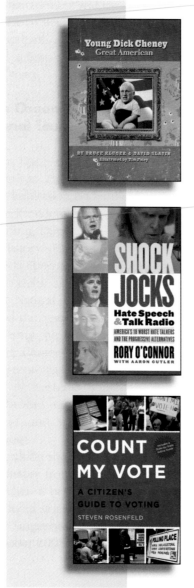

Watershed Media is an award-winning nonprofit publisher and resource center that produces action-oriented books and education campaigns about under-reported contemporary issues.

Watershed Media, 513 Brown Street, Healdsburg, California 95448, 707.431.2936, www.watershedmedia.org

Our book and outreach campaigns include:

The Guide to Tree-free, Recycled, and Certified Papers (1999)

Building with Vision: Optimizing and Finding Alternatives to Wood (2001)

Farming with the Wild: Enhancing Biodiversity on Farms and Ranches (2003)

Paper or Plastic: Searching for Solutions to an Overpackaged World (2005)

Farming and the Fate of Wild Nature: Essays in Conservation-Based Agriculture (2006)

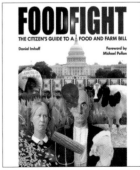

Food Fight: The Citizen's Guide to a Food and Farm Bill (2007)